ADOPTION: THEORY, POLICY AND PRACTICE

ADOPTION THEORY, POLICY AND PRACTICE

John Triseliotis
Joan Shireman
Marion Hundleby

CASSELL

Cassell
Wellington House
125 Strand
London WC2R 0BB

370 Lexington Avenue
New York
NY 10017-6550

First published 1997
Reprinted 1998, 1999

British Library Cataloguing-in-Publication Data
A catalogue record for this book is available from the British Library.

ISBN 0–304–33480–4 (hardback)
    0–304–33481–2 (paperback)

Typeset by Action Typesetting Limited, Gloucester
Printed and bound in Great Britain by
Redwood Books, Trowbridge, Wiltshire

CONTENTS

THE CONTRIBUTORS

Marion Hundleby has been a qualified social worker for over 20 years. Her experience encompasses social work practice, research and consultancy, with a particular interest in the fields of adoption and fostering and work with families. During the 1980s she was involved in two major research projects (Long Term Fostering and the Placement Outcome Survey) funded by the Department of Health. Her current post is that of Post-Adoption Specialist with the Catholic Children's Society, Nottingham. She has post-graduate qualifications from the University of Oxford and the Royal College of Art (London).

Joan Shireman is a professor at the Graduate School of Social Work at Portland State University, Portland, Oregon, where she currently is Director of the PhD in Social Work and Social Research. She has authored a book and a number of articles on foster care and adoption and has been principal investigator on a longitudinal study of adoption, from which her latest publications are drawn.

John Triseliotis is a professor and Senior Research Fellow at the International Social Sciences Institute at the University of Edinburgh. His most recent co-authored books include *Foster Care: Theory and Practice*, and *Teenagers and the Social Work Services*. He is currently engaged in a large study of foster care and foster carers. He was made an OBE in 1989.

ACKNOWLEDGEMENTS

We are extremely grateful to a number of people for their very helpful suggestions on how to improve our book. Inevitably, though, the views expressed here are our own and not those of the people consulted, who include Ratna Dutt at the National Institute for Social Work Training; Joan Fratter of Barnardos Barkingside; Gill Haworth of the Overseas Adoption Helpline; Helen Humphreys from Bury Social Services; and Julia Ridgway at the Department of Health. We are also very thankful to Familymakers, Kent, to The Bridge Child Care Consultancy, and to Ken Redgrave for permission to reproduce illustrations from their respective publications; to the Director and staff of the Catholic Children's Society in Nottingham for their continued support to Marion Hundleby; to Janet West, play therapist, and Lynn Charlton and Carolyn Oliver from Parents for Children, Durham; and to Lydia Lambert and Vivienne Triseliotis for draft readings. Finally, our thanks to Linda Morris, who ensured that the final manuscript was in a presentable shape, and to Toby Morris, who helped by converting numerous incompatible discs at short notice.

INTRODUCTION

There is no shortage of books on adoption and the question could rightly be asked 'Why yet another one?' The fact is that most of the recent publications concentrate either on the outcome of individual studies or on specific aspects of adoption policy and practice, such as open adoption, freeing children, transracial and intercountry adoption or contested adoption. What has been missing is a publication that brings together in a single volume theoretical, policy and practice issues. Students and practitioners, particularly those new to adoption work, often ask for an up-to-date reference of this kind, but there has been nothing much to recommend.

The present volume is a collaborative effort between three people with experience of adoption research and practice. Each one of us has brought something similar and also something different to the publication. Marion Hundleby's past research and current adoption practice with a voluntary agency have been a big asset. Joan Shireman's and John Triseliotis' current research work and past adoption practice brought together an American and a British perspective. Though the book is addressed to audiences in both the United Kingdom and the United States, we do not pretend that it is possible to cover in a single volume such a complex subject in all its manifestations. However, when we set out we were aware that in the field of adoption the two countries shared many common policies and practices. It is possibly one of the few childcare fields in which there has been regular and continued transatlantic dialogue and sharing of experiences.

American adoption practice and research have significantly influenced British policy and practice over the years, especially in the placement of children with 'special needs'. American studies covering the adoption of older children, transracial and in-race placements, and intercountry adoption have also exerted their influence. In turn, British research and practice have made their own contribution, particularly on questions of origins, genealogy and identity formation in adopted people.

The main differences between the two countries lie in certain aspects of law, which exist not only between the States and the UK, but also among the American states themselves. In the USA each of the 50 states is responsible for its own adoption laws and whilst these have many commonalities they also have considerable variations. A major difference between the USA and the UK is that adoption is more regulated in the latter than in the former country. For example, whilst the UK prohibits third party and private agency adoptions, these are legally sanctioned in many of the US states. As a result, a large number of infant adoptions and intercountry adoptions in the USA are independent, while older children and those with special needs are placed by adoption agencies.

Some differences between the two countries also exist in the way parental consents to adoption are dispensed with by courts and how access to original birth records is regulated. Whilst major differences will be highlighted as we go along, the emphasis will be on the great number of commonalties that unite policy makers, practitioners and researchers in both countries. Within the UK, England, Scotland and Northern Ireland have their own respective adoption laws, but differences mainly reflect legal procedures which are idiosyncratic to each country, rather than basic policy and practice principles.

A major development of the last twenty or so years, especially in Britain, has been the decided shift of adoption work away from voluntary agencies to local authority social (work) services departments. The main reason for this has been the significant decline in baby adoption and the concentration on children with special needs, who require an extensive range of resources. However, those voluntary agencies that have responded to changing needs play a vital role in placing children on behalf of local authorities and in spearheading practice developments. The focus on children with special needs has also led to the realization that adoption must no longer be practised in isolation but within the wider context of childcare and child protection. Depending on circumstances, adoption can be seen as one of the options available to all children who are looked after by local authority social services departments.

As we move from this to the next millennium, a number of important issues dominate adoption policy and practice. The parties and structures, identified earlier, will need to respond to these challenges in ways that enhance the children's long-term welfare, whilst also recognizing that the other parties to the adoption have certain legitimate interests. The main challenges and areas of debate, as we see them, include:

- making adoption policy and practice a fully child-centred

activity, respecting race, culture and religion;
- identifying the circumstances under which it is justifiable to permanently separate children against their parents' wishes;
- finding adoptive or permanent foster families for some very psychologically damaged children;
- resolving policy dilemmas in transracial placements;
- regulating and managing intercountry adoption;
- recognizing the possibilities and limitations of open adoption and developing mediation skills to help manage possible conflict;
- acknowledging the legitimate interest in adoption of single people, some of whom may be gay or lesbian;
- studying the impact on adoption of alternative orders;
- applying the concept of 'through care' by developing more uniform and high quality preparatory and post-placement support services to all those affected by adoption (see also Hughes, 1995b).

All the above, and other issues, will be discussed in the chapters that follow. Suffice it to say here that because of its nature, adoption, wherever it is practised, reflects and is shaped by social changes and attitudes to such matters as sexual behaviours, family constitution and re-constitution, non-marital births, single parenthood, racial and religious beliefs and attitudes towards methods of assisted conception and surrogacy. As an example, such changes in attitudes have contributed, along with other factors, to fewer babies being relinquished for adoption, whilst the rise in divorce and re-marriage has resulted in a significant increase in step-parent adoptions. Possible future changes in current abortion laws, or the rules governing benefits to single parents, could equally transform the present demographic picture of adoption. Furthermore, if in the past adoption was perceived as a kind of altruistic activity in the form of a 'gift', the recent advent of open adoption and adoption with contact are shifting it towards that of a more contractual arrangement. This highlights even further the fact that adoptive families are different from most families in that they are artificially constructed to provide psychological as separate from biological parenting.

It is intended that this book be a comprehensive guide of use to those working with adoption. Primarily, it should inform the policy maker and practitioner of possible directions and current 'best practice', and should explicate the practice wisdom and empirical data which underlie these foundations.

CHAPTER 1
A framework for adoption policy and practice

As a basic human experience, adoption transcends all cultures, and has existed over centuries. It is about the provision of family for those children who cannot be cared for within the families into which they are born, and it is about the experience of parenting. It is about relationships, intimacy, 'about love and loss, about concern and commitment, passion and grief' (Rowe, 1966). Good adoption practice is complex, important, and fraught with controversy.

Few social services are as consistently in the public eye as is adoption. Adoption personally touches many people: either they are part of a family formed by adoption, have lost a family member through adoption or know someone who is adopted. It is a subject about which most people have information, People feel intensely about adoption and as a result, adoption policy is responsive to political forces generated by this interest, and its practice is often subject to impassioned criticism.

Working from the perspective of two similar adoptive traditions, which have developed somewhat differently in Great Britain and the United States, the authors will attempt to identify those factors which are basic to the sound practice of adoption and to examine the theory and policy issues which shape adoption practice.

A DEFINITION OF ADOPTION

A framework for thinking about adoption properly begins with a definition of adoption, and even that is subject to change. Adoption is a legal procedure through which a permanent family is created for a child whose birth parents are unable, unwilling or are legally prohibited from caring for the child. The focus in good adoption practice is on the long-term welfare of the child. Successful adoption provides a permanent home or social base which is secure and meets the individual child's needs. At its best, adoption also meets the needs of the adopting family who have wished for a child or further children, as well as the family into which the child was born, who have willingly or unwillingly surrendered the care of the child. Legally, the rights and responsibilities of adoptive parents are the same as they would be if the child had been born to them, even if contact with the child's family of origin is maintained.

Though the legal event of adoption occurs at one point in time, adoption is a process for all parties. It begins with the identification and assessment of children needing a new family and progresses through the quest for adoptive parents for the child, and the 'match' of the capacities of a particular family with the needs of a particular child. It continues through the legal procedures, and on through the lifespan of the adoptive family. Increasingly, the uniqueness of adoptive families has been recognized and their particular strengths and difficulties identified. There is also a greater awareness of the effect that long-term grief and loss may have on birth parents and wider kin networks which, in turn, has affected service development.

One aspect of this uniqueness is the continuing role which the child's biological heritage plays in the life of the adoptive family. This is captured in the following new definition of adoption suggested by Watson (1994, p. 2):

> Adoption is a means of meeting the developmental needs of a child by legally transferring ongoing parental responsibility from birth parents to adoptive parents, recognizing that in the process we have created a new kinship network that forever links those two families together through the child who is shared by both. This kinship network may also include significant other families, both formal and informal, that have been a part of the child's experiences.

The reader will note that step-parent adoptions have not been included in this discussion. These adoptions, often important in cementing the legal and social bonds of newly reconstituted families, are outside the mainstream of agency adoption policy and practice. Typically, they are 'family affairs' and, as such, will not be considered in this book. Nevertheless, many of the basic assumptions of agency adoption practice concern these children and families as well.

THE CONTEXT OF ADOPTION

Three parties are involved in each adoption – the birth parents, the adoptive parent(s) and the child, with the adoption agency acting as intermediary. Ideally the birth parent(s) will have the opportunity to plan for the care of a child whose needs for a permanent family cannot otherwise be met (though we recognize that some parents may not see it in this way); the adoptive parent(s) will hope or expect to be able to attain the satisfactions of parenting the child; and the child should hopefully be assured a permanent home with a family able to provide appropriate care whilst recognizing the child's origins. The rights of each must be protected by good practice as well as through legal safeguards.

Extended families are also involved in the adoption. The contribution of the wider family network is being increasingly recognized as adoption practitioners are becoming sensitized by cultural groups in which the extended family is of importance. As an example, legislation in Britain has extended certain rights to grandparents such as the right to be consulted or apply for access where appropriate. However, the rights of the extended family are generally not legally protected and part of good adoption practice lies in involving these family members in the adoption process.

In Western European and American culture, and in a number of other cultures, we have believed that the family is the best place for a child to grow, and that adoption is an important option for securing a permanent home. Adoption mirrors the social changes taking place in the society in which it is practised. It evolves to reflect changes as the ethical systems and the usual ways of caring for children in the community change. It changes as the community recognizes different children in need of adoptive homes. It also changes as the needs of birth parents and potential adoptive parents change. As technology makes our world smaller, subtle historical and cultural differences, both regionally and across national boundaries, become part of adoption practice.

BRIEF HISTORY OF ADOPTION

The beginnings

The first recorded adoption in Western tradition is that of Moses, a transcultural and possibly transracial adoption in which an infant of a subjugated people was adopted by a woman of the ruling class – possibly a single parent. No agency was involved, with the birth family watching over the child until he was found. Secrecy was partially preserved in the adoption, with the identity of the birth parent being concealed from the adopting parent. The motive of the adopting parent was compassion, the motive of the birth parent the need to find a home for her child. Thus in many ways, this first recorded adoption catches elements of adoptions through time.

The history of adoption in the United States and Great Britain is interwoven, for the two countries share a common legal heritage, traditions, and one language. The result has been continued communication among those working in adoption. An historical examination of adoption practice in the Western tradition, from which British and American custom draws, reveals five distinct periods, each one reflecting the preoccupations of the time (see also Tizard, 1977).

The first period

The custom of adoption which emerged in the Greek and Roman periods was, with some exceptions, instrumental in nature, aiming to serve the interests of those adopting. Most adoptions in Greek and Roman times were of related young males to perform religious ceremonies, or arranged in order that a family might not die out, or even to cement political alliances between powerful families.

In ancient Greece, the earliest known law regulating adoption dates from 594 BC and includes reference to inheritance and relationships within the adopting family. Under Roman law, the position of the adopted person was carefully secured and the birth of subsequent legitimate children did not deprive the adopted child of his rights. The adopted sons of Roman Emperors even inherited their fathers' empire. Both Greek and Roman laws were adult-centred and Roman Law concerning adoption influenced the Napoleonic Civil Code. Thus the idea that the purpose of adoption was to provide an heir was perpetuated.

The second period

The second stage in the evolution of adoption in most of the United States and Great Britain begins with the idea of providing some security for orphaned and 'illegitimate' children. There was no common law concerning adoption, and legislation developed somewhat differently in Great Britain and the United States, as each country responded to different needs. In both countries in the nineteenth century there was a tradition of care for dependent children in institutions (often a poorhouse or almshouse) during the children's early years. Children were then indentured to the families in which it was intended that they be fed and clothed, educated and taught a trade, in return for their work on behalf of the family. Indenture was one of the principal ways in which orphanages placed children in families, a custom which may have delayed the development of adoption law (Kadushin and Martin, 1988).

However, in the United States and in Britain both the indenture system and almshouses/workhouses were, by the mid-nineteenth century, becoming overwhelmed by the numbers of destitute children needing care and education. Revelations from Dorothea Dix's 1844 inspection of almshouses about the condition of the children in these institutions, and concern about the health and welfare of children in crowded city slums in the United States, led to demands for better care for children. These demands coincided with the religious revivalism of the second part of the nineteenth century, which led to the opening, by different denominational groups and individual philanthropists, such as Dr Barnardo, of many big orphanages and institutions for the care of children. However, these institutions had serious problems with infant mortality and increasingly attempts were made to place children with families.

At about the same time a movement to board out children from urban regions into family foster homes in rural areas was inaugurated by some Scottish parishes and by Charles Loring Brace in the States. The agricultural homes of the American West could use the labour of large families and placements were free, whilst Scottish crofters welcomed the small allowance paid, which helped to supplement their meagre incomes. These foster homes were regarded as substitutes for the birth family, and in at least some a situation similar to an adoption evolved (McCausland, 1976; Triseliotis, Sellick and Short, 1995). In the absence of an adoption law, these adoptions were legalized in the United States through specific acts of legislature, a custom which became quite common during the nineteenth century (Witmer, 1963). In Britain they remained *de facto* adoptions with no legal security. Adopted children were expected to work hard, behave well and be grateful to the adopters.

The legal provision for adoption which occurred in the middle of the nineteenth century in most of the United States regularized an existing practice. The adoption statute passed in Massachusetts in 1851 became the model for subsequent adoption legislation, and provided for:

1. The written consent of the child's biological parent
2. Joint petition by both the adoptive mother and father

3. A decree by the judge, who had to be satisfied that the adoption was 'fit and proper', and

4. Legal and complete severance of the relationship between child and biological parents (Kadushin and Martin, 1988, p. 535).

Adoption seems to have been more acceptable in the frontier society of the United States than in the more stratified British society, where the first adoption law was not passed in England until 1926. The main reasons for this delay were:

- the stigma attached to non-marital births and fears that adopted children might inherit traits, including 'immorality' and 'bad habits', an attitude that limited adoption, before about 1945, mainly to the working class;
- the British courts' close guarding of the rights of parents;
- the reluctance to see inheritance passed on to 'outsiders'; and
- the maintenance of class lines based on kinship (Costin, Bell and Downs, 1991; Triseliotis, 1995).

The problems of increased 'illegitimacy' and large-scale orphanhood resulting from World War I, along with many custody disputes in cases of de facto adoption, gave the main impetus to the passage of the 1926 Adoption Act in England. The law regulated adoption, providing that it must be a judicial procedure and that the adoption order, once made, was irrevocable. This first British adoption law preserved the adopted child's right to inherit from the natural family, but specified that the adoptive family must make specific provision if the child was to inherit from them. As in the United States, the Parliamentary debates in Great Britain emphasized the need for judicial supervision over adoption for the protection of the child (Abbott, 1938). During the period between the two world wars, a number of societies were set up to arrange adoptions. In fact there was so much concern about their operation that a committee was set up to examine their operations (Horsbrugh, 1937).

In the United States, in the years between the two world wars, infant adoptions began to gain in popularity. Major factors behind the new interest were the drop in the birth rate that followed World War I and the influenza epidemic of 1918, the development of artificial feeding for infants, which made infant adoption possible, and the growing perception that environment was as important as heredity in shaping a child's personality (Sokoloff, 1993). The first agencies in the United States dedicated solely to adoption were founded during this period. These years also saw the enactment of adoption legislation in the remainder of the states, so that by 1929 all states had adoption legislation. These laws varied in provision, but continued to focus on the welfare of the child. Between 1923 and 1933 increasing numbers of regulations requiring investigations of prospective adoptive homes and trial periods in adoptive homes were written. Provision that records of adoptions be sealed and that a new birth certificate be issued for the child were designed to protect the child from the stigma of illegitimacy, as well as to make sure that the adoptive family was protected from 'interference' by the birth family. The Child Welfare League of America published its first 'Standards for Adoptive Services' in 1938.

The third period

The period following World War II marks a third stage, during which adoption was viewed as a solution to the problem of infertility and became popular among the middle classes of both Britain and the United States. Although this was a period when nurture was supposed to rule over nature, this optimism was not reflected in the practices of adoption agencies in the way they selected children for placement. This came to be known as the era of the 'perfect baby' for the 'perfect couple'. Great effort was put into matching infant and parents, in an attempt to create a family as 'like' a biological one as possible. An 'adoptable' infant was, generally speaking, white, healthy, with an acceptable background and developing normally (or at an above average pace).

Adoptive couples were subjected to intensive investigations, guided in large part by the formulations of psychoanalytic theory, particularly in the USA, in order to assess their capacity as parents. As the number of adoptive applicants began to exceed the number of infants available, the definition of the 'perfect' couple became increasingly restrictive, with narrow limits of age, specifications as to the length of marriage and residence in a community and demands for comfortable income and housing. Generally, the religion of the adopting family had to match that of the infant.

Bowlby's (1951) theories on maternal deprivation and bonding, which suggested that children separated from their parents after about the age of two would fail to attach themselves to adoptive parents, proved very influential. These writings were used, along with the Horsbrugh Report's (1937) recommendations, to justify the concentration of adoption practice on 'healthy' infants from selected back-grounds. By the late 1960s almost three-quarters of the children adopted by non-relatives in Britain and in North America were under 1 year old. Those who were older or who had even a minor disability were not even considered and were likely to be raised in residential nurseries. The characteristic feature of this period was 'a child for a home' which meant that practice was more interested in the needs of those adopting rather than in the interests of the children.

It was during this period that adoption was also recognized as a field that required specialized worker training. Social work agencies saw these services as their responsibility. In Britain this remained predominantly a voluntary sector activity until the passing of the 1975 Children Act, when most of the initiative passed into the hands of local authority social services (work) departments.

During this time of infant adoptions, it was assumed that after the legal completion of the adoption the family was 'just like any other family'. It was not expected that any further services would be needed. Based on a somewhat limited set of criteria, follow-up studies showed that the children in these adoptive homes did well, and that parents were satisfied. The cost to the community was minimal. Adoption gained popularity and respectability.

The fourth period

This period is associated with a decisive shift towards a more child-centred adoption practice. From about the mid-1960s onward in the United States and early 1970s in Britain, there has been a drastic drop in the number of young white children available for adoption. In part this can be explained by the use of new and more effective contraceptive methods, and the legalization of abortion. In part it is the result of changing sexual mores and society's increasing accep-tance of the single parent raising a child, and the increasing availability of state welfare benefits to make this possible. Demographic changes resulting in a smaller number of women of childbearing age also play a part.

As fewer infants were released for adoption, many adoption agen-cies, overwhelmed with large numbers of adoptive applicants, closed their waiting lists to those seeking a healthy white infant. Childless couples wishing to create or increase their family looked for new ways of achieving this. Many adoption societies which had concen-trated on the placement of healthy white infants closed and their records were transferred to social services departments. Social services and the remaining voluntary agencies began to expand their concept of the 'adoptable child' and who could adopt.

During the 1960s and 1970s, studies revealed that in Britain and the United States there were thousands of children who were in institutions or in unstable fostering arrangements without realistic prospects of returning to their own families. These were not the children traditionally seen as suitable for adoption, but older children, sometimes with mental or physical disabilities, children of mixed race, or groups of siblings who could benefit from the advantages of family life. Many of the children came from backgrounds of abuse and neglect. The children's families of origin had in most cases either disappeared, felt the system discouraged them from maintaining links, or were unable to make a home for them but were unwilling to relinquish them for adoption. The children were characterized as 'drifting' in residential homes and foster homes, and children's advocates mounted pressure for agencies to plan for them (Rowe and Lambert, 1973; Knitzer, Allen and McGowan, 1978). These came to be known as 'special needs' children or 'hard to place' children, or 'children who wait'. Moving children from the care system into adoptive homes proved also an attractive option to social services departments who otherwise faced many years of funding residential or foster care placements.

In both Britain and the United States, numerous projects demonstrated that, with imaginative recruitment methods, adoptive homes could be found for these waiting children, and that these adoptions could work. The search now was for 'a home for a child' moving adoption towards a much more child-centred approach. This shift was greatly helped by studies showing how well older children placed for adoption could be doing (Kadushin, 1970; Tizard, 1977; Triseliotis and Russell, 1984) and the work of Goldstein, Freud and Solnit (1973) on the reality of psychological parenting. As agencies have had success, children with increasingly severe disabilities and emotional difficulties have been placed for adoption, and adoptive homes were found for adolescents. Sibling groups were also placed. Unlike a few years earlier, an adoptable child was now defined as 'any child who can benefit from family life'. Some added 'and for whom a home can be found', but this clause restricts the definition and may provide an excuse for the presence of children without permanent homes in the child welfare systems. Transracial adoption was one of the options developed to meet the needs of children in public care, an issue that will be explored in the chapter on transracial adoption.

As a result of this work, not only was the concept of the adoptable child expanded, but the definition of the family suitable to adopt was enlarged to include families of a variety of class and economic backgrounds, those who had experienced divorce, single parents, foster parents, older parents and those with children. The special needs of some of the children needing homes stretched the economic capacity of many families who would otherwise adopt, and some families who were interested in 'hard' to place children did not have the resources to add a child to the family. To facilitate these adoptions, a system of adoption subsidies, or adoption allowances, from public money developed first in the United States, and then in Great Britain. Forced to focus on those capacities which would predict successful parenting of difficult children, adoption agencies dropped arbitrary requirements.

The fifth period

As a result of developments such as those outlined above, the fourth period in the evolution of adoption came to be seen as a more child-centred one. The belief then was, and continues to be for many professionals in this field, that every child is entitled to a permanent home. If for some reason, his own family cannot be rehabilitated, an adoptive one should be considered instead as one of the options. Permanent foster care does not provide the legality and full security of adoption, but may be right for some children. We see a fifth period emerging, which is evident, for example, in aspects of inter-country adoption and in recent attempts to de-regulate adoption in Britain, to allow 'market forces' to play a greater role, as in the United States. Additionally, the emphasis in recent British legislation and in the family preservation movement in the United States on rehabilitation of families (discussed in Chapter 3) and some of the provisions of the Children Act 1989 may lead to unacceptable delays in providing some children with new families.

In the USA independent adoptions in which a lawyer or doctor acts as intermediary, or in which birth parents and adoptive parents reach an agreement on their own, are legal in all but six states and have become increasingly important as a source of white infants (such arrangements are illegal in Britain). A broadly similar approach is followed in intercountry adoption, a process that is almost wholly adult-centred. According to the American National Association of Social Workers (quoted by Davis, 1995), the emphasis in adoption is shifting towards the rights of adults to adopt and away from requiring that services be provided by licensed professionals and approved agencies. The results are 'high fees, competitive business practices, clinical services of declining quality, litigation, distrust, and a sense of uneasiness' (Davis, 1995, p. 26).

THE LEGAL FRAMEWORK

Though the laws governing adoption differ between the United States and Great Britain, the legal framework is similar. In both countries, adoption statutes stem from a common law tradition, and there has been a history of fairly constant communication among those working in adoption in the two countries. Differences are the product of different social systems, different populations and different needs of the two societies, which have led to different court decisions and thence to different legislation. Certain common principles, though, govern adoption in both countries:

1. Adoption is a suitable alternative only for the child whose birth family is unwilling or unable to care for him or her. The consent of the birth parents to adoption must be obtained, or a judicial termination of parental rights must be made, so that the child is legally free for adoption. Birth fathers, as well as birth mothers, must consent to the adoption under certain conditions. Scotland and many states specify that when a child is above a certain age, the child must consent to the adoption. English law is moving toward this requirement.

2. For the protection of the child, there should be a social study of the prospective adoptive home. British law accomplishes this through limiting the arranging of adoptive placements to approved public adoption agencies. In the United States, both public and licensed private adoption agencies make adoptive placements. However, all but six states also allow placements made directly by the birth parent, or through an intermediary. In these independent adoptions, the court will insist on a study of the home by a licensed agency before the adoption is allowed.

3. In both countries, a child must be in the new adoptive home for a period of time, usually three months to one year: though there is no maximum, the minimum is three months before the adoption becomes final. During this time, the placing agency has a responsibility to visit to assure the

child's well-being, and to provide support to the new adoptive family. The court is empowered to remove a child from the home of adoptive petitioners, if this is found to be in the child's best interest. Adopters in Great Britain can apply for a serial number to protect their identity.

4. Provisions in the law of both countries assure confidentiality of the adoption proceedings but in Britain, unlike in the United States, adoptees can have access to their original records on reaching the age of 18. In both countries, an amended birth certificate, showing only the child's adoptive name and the names of his adoptive parents, will be issued. This birth certificate can be used for all legal purposes.

5. In Great Britain, adoption confers citizenship and for this reason there are requirements about domicile and residence which must be complied with. In the United States, conferring of citizenship is a separate procedure. This is important in international adoptions.

6. When the adoption decree is final, the child and his adoptive parents attain all the rights and responsibilities that exist between a child and his birth parents.

Member countries of the UK have their own adoption legislation, with the exception of Wales which has a common law with England, but their respective laws usually flow from a single national policy. In the US, each of the 50 states has its own law governing adoption, but there is a body of federal legislation which provides the framework for adoption services. There have been continued efforts to achieve more uniform adoption laws, but none has succeeded. However, all states have joined the Interstate Compact on the Placement of Children to facilitate the placement of children across state lines. Nearly all states have adopted procedures for the disclosure of identities to adult adoptees and birth parents, with consent, but these procedures vary by state.

The procedure of adoption is regulated to a much greater extent in Great Britain than in the United States. These regulations give a structure to the process of adoption which assures considerable uniformity. More important, adoption takes place completely within the framework of an agency service, including the assessment of step-parent adoptions. Another unique feature of the British adoption regulations is the use of adoption panels, required in all adoption agencies. These panels are responsible for making recommendations as to whether:

adoption is in the best interests of the child, whether a prospective adopter is suitable to be an adoptive parent, and whether a prospective adopter would be a suitable adoptive parent for a particular child. (Department of Health and Welsh Office, 1992)

The panels are composed of between seven and ten members and include a medical advisor and at least two persons 'independent of the agency'. Their work serves as a review of the work of the social workers. The composition of the panel ensures that varied perspectives will be brought to the issues of adoption, and the panel can become an important force in development of adoption policy. The expected Adoption Bill is likely to be more specific about who sits on these panels and their role and duties.

THEORETICAL FRAMEWORK

The main rationale for adoption, as presently conceived, is that it will promote the welfare of the child. Whilst it operates within a legal framework, much of the influence on its practice has also come from studies in child development. Over the last half century many studies have contributed to the theory of child development and how children's interests can best be safeguarded and promoted. Knowledge from these studies has influenced childcare policy and practice in general, including that of adoption. Much of this knowledge refers to the child's need for continuity of care, security and a sense of belonging to enable him or her to grow into a productive and healthy individual.

In spite of its many imperfections and despite the increase of divorce and separation, in our kind of society the family or stable households are the place where much needed continuity and relative stability in the life of a child can be provided (Triseliotis, 1993a). When the family into which a child is born cannot provide care, adoption is possibly the best available alternative. Bowlby's early work (1951) and Bowlby *et al.* (1956), emphasizing the serious damage which a young child can sustain through separation from the main caregiver(s), had significant influence on all childcare work, including that of adoption theory and practice. His warnings, though, that psychological damage occurring during the early years was largely irreversible were modified by the experience of the 1970s.

It was not until the early 1970s that the emphasis in adoption shifted towards the placement of older children who needed permanent homes. One reason, among others, for this shift, was research showing favourable outcomes for children adopted when older. These studies were beginning to show that, contrary to Bowlby's (1951) pessimistic view, many older children could recover from early trauma and could make secure attachments within adoptive families (Kadushin, 1970; Tizard, 1977; Triseliotis and Russell, 1984). These and other studies, for example that of Clarke and Clarke (1976), forced the re-evaluation of many of the psychoanalytic theories which suggested that basic personality patterns were laid down in very early years, and opened the way to theories based more on current functioning and coping patterns.

A further theoretical development resulted from the work of Kirk (1964). Kirk took the results of his series of studies of adoptive families and presented the data within the framework of sociological role theory. His conclusion was that, by denying the fact of adoption and pretending to be 'just like' all families, the adoptive family created for itself a series of role handicaps which led to difficulties. For the first time, the challenges and dilemmas which an adoptive family faces were outlined. The theory suggested that 'acknowledgement of differences' (from the biologically formed family) would be 'conducive to good communication and thus to order and dynamic stability in adoptive families' (p. 99).

Another strand of theory which has had its impact on adoption practice in the last quarter of a century is the increasing recognition of kinship networks, biological identity, and the importance of 'roots' in identity formation. Though clinical observations and McWhinnie's (1967) study had alerted us to these important facts earlier, studies carried out by Triseliotis (1973; 1984), Haimes and Timms (1985), Brodzinsky (1984) and Tizard and Phoenix (1993) pinpointed more precisely the importance of origins and roots and highlighted their contribution to identity formation. Like Kirk's theory concerning the 'acknowledgement' of difference by adoptive parents, based on our studies, we would like to suggest that the resolution of identity issues in the adopted person relies, amongst other things, on the acknowledgement, rather than denial, of his/her biological roots and heritage, including race and ethnicity.

Further weight has been given to this important aspect of adoption work by counselling adopted adults searching for personal information and/or seeking members of their birth families.

The highlighting of the importance of roots, origins and identity raised also consequent issues of loss, rejection, grief and of resultant stress as part of any adoption (Triseliotis, 1973; Bourguignon and

Watson, 1987; Brodzinsky, Schecter and Henig, 1992). These developments have provided us with a unique long-term insight into the circumstances and feelings of many adopted people and have helped us to piece together a beginning psychology of adoption which is outlined as part of the next chapter.

THE CURRENT STATISTICS OF ADOPTION

Statistics on adoption are centrally collected in Great Britain and centrally reported. However, the absence of detail in the published statistics of recent years makes them of little value. In the United States, there have been no nationally collected adoption statistics since 1975. Nevertheless, sufficient data are available to identify broad trends, and to make broad comparisons between the United States and Great Britain. In both countries, the number of adoptions has been declining in the last quarter of a century.

In Britain, in 1968, around 27,500 children were adopted. By 1977 the number fell to around 15,000 and in 1991 it stood at around 8000, with around half of these being step-parent adoptions (Department of Health, 1993; Registrar General for Scotland, 1992). It is assumed that adoption numbers may have now stabilized.

In the United States, the number of adoptions peaked in 1970, when there were 175,000 adoptions (Stolley, 1993, p. 29). In 1990 there were only 118,779 adoptions (Flango and Flango, 1994, p. 317). As in Britain, about half of these adoptions were relative adoptions, most commonly by step-parents (Stolley, 1993; Department of Health, 1993; Registrar General for Scotland, 1992).

The number of adoptions of infants and very young children has, in both countries, become a smaller proportion of the total. In England and Wales only 12 per cent of adoptions in 1991 were adoptions of children under 1 year of age compared to around 75 per cent in 1968 and 23 per cent in 1977 (Department of Health, 1993). The most recent data available in the United States on this dimension were collected in 1986. In that year about a quarter of adopted children were under 2 at the time the adoption was finalized (National Committee for Adoption, 1989). It is probable that the proportion has declined in subsequent years. The trend in the two countries is similar. About a third of the unrelated adoptions in the United States are those of 'special needs' children (National Committee for Adoption, 1989). In both countries a significant number of these adoptions will be made with a subsidy, or adoption allowance, to help the adoptive family with the extra expenses of the adopted child.

SOME OTHER CURRENT ISSUES

Adoption has changed and evolved over the years, reflecting the changes in the society which it serves, and new empirical knowledge and new theory. The scarcity of infants available for adoption resulted in a shift toward the placement for adoption of older children with 'special needs' and in increased interest in international adoptions. These developments, in addition to new theory about the adoptive family and the adopted person, have encouraged the development of post-adoption services to support the adoptive family and other members of the adoption triangle. Other issues in current adoption practice concern the auspices under which adoption takes place, the rights of parents and children in contested cases, and the 'open' or 'closed' structure of adoption.

Older children placed in adoptive homes bring with them a 'baggage' of memories and adaptive responses learned in the families which were, in the end, unable to care for them. As child welfare services have, in recent years, increasingly emphasized rehabilitation of birth families, the children who are eventually released for adoption have tended to come from more disturbed homes and to have had increasingly difficult experiences within the public care system, compounding their initial difficulties. As a result it has been necessary for agencies to provide continuing support services to their adoptive families in order to maintain the adoption. There is recognition that these adoptions present both family and child with additional challenges and that agency services may be needed for many years.

The structure of adoptive families gives rise to other current issues. Children are adopted by single parents, both men and women, though most agencies give preference to married couples. Gay and lesbian couples are beginning to be able to adopt openly in a few places and this will probably become more common. Increasingly, foster parents adopt the children for whom they have cared and with whom a mutual attachment has formed.

Another dimension, important to the process of adoption, is the degree of involvement which birth parents and adoptive parents have with each other. Historically, adoptions have been 'closed', with the adoptive family and birth family not knowing each other's identity. This secrecy was then thought to protect the integrity of the adoption. Open adoptions range the continuum from the sharing of information and the exchange of a few pictures as the child grows, to adoptions in which the birth parent and family become a part of the family life of the adoptive family.

We know perhaps least about the characteristics of the birth parents for whom adoption planning is most appropriate, but we are beginning to learn more about the continuing struggles, anxieties and sometimes grief which may follow this decision, and the kind of help which is needed for some. Adoption planning may continue to be a solution for the birth parents who do not have sufficient family and community support to successfully raise the child themselves. But the dimensions of this support, and the ways in which it is best provided, are being worked out in the daily process of the delivery of child welfare services, not always successfully.

CONCLUDING REMARKS

This chapter has been introductory, presenting many issues in broad outline and raising some important questions of current adoption practice. All of the changes described create controversy, and they will be taken up one by one and explored at greater length in the chapters that follow. It is the hope of the authors that the resultant book will provide the adoption practitioner with ideas about how to best accomplish the goals of practice, and will also provide understanding of why these methods are effective. It is our hope, too, that the book will provide a source of information and understanding for those scholars and researchers in adoption who wish to approach the subject from the perspective of the daily practice of adoption.

Five key points

1. Adoption is a suitable alternative only for the child whose birth family is unwilling or unable to care for him or her. Its practice should be based on what is known to be good for the long-term welfare of children. The increasing de-regulation of adoption poses a threat to the child's long-term welfare.
2. Adoption takes place within a legal and theoretical framework, influenced by community values and by research.

3. In the United States and Britain there has been a concerted effort over the past quarter of a century to place older children, those with disabilities or handicaps and sibling groups; most agency based adoption is now adoption of older children.
4. In both the United States and Britain political, moral, policy and empirical arguments are put forward either to support or to refute transracial and intercountry adoption.
5. Compared to the past, adoption is now being practised with much greater openness and it is recognized that an adopted child's genetic heritage must be acknowledged and fostered by the adopting family.

CHAPTER 2
Outcome studies

Adoption is one solution that has developed to meet the needs of children who cannot grow up with their birth families. The legal protection which surrounds adoption guarantees the adopted person the same permanency which the child has in the family of his/her birth. Besides permanency, adoption offers committed parents prepared to nurture, guide and protect. By being such a unique human experience, adoption has attracted the attention of many diverse groups of researchers keen to study its various manifestations from their discipline's perspective. Insights from psychology, psychiatry, medicine, law, sociology, anthropology, social policy and social work have all contributed to the better understanding of various aspects of the adoption process and its outcome. A key question asked by many studies is 'How successful a solution is this form of psychological parenting to the care of children?' Some of the themes covered by research have included: the organizational context; the placement process; issues of adjustment and outcomes for all parties; the effects on the family of origin; the experience of adoption; who can successfully adopt and who can successfully be adopted; the relative influence of heredity and environment; the importance of early adverse childhood experiences on later development; the disclosure of adoption; and the concept of origins and identity formation.

All studies involving human beings are complex and difficult to carry out. For example, it is difficult to provide for controls to ensure that like is compared with like. Equally problematic is the identification of outcome criteria and of suitable measuring tools. Knapp (1989) has defined outcomes as the effects of a process (for example receiving a service, in this case adoption) which can be attributed to the process. Some child welfare studies concentrate on what are seen as intermediate outcomes (for example, when the children are 5, 11 or 15), whilst others may follow the children into early adulthood. Their main aim usually is to establish the adoptees' quality of life based on a number of dimensions such as adjustment, health, education, employment, behaviours, identity and self-esteem and contrast them, where possible, with that of the general population. There is then an effort to relate these outcomes to the decisions made five, ten or even twenty years ago and identify which decisions contributed to positive or negative outcomes. In practice this is much more difficult than it may appear.

Questions of definition and measurement can be asked about all outcome studies that aim to establish such intangibles as adjustment, identity, self-esteem and sense of security and well-being. All the methodological approaches used by different researchers – including interviews, standardized tests, self-rating questionnaires and self-reporting have their strengths and weaknesses. No research can be free of value biases and adoption studies are no exception. Prevailing psychological and sociological theories, government policies and funding sources can all exert their influence. In addition, prejudices and biases can enter research at all stages, including when the problem is being identified and defined, in the design of the study, during the data collection and in the analysis and interpretation of the data. To compound the problem, some studies are based on clinical, volunteer or self-identification populations, or experience such big sample losses that comparisons are not often possible.

Furthermore, different researchers have studied adopted children at different ages and stages, with some basing their judgements on reports solely by parents or by parents and teachers, sometimes in association with a range of 'objective' tests. Only more recently have researchers started asking adoptees about their personal experiences and thoughts on the subject. Retrospective studies of adult adoptees, though, have their own limitations as it is often difficult to separate problems of outcome that are related to adoption from the rest of life's experiences, which may be unconnected. Because of all these difficulties, caution is always required when quoting from or contrasting research studies. Nevertheless when a number of studies are agreed, and there are by now a number of areas in which adoption research has been replicated many times over, then confidence in the findings is increased.

Because of the importance of age as an outcome variable in adoption, this chapter discusses first the outcome of early placement adoption before it moves on to examine that of older children. In the case of older children special reference will be made to the so-called 'permanency movement' which was concerned with the placement of children with 'special needs'. The chapter ends by examining the contribution made by studies to the emerging psychology of adoption.

THE ADOPTION OF YOUNG CHILDREN

There is no shortage of studies of early adoption and only selective reference will be made to them here. A summary of a number of American follow-up studies covering a total of 2236 adoptions found that success rates, as defined by each study, varied from 74 to 85 per cent, depending on whether one included the fairly successful in the success group (Kadushin, 1970). Family members rated retrospectively about 85 per cent of adoptions as 'successful'. Some 15 per cent were definitely unsuccessful, which is about the same as with children growing up in their own families. In an up-date, Kadushin and Martin (1988) provided another comprehensive review of studies in tabular form, concentrating this time on disruptions. They reported an infant adoption disruption of 1.87 per cent and a disruption rate for 'special needs' children of 11.3 per cent. As we shall see later, when it comes to special needs children, averages do not reveal the full picture.

Based on Kadushin's review referred to above, Brodzinsky, Schechter and Henig (1992) concluded that 'the vast majority of adoptees do perfectly well in all of the ways that society measures success' (p. 9). The writers add that adoptees do well in such areas as the process of growing up, marrying, having children, relating to their friends and their adoptive families, holding down jobs, having hobbies and having good and bad moments. In subsequent writings Brodzinsky (1993) also concluded that studies focusing on the under-5s have not found differences between adopted and non-adopted children in temperament, mental and motor functioning, communication development and mother–infant attachment. Only a minority of adoptees, in his view, present evidence of 'clinically significant symptomatology'.

Bohman's (1970) and Bohman and Sigvardsson's (1980 and 1990) prospective longitudinal studies of 168 adopted infants in Sweden provide possibly the most consistent and interesting findings. This is one of the best documented studies of its kind, along with the British National Child Development (NCD) one to be referred to later. The children in the Swedish study were assessed at ages 11, 15 and 18 and compared at each stage with controls. At the age of 11, interviews with teachers showed that the adopted boys displayed a higher rate of nervous and behavioural disturbances compared to the control children in their classrooms. Twenty-two per cent of the adopted children were classified as problem children, compared to 12 per cent among their class controls. There were, however, very few among either the adoptees or the controls who could be classified as presenting conduct disorders in comparison with the children who were reared by their mothers or who were fostered. Four years later at the age of 15, the differences between adopted children and their classmates were further diminished. There was a slight tendency for the adopted children to have lower scores for adjustment and lower school grades, but these differences were very small and only occasionally significant. By age 18, though, the few problems presented by the adopted group disappeared when compared to the rest of the class and they were doing better than the other two groups. Thus, their early placement for adoption appeared to have been a good solution for this group of children.

The British NCD study covering children born in one week in 1958, some of whom were adopted, has yielded some very useful material (Seglow, Pringle and Wedge, 1972). The children were studied at ages 7 and 11. At the age of 7 adopted children were generally as good, or slightly better in abilities, educational attainments and social adjustment than other children, and significantly better than children who had been born 'illegitimate' but had not been adopted. As far as social adjustment at school and home was concerned, the adopted children gave some indication of showing similar behaviour difficulties as the children born and kept by unmarried women. By the age of 11, adopted children were significantly better at reading than other children, they were doing as well in maths, and their social adjustment was not worse. Much of the benefit was attributed by the study to the exceptionally favourable circumstances in which the adopted children were living. Compared, however, to age 7 the adopted children's adjustment at age 11 had deteriorated somewhat. A follow-up report when the children were aged 16 showed that their adjustment and achievements had in fact improved, although these still lagged slightly below those of their non-adopted classmates.

A number of other studies confirm the NCD's findings that problems in adoption arise mostly between the primary school years and in adolescence (Brodzinsky, Schechter and Henig, 1992). These problems are summarized as low self-esteem, academic problems and 'acting out' behaviour such as aggression, stealing, lying, hyperactivity, argumentativeness and running away. This conclusion led Kirschner (1980) to put forward the idea of an 'adopted child syndrome' being present but Brodzinsky, Schechter and Henig (1992) comment that few professionals would give credence to such a syndrome: a reminder again of Bohman's (1970) and Bohman and

Sigvardsson's (1980 and 1990) studies, which, whilst noting more problems amongst adoptees at age 11, showed that these apparently were transient and disappeared by the time the children reached their late teens and early twenties.

Raynor (1980) in her British study talked to adoptees who were placed when mostly less than 1 year old and who were 21 and over at interview. The study also obtained separately the views of both the adopters. She found that overall, 86 per cent of the parents rated the experience of adoption as very satisfactory or reasonably satisfactory, leaving only 14 per cent definitely dissatisfied. Among the adoptees, 70 per cent were found to be making good or excellent life adjustment as adults, and 30 per cent were either poorly adjusted or very much at risk. Though some of the adoptees displayed a range of emotional and behavioural problems during childhood, by adulthood behaviours such as criminality or psychological disturbance were no higher than the average among the rest of the population.

Stein and Hoopes (1985), in a study which contrasted adopted with non-adopted adolescents, did not find evidence to sustain the view that those adopted would have greater difficulty with the tasks of adolescence. Adopted adolescents were also found to score higher than children of single parents on self-esteem, confidence in their own judgement, self-directedness, positive view of others, and feelings of security within their families (Marquis and Detweiler, 1985). Benson, Sharma and Roehlkepartain (1994) claim from a study of 881 adopted adolescents and 1262 adoptive parents that children who were adopted fared as well as or better than a national sample of non-adopted adolescents, in self-esteem, mental health and school achievement. In answer to the statement that 'there is a lot of love in my family' 78 per cent of adopted adolescents agreed, compared with only 70 per cent of the national sample. In answer to another statement that 'my parents attend meetings or events at my school', 52 per cent of adoptees but only 36 per cent of the national sample agreed.

TRANSMISSION OF BEHAVIOUR DISORDERS

A question which is often asked relates to the extent to which aspects of behaviour, handicaps or difficulties are transmitted from one generation to the next and the processes involved. In other words, whether such processes, where they operate, are genetically or environmentally transmitted. Some studies have examined behaviours, such as crime and alcohol abuse, by contrasting adopted with non-adopted people. As an example, Crowe (1972) and Hutchings and Mednick (1974) claimed to have found a significant correlation between criminality among adoptees and their biological parents. In the researchers' view, as the children had been adopted very young this could only suggest a genetic transmission. Yet Bohman (1978) found no such relationship from his longitudinal study, as adoptees born to biological parents registered for criminality were not recorded more often for criminality than adopted controls with a non-criminal heritage.

Other studies, which looked at possible links between alcoholism and genetic transmissions, found alcohol abuse among adoptees and similar behaviour in the biological families (Goodwin et al., 1973; Cadoret and Garth, 1978; Bohman, 1978). Bohman and Sigvardsson (1990), however, point out that in regard to both criminality and alcohol abuse among the biological parents 'the conclusion is warranted that adoption largely reduced the risk of social incompetence and maladjustment' (pp. 104–5). In fact, by age 23, no differences were found when adoptees were compared with control groups.

A number of studies have also tried to identify possible gender differences in the display of behaviours. For example, one study suggested that boys adopted early are likely to display significantly more behaviour problems in adolescence than other boys or adopted girls, but not if they came from 'stable adoptive homes' (Cadoret and Garth, 1978). This may not be surprising as there is considerable agreement in the general literature on delinquency that aggressive and delinquent behaviour is more common in males, while girls react to loss and stress by more internalizing behaviours.

TRANSMISSION OF PSYCHIATRIC DISTURBANCE

Another question often examined is whether adopted people are over-represented amongst those seeking psychiatric help. Though clinical studies suggest that adoptees display a disproportionate rate of psychological problems when compared with non-adopted people, Brodzinsky (1993), like others, urges caution. He suggests that the findings may reflect, in part, differential patterns of referral and differential use of psychological and psychiatric facilities by adoptive parents, as opposed to increased rates of disturbance. As an example, Warren (1992) found that the same behaviour was viewed as more problematic when manifested by adopted that non-adopted children.

Psychiatric disturbance and its possible genetic transmission has mostly been examined in relation to schizophrenic illness. The best known studies involving identical twins have been carried out in Scandinavia by Kety *et al.* (1968) and Rosenthal and Seymour (1968). These and other studies tend to show that psychological disturbances are transmitted to adopted children from biological parents (Kendler, Gruenberg and Strauss, 1982; Cadoret, 1990; Tienari, 1991). Tienari (1991) contrasted children of schizophrenic women in Finland who were adopted by non-relatives before the age of 4 with children of non-schizophrenic women who were also adopted by non-relatives. Of the 15 psychotic adoptees in the total sample at the time of the study, 13 were offspring of schizophrenic women and only two of control offspring. Tienari concluded, in addition, that 'being reared in a healthy family may also be a protective factor for a child at risk' (p. 465).

However, Marshall (1990) calls into question the findings of these studies and concludes that careful examination of the genetic evidence suggests that the methodologies, statistics and inferences employed in the research fall short of what should be required in a matter of such importance. He acknowledges that inherited factors are relevant but questions the degree of linkage between genetics and schizophrenia and believes that the tendency to emphasize the high genetic contribution is unwarranted. Assarnow's (1988) evaluation of high risk studies, which considered social and environmental factors in addition to genetic ones, lends support to Marshall's studies.

All the studies that claim a strong genetic link operating in schizophrenia are at pains to indicate that the development of these conditions in the offspring is not inevitable. Bagley, Young and Scully (1993) illustrate this point by quoting from Lowing, Mirsky and Pereira (1983) who say that the incidence of schizophrenia in the general population is about 1 per cent; in an adopted child of a schizophrenic parent it is about 3 per cent; but in a child reared by a schizophrenic biological parent it is 10 per cent. Like others before them, the writers conclude that 'adoption greatly diminishes the risk of developing schizophrenia in an individual with some genetic proneness for the disease' (p. 46).

In Clarke's (1981, p. 28) view, because adoptive families are selected and prepared, they are offering 'better than average opportunities for their children and almost certainly mitigating to an unknown extent risks which otherwise result in children becoming deviant in one way or another'. Triseliotis and Russell (1984), too, concluded from their study that even in situations where genetic factors might be at play, it did not follow that familial disorders would find expression. After all, genetic theory predicts parent–offspring differences as well as resemblances. Subsequent social stresses and the quality of care may determine to a large extent whether the resemblances will dominate or not.

EARLY ADOPTION AND INTELLECTUAL ABILITY

As with the debate surrounding the possible genetic transmission of behaviours, studies on the relative influence of heredity and environment on cognitive and intellectual ability are not very precise. Munsinger (1975), who reviewed a number of studies, concluded that both heredity and environment play a part in influencing intellectual development. Clarke (1981) from her review of a number of studies puts the emphasis on hereditary factors as being a very significant cause of variation in IQ among adopted children, and therefore among children generally. In her view the IQs of children correlate with the birth parents' IQs or educational status rather than with that of their adoptive parents, despite selective placement.

Many studies suggest that favourable environmental influences can help develop the child's potential to the full and can improve IQ performance by up to 10 or 12 points (Capron and Duyme, 1989). Another French study by Schiff *et al.* (1978), which contrasted siblings who were adopted with those who stayed with their biological parents, found that in terms of school attainment the two groups were typical of their rearing environments. The children reared by their biological parents had an average IQ of 94.5 and those adopted 110.6. On another test, the IQs were 95.4 and 106.9. In an assessment of the Capron and Duyme study, McGue (1989) remarked that the work showed clearly that IQ is influenced by both biological background and the circumstances of rearing. Maughan and Pickles' (1990) British research, showed that children of disadvantaged parents adopted into middle-class homes had, by their early adult years, 'acquired cognitive and intellectual styles close to those of non-adopted, middle class children' (p. 41).

ADOPTION ADJUSTMENT AND THE CHARACTERISTICS OF THE ADOPTIVE PARENTS

As far as young children are concerned, characteristics of their parents such as age, religion, wealth and years after marriage before adopting have not been found to be relevant to how adoption works out (Triseliotis and Russell, 1984). Though it is too early yet to be definitive, adoption involving some form of contact between the birth and the adopting family does not appear to constitute a threat to the placement (McRoy, 1994). Placing siblings together not only does not constitute a threat to the placement of young children but on the contrary, other things being equal, can promote stability (Wedge and Mantle, 1990).

THE ADOPTION OF OLDER CHILDREN

In 1951 Bowlby published his seminal work on 'maternal deprivation and mental health' on behalf of the World Health Organisation, which was to prove a big landmark in our knowledge about the impact on children of separation and loss from people they are attached to, including their sense of loss and grieving. Both he and others also drew attention to the harmful effects of institutionalization, especially for young children. However, Bowlby went further than this to say that children who experienced such separations and deprivations in their early life would never recover from this trauma, especially if the experience was prolonged.

As we have seen in the introductory chapter, in the case of adoption Bowlby recommended that children should be placed before the age of about 2. Early placement, in his view, would make possible re-attachment to new carers, otherwise the children would not recover from the experience of separation and of other possible adversities. Subsequent studies were to show that whilst separations and deprivations are not good for children of any age, nevertheless children are resilient. Given an accepting and loving home, many have the capacity for recovery from adversities, unless these were too severe and prolonged. Clarke and Clarke's (1976) review of a number of case and research studies, all involving children who had been exposed to extreme deprivations and forms of institutionalization, supported this optimistic view. The authors concluded that:

> children have the potential for recovery from physical, emotional and social deprivations, provided that they are removed from the depriving environment and placed in a nurturing, caring and stimulating one.

At least three adoption studies, unconnected with the permanency movement, found that the great majority of children who had experienced separations and physical and emotional deprivations and who were adopted when older, were able to recover, displaying behaviours not different from the rest of the population (Kadushin, 1970; Tizard, 1977; Triseliotis and Russell, 1984). Tizard (1977) concluded that the subsequent development of the early institution-alized child depends upon the environment to which he is moved. In other words, a loving and stimulating environment will help the child to overcome previous negative experiences. Triseliotis and Russell (1984) added that the adoptees' current personal and social circumstances and adjustment demonstrated that positive adoptive parenting could help to reverse past adverse physical and emotional experiences. The earlier of these studies acted as an encouragement to adoption agencies to depart from previous policies and engage in the placement of older children and those with special needs.

Emerging research from intercountry adoption, to be discussed in Chapter 8, also supports the view that children, especially those placed when younger, and who have experienced physical, social, linguistic and emotional adversities in their earlier lives, have the potential for recovery provided they experience a new, loving and accepting environment. With children placed when over about the age of 8 or 9 achievements are more qualified. Studies of children adopted intercountry lends considerable support to these findings.

THE 'PERMANENCY MOVEMENT'

By the permanency movement we refer to the concerted efforts made in the USA and in Britain after about the mid-1970s to place older chil-dren, often with brothers and sisters, and those with physical or mental disabilities in adoptive homes. These children came to be known as 'special needs' children or 'hard to place'. They were usually placed in adoptive homes from residential establishments, having previously experienced many moves from one institution to another or from one family foster home to another. Overall they had experienced disrup-tions in their continuity of care, cumulative experiences of rejection and loss, insecurity and uncertainty. Many were displaying the effects of such instability through disturbed behaviours, low self-esteem or other psychological problems. Adoption workers in seeking new and permanent families for these children were very much influenced and encouraged by the studies quoted earlier, that is those demonstrating children's capacity to overcome, through positive parenting, psychological, social and medical adversities.

There are now a number of British and many American studies which have followed up such children after adoption, which will be quoted later on. They show on the whole that for 'special needs' children placed for adoption under about the age of 10, the disruption rate is around 10 per cent. However, after that there is an increase in breakdowns which is closely related to the children's older age. Beyond the age of about 9, the older the child the more likely it is that the adoptive arrangement will fail. The breakdown rate reaches sometimes 50 and 60 per cent with adolescents. Rosenthal (1993), who reviewed some similar and some different studies to the ones reviewed here, reaches a more optimistic view adding that taken on balance the 'disruption rate may be about 10% to 15% for children placed when older than 3 years'.

In Britain the overall disruption rate of special needs children has stabilized at around 25 per cent but considerable variations exist between adoption agencies. Older age, of course, is often accompanied by greater emotional and behavioural difficulties. There are obviously many risks involved in placing older children. Research has shown that what usually helps in placing special needs children is good preparation of the adopting family and the child, good matching between the child's needs and what the family has to offer and post-placement support to the adoptive parents and the child.

Most of the studies covering the placement of children with special needs have concentrated on establishing disruption rates after placement, and/or after a number of years following the granting of the adoption order, and then identifying factors in the child, the new parents or the agency contributing to breakdowns or stability. Obviously studies that focus on disruptions following adoption fail to take account of the number of children disrupting before an adoption order is made, resulting in more favourable outcomes.

American studies

Taking some key American studies first, Tremitiere (1984) reviewed around 2500 adoptions from 1979 to 1983 and found that 6 to 12-year-old children had a disruption rate of almost 10 per cent and 12 to 18-year-olds of 13.5 per cent. Boyne *et al.* (1984) identified a mean disruption rate of 23.2 per cent amongst 219 'special need' children with disruption rates of 9, 15, 25 and 47 per cent for age groups 0–5, 6-8, 9–11 and 12–17 respectively, thus showing the relationship between increased breakdown rates and increased age. A study by Barth and Berry (1988) which surveyed 900 children placed in the early 1980s again demonstrates the increased risk of breakdown with older age. Disruption for children aged 3 to 5 was 5 per cent, 6 to 8 years 10 per cent, 9 to 11 years 17 per cent, 12 to 14 years 22 per cent and 15 to 18 years 26 per cent. Kagan and Reid (1986) reported around 50 per cent adoption disruption of 'emotionally disturbed' teenagers and Nelson (1985) recorded that seven (or 28 per cent) out of 25 children placed when 8 years of age and over broke down within a year of the adoption order.

An important study by Rosenthal and Groze (1992), instead of looking at breakdown rates, reports findings from a longitudinal study of 302 predominantly 'special needs' children in intact families where the main aim was to assess change on several measures of adoption outcome. The mean age of the children at the first survey was 10.2 and at the second 13.5 years. The children's mean age at initial placement was almost 5 years old. They note that many of the children had been placed initially as foster children, before they were later adopted. Approximately three-quarters of the parents reported that the impact of adoption on the family was positive to very positive. Only 6 per cent reported it as mostly negative or very negative. They do confirm though, that problems for some special needs adoptees do not 'disappear' over time.

As in Britain, those who adopt 'special needs' children in the USA come from a much broader social background compared with the predominantly middle-class one of those adopting young, healthy babies.

British studies

Turning to some British studies, Thoburn and Rowe's (1988) large survey covering 1165 children placed between 1979 and 1984 found that between 18 months and five years after placement there was an overall breakdown rate of 22 per cent. However, for those placed when under the age of 9, the breakdown rate was only around 11 per cent, compared to 34 per cent for those aged 9 to 11 and almost 40 per cent for those aged 12 and over. Thus the biggest jump in breakdowns was for those aged between 9 and 11. Significantly higher breakdown rates were found by a Strathclyde study (1991). An average of 43 per cent breakdowns was identified over a period of three years after placement, but for those placed under 12 the average was only around 25 per cent and for those aged 12 and over around 60 per cent. Another British study by Borland, O'Hara and Triseliotis (1991), monitoring 194 placements made by one authority over a three-year period, found a mean breakdown rate of 21 per cent, but again there was considerable variation between different age groups. The disruption rate rose from 6 per cent for those placed when under 9 to 31 per cent for those aged 9 and over at placement. However, none of those placed when aged 15 and over disrupted, suggesting that practitioners should not be put off by the older age of some children, provided all are committed to the plan. The highest breakdown rate was amongst those aged 11 and 12 at placement. Most breakdowns seem to happen during the first twelve months. Equally, many children whose first adoption placement breaks down can be successfully placed in another adoptive family.

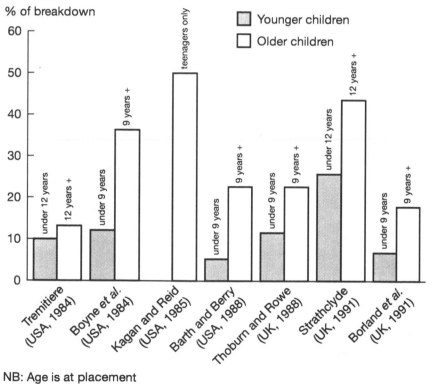

NB: Age is at placement

Figure 2.1 The relationship between increased age at time of placement and higher breakdown rates of the adoption

Most of the studies referred to are agreed that special needs adoption works well for most children and their families. The studies are also agreed that the quality of preparation and of post-adoption support, including adoption allowances, offered to new families can be crucial to the stability of the placement (Hill, Lambert and Triseliotis, 1989; Rosenthal, 1993).

Looking at the disruption rates identified by studies of 'special needs' placements in the 1970s and early 1980s, that is during the early years of the permanency movement, and contrasting them with those in the late 1980s and onwards, it is evident that the breakdown rates increased significantly.

This is possibly due to the greater risks taken by adoption agencies and the more problematic qualities of the children requiring placement. It is also possible that the more optimistic findings recorded, particularly by American studies monitoring the 'permanency movement', have been augmented by the inclusion of many children who were adopted by their foster families and by relative adoptions.

By the late 1980s the climate around the adoption of special needs children began to change. Agencies became far more cautious, especially about the placement of older children, and so did prospective adopters. The enthusiasm of the 1970s and early 1980s that every child was adoptable and every family had something to offer, and the altruism displayed by many families then, was gradually being replaced by a more tempered approach (Lunken, 1995). The belief that given unlimited love and attention most children would be able to recover from some very negative, rejecting and destructive past experiences was perhaps over-optimistic. Possibly as a result of the more recent studies and a number of other factors to be discussed later in this book, the placement of children with special needs has been in some decline.

British outcome studies in progress at the time of writing include:

D. Quinton and A. Rushton at the Maudsley Hospital. This is a study of 29 girls and 32 boys placed between the ages of 5 and 9 with follow-ups at three and twelve months. A special feature of this study is the social work input in placements.

D. Howe at the University of East Anglia is studying 120 adopters who, between them, adopted 300 children of different ages, now in their late teens and beyond. A particular focus is the exploration of the concept of attachment.

J. Thoburn and her colleagues, also at the University of East Anglia, are following up black children some of whom were placed transracially and others in-racially.

M. Rutter at the Maudsley Hospital is following up a group of Romanian children placed with adoptive families when under the age of 42 months. The focus is on the children's progress covering physical, intellectual and emotional development.

For a summary of key American studies in progress see *Adoption Research Newsletter* 3 (Winter 1996).

The studies referred to earlier have identified factors contributing to greater stability in the adoptive placement. They include:

Factors associated with the child

- The younger at placement the better, but many older placed children can do well and some very well
- Not having a history of extreme rejection and deprivation
- Not being too disturbed at time of placement, especially for children over the age of 9
- (For the older child) maintaining some form of contact with a parent and/or sibling, or grandparent after placement
- Being placed with a sibling, though much can depend on the relationship between them (not all studies are agreed on this)
- (For the older child) being actively involved in the placement and being well prepared beforehand, especially over expectations, past and current circumstances and origins

See also Thoburn (1994).

Children who have been abused, rejected or grossly neglected, some of whom may later be adopted, can display a range of behavioural and emotional difficulties. Though the evidence suggests that, given optimum conditions, some of these difficulties may decline or disappear over time, others may still persist depending on the extent of the damage. The areas in which such children can be vulnerable were summarized by Cicchetti and Toth (1995), with respect to (1) *the regulation of emotions* – control of anger and frustration, and emotional responses to anger between others; (2) *the development of attachment* – particularly in the development of secure attachments and stable internal models of attachment figures; (3) *the development of self-system* – identity and self-esteem; (4) *the quality of peer relationships*; and *adaptation* (5) *to school*.

Factors associated with the adopting family

- Childless and parenting young children
- Having own children and parenting older children

- No own young children when placing young children
- Not over-stressed as a family
- Strongly motivated to provide a home for a child
- Stability in couple relationships, quality of parenting skills, tolerance of difference, flexibility of roles and rules
- Realistic from the start about possible difficulties
- Inclusive of the family of origin and of the child's past links, including where necessary the acceptance of contact
- Open to seeking and receiving support and help from outside

Factors associated with the agency

(Variations in breakdown rates between agencies cannot be explained solely by the type of child placed, but also depend on the quality of services offered.)

- Staff who are knowledgeable and skilled in child placement and family finding work
- Comprehensive preparation of children and adopters. Adopters knowing what they are taking on, especially how damaged some children are. Their satisfaction may have to come from small gains and from offering the older child a base in life.
- Preparing families to recognize that love is not enough
- Careful matching of children's needs with the new parents' parenting skills
- Seeking especially the older child's views and heeding them
- Building into the new arrangements important emotional links from the child's past
- Comprehensive post-placement support available over 24 hours where necessary
- Availability of adoption allowances or subsidies
- Access to specialist advice, such as educational and psychological services. Also the opportunity for counselling.

TOWARDS A PSYCHOLOGY OF ADOPTION

Besides mainstream research in outcomes and adjustment, there was a third type of adoption study, the main value of which has been to throw new light on issues of genealogy and identity formation in the adopted person. These studies benefited greatly from obtaining initially the views of adoptive parents and subsequently those of adoptees about such aspects as disclosure, background information, origins, access to genealogical information and notions of self-concept and of identity formation. More recently the studies have expanded to obtain the perspective of the birth parent(s) and the impact on them of the decision to part with the child. Taken together, all of the studies have contributed towards a much greater understanding of the adoption experience, especially in the area of identity formation. Along with other studies they have contributed towards the gradual building of a psychology of adoption. A central feature of this new empirically based theory is the way it has brought together the additional tasks faced by members of the adoption triangle. These will be discussed in relation to each member.

Adopted people

Difficulties are not inevitable with adoption. Nevertheless, unlike children growing up with their birth parents, those adopted have to accomplish or be aided to accomplish a number of additional psychological tasks, which most of them do successfully. These tasks include:

1. Re-attachment to new parent(s);
2. The awareness of being adopted, which in turn involves:
   (a) the knowledge of being adopted and the gradual understanding of its meaning and implications;
   (b) access to genealogical and other related information;
   (c) the notion of two sets of parents and the acknowledgement of the differences involved;
   (d) dealing with the sense of loss of the original parents and the element of rejection that it conveys.
3. The formation of an identity that includes the above attributes.

1. The process of re-attachment

The concept of attachment is a complex one and, though a lot has been learned, much more work is required, especially how to recognize it and measure its strength (Bowlby, 1969, 1973, 1979 and 1980; Schaffer, 1990; Howe, 1995). In spite of these limitations, the first task faced by adopted children is to attach themselves to their new

parents. It goes perhaps without saying that for satisfactory development all children require a warm, caring, secure and stable
environment within which to grow up. Children, the younger the
better, can attach themselves to new carers and, equally, carers can
bond with children they have not given birth to. Except for babies
placed directly from birth with adoptive parents, for the rest adoptive placement usually follows after one or more previous
placements with either foster carers or in residential establishments.

Though uprooting and re-attachment carry many risks, nevertheless the studies quoted earlier suggest that the majority of children,
especially when under about the age of 9, seem to re-attach themselves to new families and do well. Psychological parenting, in other
words, is a reality and 'a blood tie' is not necessary for children to
attach themselves to new carers. Brodzinsky, Schecter and Henig
(1992) add from their studies that 'the adoptees taken as a whole
were essentially just as secure in their attachments to their mothers
as were the non adoptees' (p. 54). Similarly, the evidence suggests
that the quality of this relationship is possibly the paramount factor
which appears to over-ride all other considerations and factors,
including colour and ethnicity (Clarke and Clarke, 1976; Tizard,
1977; Triseliotis and Russell, 1984; Schaffer, 1990; Brodzinsky,
Schechter and Henig, 1992; Tizard and Phoenix, 1993).

It is also arguable whether 're-attachment' is the right word to use
for the child who is adopted over about the age of 10 since this is usually
the time when children begin to separate from parental figures rather
than trying to get attached to them. The best that can be expected
under such circumstances is the establishment of mutually satisfying
relationships. This will avoid having unrealistic and possibly inappropriate expectations either of the older child or of the adoptive parent(s).

2. The awareness of being adopted

The awareness, knowledge, and understanding of being adopted
also leads to the additional tasks (p. 35) that are not faced by all other
children, although those in re-constituted families and those born
through methods of assisted reproduction share several aspects of
this experience. These include:

- the element of loss, rejection and grief that adoption
  inevitably conveys;
- the acknowledgement of the difference between biological
  and psychological parenting;

- and the incorporation in the developing self of the concept of having more than one family.

(a) The knowledge of being adopted

Studies across diverse cultures suggest that people generally want to know the truth about themselves and about their background and circumstances. In this respect, adoptees are no exception. The adoption disclosure usually starts from the time children begin to ask questions about babies and sex. Adoptive parents use a range of ways for introducing the idea of another family, including the telling or reading of relevant stories (see Craig, 1991). The disclosure introduces the young child to the idea of something different about himself, though he does not yet understand how and why. The concept of two families, of a biological and a psychological one, becomes central to the explanations, whilst stressing also the permanency of the arrangement. It is the responsibility of adoptive parents to make the disclosure:

> 'Hearing it from the people you grow up with does not make you feel that it is something wrong or awful.'

Disclosure has to be part of a process rather than a once and for all occasion. Neither should parents wait for the child to ask questions. The responsibility lies with them to take the initiative in explaining, discussing and sharing information (Triseliotis, 1973). More recent studies such as Craig (1991) suggest that most parents now seek opportunities to talk and explain to the children about their adoption. The reluctance of some to take the initiative is summarized in the following comment.

> 'Maybe my parents waited for me to ask and I waited for them to take the initiative and eventually we never talked about it.'

A balance has to be struck between what Kirk (1964) describes as an 'acknowledgement of difference' and 'the rejection of difference', sharing information and being honest and truthful but going at the child's pace, without bombarding the child with information. Overstressing adoption could equally convey the feeling of something strange or wrong (Triseliotis, 1973). Some parents are put off quickly if the child shows some reluctance to listen, yet whilst avoiding oppressing the child with their insistence, parents have to use appropriate opportunities to return to the subject. There is no doubt from Craig's (1991) evidence that some children refuse to listen until they feel ready and this has to be respected. Eventually though, the adopted person cannot reach a positive resolution of the duality of his parentage without acknowledging it and integrating this difference into his developing personality.

For children adopted very young and with no previous memories, Brodzinsky (1984) and Brodzinsky, Schecter and Henig (1992) rightly distinguish between knowing and understanding and add that it is not usually until the age of 6 or 7 that children cognitively begin to grasp the meaning and implications of adoption. They may use the word 'adopted' over and over, but it does not follow that they also understand its meaning or full implications. This comes more gradually. Disclosure, though, has to start much earlier so that the child can feel that he/she 'always knew'. Many adopted people will say 'but I always knew' as far back as they could remember. This is true, but knowing and understanding are not the same. With the onset of adolescence the adopted child begins to consider the full implications of adoption, such as the element of loss and rejection involved, the grief that goes with it, and how this fits with his total circumstances.

In all the research studies we carried out, it was very rare indeed for an adopted person to say that they would rather not know the truth about themselves. They saw this, along with other information to be discussed later, as part of their birth right. Knowing as much as there is to know, far from undermining the relationship between the adopted person and the adoptive parents, helps to cement it. On the other hand, evasion, secrecy and lying undermine the adoptee–adoptive parent relationship. A typical comment from one adoptee representing those of many others:

'Truth is always better than deception. No-one should have the right to erase part of yourself, even if it is only a very minor part.'

(b) Access to genealogical and other related information

We now know that it is not enough for the adopted child to be told of his or her adoption. The child also needs to have gradual but detailed information about his background, genealogy, circumstances of adoption and, where appropriate, become aware of his race, ethnicity and cultural heritage. All this information and the way it is made available are closely linked with the formation of identity and self-concept (McWhinnie, 1967; Triseliotis, 1973; Triseliotis and Russell, 1984; Haimes and Timms, 1985; Craig, 1991; Walby, 1992; Brodzinsky, Schecter and Henig, 1992). All individuals during their growing up years have the opportunity to develop a sense of themselves and who they are, based also on what they come to know about their parents, ancestors, place they were born and the history of their country and ethnic group. As Giddens (1992, p. 53) puts it:

> it is the self as reflexively understood by the person in terms of her or his biography. Identity here still presumes continuity across time and space ... to be a 'person' is not just to be a reflexive actor, but to have a concept of a person (as applied both to self and others).

Like others, adopted people too have to establish who they are if they are to become whole and complete people. They need to have the kind of information and opportunities to establish both their psychological self and their physical self. The search for self for adopted people is no more pathological than the search for identity by those who are not adopted. For adoptees it is, though, somewhat more complicated. To accomplish these tasks satisfactorily they need to have answers to questions such as: Why was I put up for adoption? Who were my birth parents and what kind of people were they? Finally they must find their own answers to the question of 'Who am I?' The adopted person's family of origin, race and culture may represent only one aspect of personal and social identity, but it is nevertheless a vital one. The assimilation of this information and the full realization of what it means seem to put some extra strain on adopted children. For those adopted intercountry there can be additional difficulties, depending on how well the adoption was arranged and how carefully detailed background information together with such things as photographs, letters and videos were gathered.

The value of open adoption, discussed in Chapter 4, is that the adoptive parents will have the opportunity of meeting the birth parents and be able therefore to obtain and later convey more direct information to the child. Where of course there is continued contact between adoptive and birth parents and child, there can be less secrecy and the child will have the opportunity of obtaining information from the birth parents himself or herself. The physical reality of the birth parents and first-hand explanations of why they had to give up the child should, theoretically, lessen the possibility of identity confusion in the adoptee.

(c) The notion of having more than one family and the acknowledgement of the difference involved

The disclosure of adoption and the sharing of background information leads also to the realization by the child that he/she has more than one family or two sets of parents. The idea of more than one family is a difficult and an evolving one, but its positive acknowledgement and resolution is gradually assimilated and becomes part of the developing self. Those adopted transracially and/or inter-country have the extra task of acknowledging their different racial, cultural and ethnic background, where appropriate. This form of biculturalism does not seem impossible (Tizard and Phoenix, 1993).

(d) The sense of loss and rejection

The full grasp of the meaning of adoption leads inevitably to the realization that adoption involves a sense of loss and rejection, which can affect the individual's feelings of self-worth (Triseliotis, 1973; Triseliotis and Russell, 1984). The loss and its accompanying grieving is that of the original family, heritage and/or culture or ethnic group. People are often missing from an adopted person's conception of genealogical family, such as fathers who have failed to register, or grandparents or siblings. There is, then, the inevitable sense of rejection by parents and grief irrespective of the circumstances that led to it. The question almost all adoptees ask – Why was I given up for adoption? – hides behind it a second one:

Was I wanted and loved before I was given up?

To feel that you were not wanted or loved by your birth parents or even country (though more needs to be known about the latter) can be experienced as traumatic and have an impact on the adopted person's sense of self-esteem and self-worth. Such feelings are sometimes accompanied by anger about what had happened. The strength of the anger is often in relation to other events that have occurred in the adoptee's life.

Brodzinsky, Schecter and Henig (1992), who suggest that this sense of loss rarely comes before the age of 5, looked at the two crucial processes that face adoptees in life, that of the search for self and the experience of loss, and have come up with what they call a psychological model of adjustment. Using Erikson's (1963) psycho-social stages of development, they outline the different tasks facing parents and children at each stage and then outline the additional ones facing adopted children and their parents. They then discuss how positive resolution could be achieved at each stage. The love and care of the adoptive parents can go a long way to help towards the healing of these wounds. What has been found, though, is that when new important losses occur in adoptees' lives, they may awake feelings related to the initial losses (Triseliotis, 1973; Triseliotis and Russell, 1984; Bouchier, Lambert and Triseliotis, 1991).

3. The formation of an identity

The quality of family relationships, information and knowledge about the past, positive community attitudes and the successful resolution of feelings of loss and rejection all contribute to the formation of personality and identity in the adopted person. In no way is this meant to imply that identity is in some ways given by the birth and adoptive parents to the adoptees. On the contrary, as Giddens (1992) reminds us, people take an active part in the construction of their identity:

> Self identity, in other words, is not something that is just given, as a result of the continuities of the individual's action system, but something that has to be routinely created and sustained in the reflexive activities of the individual.

Neither is identity fixed. Adoptees, like others, 'live' their biographies in a process of continual development. Barbara Hardy (1968) captured this process by her reference to the 'narrative' of life. The life story books prepared when children move to new families (see p. 125) is one way of keeping the narrative of these children's lives after they grow up.

Marcia (1980) refers to identity as 'a self-structure - an internal, self-constructed, dynamic organization of drives, abilities, beliefs and individual history'. Depending on how well this structure is developed, individuals can feel whole and unique or confused and different. Erikson (1968) described a positive identity as:

> a sense of psychological well-being, a feeling of being at home in one's body, of knowing where one is going, an inner assuredness of anticipated recognition from those who count.

Mead (1934), writing earlier from a sociological perspective, remarked on how identity begins by what he calls 'role-taking', namely taking the attitudes and views that others have of us as our own by learning to see ourselves through their eyes and acting by means of their standards. Others, such as Goffman (1969), agree with Mead that as a result of this social process we may come to perceive ourselves as 'best' or 'second class' or 'bad' or 'dull'. A sense of spoiled identity usually develops from the receipt of consistently negative messages. Though in some respects we can intervene in the process of self-building and resist attempts by others to affix to us a certain identity, nevertheless children, because they are in a formative stage of development, have less power to resist consistently negative messages. As one adoptee put it:

'When my in-laws heard that I was adopted they said they didn't expect that and had to think about it, as if I was different just because I was adopted.'

Instead of identity, Brodzinsky, Schecter and Henig (1992) use the term 'self' and refer in their writings to 'the physical self', the 'psychological' and the 'social self'. The *physical self* includes awareness and perceptions of one's own body: how it looks, how it feels, how it sounds, smells, tastes. The *psychological self* includes notions of our own intangible qualities, including what we call personalities: our view of our intelligence, our capacity for empathy, our ability to control impulses, our generosity or lack of it. The *social self* includes our awareness of ourselves in relation to others and our view of how others see us. Finally, the authors add:

there is the overriding, evaluative component of the self that integrates the other three: the part called self-esteem. This represents our judgements about whether aspects of our selves are good or bad, likeable or dislikeable, valuable or not. Self-esteem plays a major role in patterns of psychological adjustment. (p. 13)

There can be a range of identities such as personal, social, cultural or ethnic. Yet they must all add up to a coherent whole. How far identities can compensate for each other is not clear. For example, would gaps in one identity, such as genealogical, ethnic or physical, be compensated for by strengths in other identities? There are those who claim, for example, that the lack of ethnic identity does not affect self-esteem (McRoy and Zurcher, 1983; McRoy, 1990; Tizard and Phoenix, 1993).

ADOPTIVE PARENTS

Having identified the additional tasks expected of the adopted child, we now turn to those expected of adoptive parents. The main expectation is the acknowledgement that they are only the psychological and not the biological parents of the child. In other words, that the child was not born to them (Kirk, 1964). This acknowledgement appears simple but is emotionally fraught. In addition, the acknowledgement carries a number of obligations towards the child, particularly to help him to accomplish successfully the extra tasks described earlier.

Acknowledging and accepting that being an adoptive parent is different from being a biological one is something that would-be adopters can be helped to explore and understand during the assessment and preparatory period. Recognizing the difference also implies openness not only in disclosing the adoption, but also in being inclusive of the family of origin, race, ethnic group and culture, where relevant. This involves communicating background information to the child as part of a process and providing background details. Depending on the agreements reached, it could also involve the periodic exchange of letters and photos with the birth family or even periodic or more continuous contact. At the same time adoptive parents need to feel that they are in charge and in control (Tizard, 1977). Though more needs to be understood about the concept of 'being in control', it is doubtful whether adoptive parents can convey a sense of security to the child, unless they themselves feel secure as parents to the child.

Adoptive parents will convey feelings of inferiority or second class citizenship to a child if they feel that adoption is second best, or if they feel shamed by acknowledging the adoption because it is often connected with childlessness (Triseliotis, 1973). In some societies childlessness still carries certain shame and stigma. Similarly, adoptive parents can antagonize the child if they feel hostile and rejecting towards the child's roots, heritage and race. The growing child needs to be helped in his or her struggles to establish a positive sense of self through having a positive view about his or her background and heritage. The fact that a biological parent may have a criminal record, a mental illness or a wayward life, should not be a reason to be critical of them.

A project set up in Scotland in the early 1970s has demonstrated how much can be achieved by adoption agencies who take the trouble to prepare adoptive parents on how to disclose adoption, make it part of a process, share background and genealogical information and not to be alarmed if their child shows interest in his birth family or seeks to meet a biological parent. Twenty years later the study found how worthwhile this preparation was and how satisfied both the children and the parents were with the adoption outcome (Craig, 1991). Based on the findings of the studies discussed earlier, adoptive parents can be reassured that they have nothing to fear from being truthful, open and honest with their child and equally do not need to worry that they will lose their child's love if he/she shows interest in their birth family. If love is there, then there is no danger of losing it (Triseliotis, 1973; Haimes and Timms, 1985; Craig, 1991).

Preparation for open or semi-open adoption should facilitate the acknowledgement of difference on the part of the adoptive parents and the acceptance of the reality of the biological parents (Mullender, 1991).

With the emphasis in recent years on the adoption of special needs children, adoptive parents are being faced with additional tasks compared to those involved when adopting infants and young children. They include making role, rules and boundary adaptations to their family system; the provision of parenting to children who already have a history of parenting and substitute parenting experiences; and the capacity to accommodate contact and possibly visits by members of the original family. With much younger children there is a gradualness and more time, which is not always available with the older child.

No doubt much more needs to be understood about social and psychological parenting in adoption, but a start has been made. The research and writings of recent decades which focus on differences and similarities in parenting and role performance by biological parents, and on the changing role of fathers, have not yet been explored with regard to adoption. Neither have similarities and differences in motivation between male and female adopters been pursued from the perspective of single-parent adoption.

BIRTH PARENTS

Birth parents, or most usually the birth mother, are the third party making up the adoption triangle. In Chapter 5 on biological parents research studies are quoted to describe the psychological impact on the parent who gives up a child for adoption. To summarize, the evidence suggests that birth mothers who have parted with a child for adoption do not usually find it easy to forget the experience. On the contrary, for many the experience is a constant preoccupation. There is apparently no clean break with the past. Researchers have found amongst their sample of birth mothers unresolved anger, pathological mourning, guilt, searching in waking life or in dreams and memories, being stirred by anniversaries such as the child's birthday. Continuing distress, cycles of blame, guilt and personal anguish arising from the parting decision are some of the lingering feelings (Pannor, Baran and Sorosky, 1974; Winkler and Keppel, 1984; Bouchier, Lambert and Triseliotis, 1991; Howe, Sawbridge and Hinings, 1992; Wells, 1993). When relinquishing mothers were compared with a matched sample, they were found to have significantly more physical and/or psychological difficulties and to be much more prone to depression (Winkler and Keppel, 1984).

The adopted person, as we saw earlier, has to resolve feelings of loss, rejection and grief. The birth parent, too, needs to come to terms with some similar and some different feelings: loss, guilt and self-blame. Parting with a child for adoption seems to undermine a birth parent's view of himself/herself as a person. Such feelings seem to be reduced, as far as mothers are concerned (we do not know enough about fathers), when the decision was freely made or she felt she had a choice and that the decision was hers rather than imposed on her. Some of the available evidence also tends to suggest that open adoption reduces some of the negative feelings associated with relinquishment. However well the various procedures and preparation are carried out with the birth parent(s), they still have to recognize and emotionally accept that they are the child's biological but not psychological parents. This does not exclude the possibility of some sharing of the psychological parenting role. (See Chapter 11, pp. 227–9.)

CONCLUDING REMARKS

Adoption need not be problematic. Studies confirm that the great majority of adoptive parents and adopted children are satisfied with this form of psychological parenting and it is not a problem to them. The placement of special needs children, which has been a feature of adoption policy and practice for the last quarter of a century, has tapped qualities of parenting that had previously gone unnoticed. It also demonstrated that given good parenting, many children can recover from some awful past experiences. There are limits, however, to such recoveries and this may help to explain the greater cautiousness shown by agencies in the last five or so years in the placement, particularly of children over about the age of 9, who have been badly damaged psychologically.

Five key points

1. Studies show that the great majority of young children in adoptive families do well and many very well.
2. Many older children placed can benefit considerably from adoption and are able to overcome many early emotional adversities through positive new parenting experiences.
3. The adoption of adolescents and of very emotionally disturbed children carries high risks and such adoptions require much more preparation, better matching and more intensive post-placement support.
4. A number of criteria have been identified which highlight factors contributing to success or failure in adoption.
5. Studies in origins and identity formation, along with those of adoptive parenting and of studies monitoring the experiences of birth parents who parted with children for adoption, have contributed to an emerging theory of the psychology of adoption.

CHAPTER 3
The children and the childcare system

Adoption, part of the childcare system, exists as a means of providing permanent homes, capable of nurturing and guiding children whose birth parents cannot care for them. Legislation gives recognition to the child's need for continuity of care, for permanence and security, by making it possible for children whose families cannot manage their care to be adopted. The undergirding principles of the childcare system and of adoption are (1) meeting the needs of children and (2) determining the best interests of children. In this chapter, these concepts will be explored.

THE NEEDS AND THE BEST INTERESTS OF CHILDREN

Needs

Decisions within the childcare system are made to meet the needs of the child, and to act in the child's best interest. Though each child's specific needs are unique, and vary over time, it is possible to construct a framework within which needs can be evaluated. Guided mostly by empirical studies, Pringle (1972) concluded that there are four basic emotional needs which must be met if children are going to grow up into capable and confident adults.

1. The *need for love and security*, probably the most important, in terms of forming the basis of developing a positive identity and the capacity to make rewarding relationships with an increasing number of people. Love and security involve experiences of good physical care, protection from danger, affection, continuity of care and an environment within which the child feels secure and a sense of belonging. (The concept of attachment and bonding between child and primary carers is implicit in this statement.)
2. Children have a *need to explore and to be stimulated* by increasing information and new experiences in order to

develop intelligence, confidence and a sense of control over the world in which they live. Thus the child needs opportunities for play, social interaction and language development.

3. The *need for praise and recognition*. Growing up into a socially able adult requires a vast amount of emotional, social and intellectual learning. Praise and recognition can help children through periods of frustration, conflict, disappointment and sometimes confusion. Inappropriate demands may lead to anger or withdrawal.

4. Children *need to develop a sense of responsibility* through personal independence. In order to express this in a socially acceptable way, limits and controls must first be established by those who are important to the child.

Pringle makes the point that meeting these needs must be geared to the characteristics, personalities and capabilities of individual children. However, the needs are universal.

Particularly important in a discussion of adoption is the identification of the child's need for continuity of care within an environment in which he feels secure and develops a sense of belonging. A permanent family home, either the child's own home or an adoptive home, best meets these needs. Relative permanency can also be achieved in other forms of substitute parenting, such as in long-term foster care and custodianship, but these lack the legality and security offered by adoption (Hill, Lambert and Triseliotis, 1989).

Best interests

The concept of the best interests of the child reflects empirical evidence, where available, and legal decisions over time which have established that children cannot be treated as property, have rights, and that the privacy of family life may be invaded by the state when it is in 'the child's best interests'. It further reflects the idea that the state's primary concern is with the welfare of the child throughout the growing up years and beyond. However, in the individual situation, when the particular needs of the child are considered, there is often considerable disagreement about where the best interests of the child lie. This disagreement is often at the core of decision making about adoption.

Children become available for adoption in two ways. First, for some children adoption is planned by their parents, with the mother often taking a leading role. These are usually young infants whose parents (often single mothers) are, for a variety of reasons, unable to rear them. The law establishes safeguards to ensure that relinquishment of parental rights is voluntary, but how free parents are when making an adoption decision is a point of considerable debate to which we shall be returning in Chapter 5 on birth parents. The relinquishment, if legal procedures have been followed, is permanent.

The second route to adoption is via the state childcare system. These are children who come under the protection of a childcare agency and who eventually cannot return to their families. These children may become available for adoption when the court terminates the rights of the parents and/or dispenses with their consent to adoption, after they have been found incapable of caring for their children. In other cases parents come to recognize for themselves that they are not able to resume care for their children and voluntarily relinquish them. These are usually children who have had seriously traumatizing experiences in their homes, and have had one or more foster and residential placements while social workers attempted to rehabilitate their birth homes for them. When parents are demonstrably unable to continue to care for their children, the plan is to provide the child with a new and permanent family through adoption. As we shall be discussing in the next chapter on the birth family, parents often contest the state's plan to place their children for adoption. Courts tend to protect the 'blood tie' of biological families, and the legal process of involuntary termination of parental rights/consents can be complex and difficult for everybody involved in the process.

Though the first route of voluntary adoption planning is generally easier for both adoptive and birth family, and much easier for the child (if old enough to be involved in the planning), nevertheless even in these adoptions there are sometimes disagreements about the best interest of the child. When children come to adoption through the second route, this disagreement can be intense, and can be resolved only through careful evaluation of the needs of the particular child, and evaluation of the soundness of the plans to meet these needs. In this evaluation, both the childcare system and the legal system are involved.

THE PLACE OF ADOPTION IN THE CHILDCARE SYSTEM

The childcare system

In both Britain and the United States, there is recognition that a network of services is needed to support and sustain families in the care of their children. This network was in great part supplied by extended families, by churches, and by local, private charity in the past. Three factors have modified this, and have resulted in increased public involvement in family support. The first is the growing urbanization, mobility, complexity and depersonalization of our society, isolating families from these formerly supportive networks. The second is the increase in marriage breakdown. The third is recognition of children as individuals with rights, and in consequence the increasingly high standards of childcare which are demanded. No longer do Western, industrialized countries tolerate children labouring in factories, children being severely neglected or abused in their homes, or children being disposed of as property. As children are relatively powerless, large public child welfare organizations have been set up for their protection.

The childcare system has been developed, albeit within a climate of limited resources, to protect children through supporting their families and ensuring that their childcare meets minimally adequate standards. Increasingly, under the stress of limited budgets and community demands for child protection, public child welfare agencies have focused on their protective rather than their support-ive role. A number of writers have drawn attention to how child protection, in recent years, has diverted childcare workers from their more fundamental task of strengthening families to child protection work (Marsh and Triseliotis, 1993; Lindsey, 1994; Barth *et al.*, 1994).

A range of services need to be made available to families and children who go through a crisis, are under stress, or have difficulty coping with the demands of family life. The intention is to strengthen families to enable them to care for their children, and to remove children from their parents only when safety demands it. These efforts have received new impetus with the development of the promising techniques of the family preservation movement, and in the Children Act 1989. (For an exposition of preventive and rehabilitation services to families and children in Great Britain, see Marsh and Triseliotis, 1993. Family preservation models in the United States are reviewed and evaluated in Nelson and Landsman, 1992.)

While all these services prevent many adoption placements, there are situations which necessitate the removal of a child from its family for short or longer periods. Temporary removal can be intended to provide protection for a child, to provide respite for carers, and/or to give social workers time to rehabilitate homes for children as part of the prevention of permanent family breakdown.

Whatever the reasons, the separation of children from parents almost always causes distress and pain.

Why some families fail

The root causes of family failure are usually complex and hard to pinpoint. It is often easier to identify the crisis which precipitates the final break-up than the complex reasons that led up to it. Poverty and the lack of economic opportunity, poor housing, ill-health, customs and ideas of approved behaviour, parental inability to maintain stable relationships, all create stress on family life. The continued presence of racism and discrimination create stress for black and ethnic minority families and lead to tensions within the neighbourhood. When the extended family and community cannot provide the supportive resources to offset these stresses, families may not be able to care adequately for their children.

Though attitudinal factors operate in some cases, nevertheless the problem of family breakdown has much of its origin in situational factors such as low income, lack of economic opportunity, and lack of supportive services to enable families to carry out their parenting satisfactorily. What sometimes is seen as personal and family inadequacy often derives from the continued impact of the deficiencies described above. Long-term poverty or unemployment can have a demoralizing effect and can destroy a family's way of functioning. Chronic disadvantage can act as a serious stress factor which may produce negative changes at various levels of the family coping system. Public ills thus become private pains. In studies by both the European Commission and the Washington-based Joint Center for Political and Economic Studies, Britain has the distinction of having experienced the sharpest increases in poverty and income inequality in the 1980s. Between 1979 and 1990–91, the average real income of the bottom tenth of households fell 14 per cent, whereas the richest tenth saw a 50 per cent increase. Between 1974 and 1991 the number of children under 16 dependent on benefits has quadrupled (analysis provided in *The Times*, 28 December 1995, p. 25). Put another way, in 1989, over one-fifth of all children were living in poverty compared with only 11 per cent in 1979. Furthermore, 76 per cent of children living with a lone parent (estimated at one and a half million) were living in poverty, compared with 13 per cent of those living with two adults (Oppenheim, 1993). And again, 75 per cent of lone parents were living on income support in 1992 (Glendinning and Millar, 1992). Unsurprisingly, most childcare and child protection problems occur among the poorest families, which include single-parent families and those of mixed parentage (Bebbington and Miles 1989; Lindsey, 1994).

There is a developing debate about whether the changes in the structure of our society itself in the last decades may have undermined the ability of the family to care for its children. A usual reaction is to condemn these changes, attributing individual or family pathology, instead of recognizing them as social phenomena and providing the necessary support systems, such as in the case of lone parents. As Richards (1995) also points out, it is not always clear exactly what the changes are that are usually being condemned or, indeed, how they might be resisted. Nevertheless, a revolution in sexual mores and an increase in the autonomy and independence of women have in the last three decades produced a more than three-fold increase in the number of children living with one parent in both the United States and Britain. Lone parents now account for almost one-fifth of all family households in Britain. More than four-fifths of these households are headed by women, and lone mothers and their children constitute the largest social group living in poverty (Lindsey, 1994; Long, 1995).

The divorce rate in Britain seems now to have stabilized to around one in three marriages ending in divorce, but it is still one of the highest in Europe. About one child in every six aged under 16 lives in a reconstituted household. Young people whose families undergo disruption and who are looked after in care are more likely to experience social, educational and health problems than those whose families remain intact (Triseliotis *et al.*, 1995). Tragically, some children are born to teenage parents who are neither developmentally or economically ready to care for them. Girls who become part of a step-family by the age of 16 years run twice the risk of becoming teenage mothers and giving birth to their baby outside marriage (OPCS birth statistics FM1 and *Population Trends* 73, *1969–1991*).

Abuse and neglect of children

Most children who may later be candidates for adoption are in the care system because their parents fail to provide a minimally adequate level of care. A parental history of disturbed attachments, emotional deprivation, alcohol and drug abuse, as well as lack of the social skills and emotional resources needed to create stable relationships, usually interact with the socio-cultural factors outlined in the preceding paragraphs to produce the frustration, depression, self-depreciation, and sometimes aggression which lead to abuse and neglect of children (Vondra, 1990).

Alcoholism has always been a problem in families, crippling the ability to support a family and acting as a 'dis-inhibitor'. Not infrequently it is accompanied by physical and sexual abuse. Drug abuse has now become a major problem and its effect on childcare is often that of neglect. Pre-birth damage to the foetus can also be a factor when parents abuse alcohol or drugs. These families are extremely difficult to rehabilitate, and there is speculation that it is this increased substance abuse which has led to larger numbers of young children entering care and staying longer. Though difficult to prove, a final societal factor in child abuse is often said to be the increasing degree to which violence is presented in the entertainment media, and its presence on the streets and in the home. Though domestic violence and child abuse are linked, and though studies have shown that exposure to violence increases the probability that a child or young adult will see its use as a solution to problems, the exact role which exposure to violence plays in the inability to care appropriately for children is unclear.

Other reasons for placement

Other children and young people come under the protection of child care agencies because of:

(a) their parents' material, social and/or personal circumstances;
(b) a child's illness, either physical or mental, which makes it impossible for parents to provide care or which necessitates respite care; or
(c) the child's own behaviour such as delinquency or being beyond parental control.

MEETING CHILDREN'S NEEDS WITHIN THE CHILDCARE SYSTEM

Social work services provided by public and voluntary agencies must be individually planned to meet the unique needs of each child and family. Services such as residential care, foster care and adoption are available to every child looked after in care, depending on what is thought to be best. Placement decisions must be based on an understanding of the needs of the particular child and on an understanding of what various placement options, in general, offer children. Obviously, as many studies (for example, Millham *et al.*, 1986; Barth *et al.*, 1994; Triseliotis *et al.*, 1995) have found, there are often wide discrepancies between intentions and actuality.

All children whose family life has been disrupted and who are looked after in public care, require good quality care which is crucial to the development of a secure personality and a strong sense of self-worth. They may, if they have experienced serious problems in their own families, need specialized treatment services both from professionals and within their living situation. In addition, black and Asian children looked after in care require suitable role models which may not be available in a system with predominantly and sometimes exclusively white staff. The children also need help to develop self-knowledge about their background, genealogy, race and ethnic group (where relevant), including also knowledge about the circumstances of coming to live with substitute carers. All these are necessary for the development of a secure social identity. If they are to return home, visits from parents are important in maintaining family ties, and there is some evidence that such visits are helpful also for children moving toward permanent foster care or adoption (Meezan and Shireman, 1985; Triseliotis, 1991b; Fratter, 1995). Timely planning is crucial, so that children know what is happening and have, as soon as possible, the advantages of a permanent home.

Building a case record

Each child in the childcare system will have his own case record (the record of the plans made and actions taken for the child), which must be reviewed at regular intervals. Some states in the United States have time limits for rehabilitation, after which alternative placement arrangements can be pursued. The record of the social worker's efforts with a family is particularly important when a child is removed from his home and placed in substitute care, and may become crucial if the social worker has to ask the court to terminate the rights of parents and free a child for adoption. It will also be important later for research purposes or should services be transferred from one worker to another, for any reason.

The Children (England and Wales) Act 1989 has encouraged some creative social work. This is done through engaging clients, in this case, in the assessment and documentation process, creating a record together through which both client and worker can recognize and act on service plans and accomplishments. There is no doubt that careful assessments are also needed for good practice in the case of older children. Obviously assessments are not objective records; rather they present the analysis of data provided by experts such as the social worker, the medical doctor and perhaps a psychologist or psychiatrist. A good assessment of the child needs to be completed before he/she is placed and is essential for the selection of a home that best meets these needs.

Depending on age and understanding, the following areas are suggested for consideration when assessing the child's circumstances and needs (these have been adapted from an outline by Fitzgerald (1991) and BAAF's form E):

- a detailed chronological history of the child's experiences, including numbers and changes of carers and levels of physical and emotional care;
- a full developmental history, which includes the child's levels of attachment to former and current carers
- a detailed history of the child's educational experiences
- a detailed medical history and past or current psychological help, together with medical and any other specialist reports
- full details of the circumstances and type of possible abuse experienced
- a record of the child's own views and perspectives in relation to his or her own life, and how this was obtained
- a record of the parental views and perspectives in relation to the child's life

Other relevant information usually includes:

- the child's legal status
- a profile of the child, such as a brief description of his/her personality, preferably with a photograph attached
- type of placement needed
- siblings and grandparents (where available)

Assessments require reviewing and need to be followed by a clear statement of future plans.

Foster care as an option

Foster care involves the temporary placement of children with families who are paid to look after them. The families are asked to care for the children, whilst acknowledging that the child has his own family to which it is hoped he or she will return. The ultimate aim of most foster care is the return of the child to its own family, though this does not always happen because the birth family may be unwilling or unable to resume care or the child does not want to return home. In both Britain and the United States social workers are expected to give priority to the fostering of a child with relatives before placing him/her with strangers, and for those under the age of 10, to foster care placement with non-relatives before considering residential care. Increasingly, good practice is recognizing that foster care placement in the child's own neighbourhood, so that school and friendships are not disrupted, can be important. Foster care may last for a few days or a few months, until the child can return home or until a permanent family is arranged. When a child cannot return home and family ties preclude adoption, the foster home will become the home in which the child grows up. Because of the scarcity of babies to adopt, some families deliberately put themselves forward to foster in the hope that the placement will develop into adoption (Thoburn and Rowe, 1988). Such motives can lead to confusion, distortion of roles and eventual disappointment.

When considering foster care, it should be recognized that each individual home differs in the needs it can meet. The reality is that very often there is only one foster home to choose from. The usual aim of foster care placement is for the child to have only one foster home. In practice children still move frequently (Rowe, Hundleby and Garnett, 1989). In the United States, children under 4 years of age constitute a rapidly growing proportion of the children being placed in foster care, now estimated to be about 20–25 per cent of the total, and these children may remain in foster care for almost three years while attempts are made to carry out permanent plans (Schwartz et al., 1994). Older children come to public care having had difficult experiences in families which could not care for them, and will present a variety of emotional and behavioural problems. School-age children may need adoptive homes if their own homes cannot be rehabilitated, whilst many adolescents are more likely to need long-term family foster care or a lodging type arrangement with an approved carer. These unique needs must be understood before a foster home is selected and a placement is made. (For a detailed discussion of the place of foster care within the childcare system see Triseliotis, Sellick and Short, 1995.)

It is estimated that a third of the children in Britain and the United States are fostered by relatives. In both countries the numbers of children placed with relatives has grown in recent years, partly as a result of increasing focus on the importance of family to children and partly as a result of a shortage of traditional non-related foster homes. Except for Rowe, Hundleby and Keane's (1984) study, little is known about foster care by relatives in Britain. American studies suggest that relative foster parents are older, a higher proportion are single women, a higher proportion of minority race, and they have lower income than traditional foster parents (Berrick, Barth and Needel, 1994; LeProhn, 1994). The same authors, who compared relative foster homes with non-relative ones in the United States, found that a great strength identified was that the placements were stable, relatives had a commitment to the children and that the children had considerable contact with birth parents. Adoption by relatives is often complex, because of strained family relationships. The authors confirm that children placed with relatives seem to present the same range of health, behavioural, and emotional difficulties as those placed in traditional foster homes, but that such foster homes receive fewer services (such as respite care, support groups, training) than do traditional foster homes (see also Rowe, Hundleby and Keane, 1984).

In the last fifteen or so years, it has been recognized that foster homes which expect to give long-term care to a child were also a good resource as adoptive homes if the child could not return to his birth home (Hill, Lambert and Triseliotis, 1989). This transformation is not as natural and automatic as it might seem, however. Foster carers report feeling pressured by agencies which are trying to make permanent plans for children and being told that they must either adopt the child or he/she will be moved (Meezan and Shireman, 1985). On the other hand, foster carers at times become embroiled in intense court battles with childcare agencies when they wish to adopt a child who is either not free for adoption, or whom the agency wishes to place elsewhere. Recognition of the psychological bond which children form with care givers has resulted in foster carers attaining some rights to custody of children (see Children Act 1975). Nevertheless, as we say elsewhere, long-term and even permanent foster care are not experienced as secure as adoption (Triseliotis, 1983; Hill, Lambert and Triseliotis, 1989).

THE MEANING AND IMPORTANCE OF PERMANENCE

From the late 1950s onwards, studies of children in both Britain and the United States were discovering high breakdown rates in foster and residential placements and that children were often drifting for long periods of time with no effort being made to reunite them with their own families or to find alternative more permanent arrangements (Maas and Engler, 1959; Rowe and Lambert, 1973). Though many foster homes seemed to be providing well for the children, there was only relative security and permanency (Triseliotis, 1983). Too often a child was moved because of changes in the foster family's circumstances, or because of difficulties which arose between child and foster family. As a result, some children grew up without permanent ties to any family. Some of those growing up in residential care during these years had a rather more stable residence than the children in foster care, but did not enjoy the advantages of life in the family and community.

The start of 'the permanency movement' is therefore associated with the early 1970s. Its basic premise was that a child accommodated within the care system was to have a plan made for return home or else a permanent home, and any other type of care was to be of as short duration as possible. Child advocacy organizations, initially in the United States and later in Britain, took up this cause with impassioned writing which demonstrated how destructive long-term residential care or uncertain foster care could be (Rowe and Lambert, 1973; Goldstein, Freud and Solnit, 1973 and 1980; Adcock, 1980). Permanency planning emphasized maximum co-operation with parents for a limited period to be followed by a shift to a permanent alternative family if parenting did not significantly improve (Holmes, 1980; McKay, 1980). As noted also in Chapter 2, these efforts were boosted by research findings demonstrating that the trauma of early experiences could be overcome, especially with children placed when under the age of about 10. Project after project demonstrated that adoptive homes could be found for progressively older children and those with disabilities and handicaps (Triseliotis, 1980). This was an exciting period and much was accomplished. As with many other pioneering initiatives, mistakes were also made and the 'motto' that every child was 'adoptable' was to be tempered by the early 1990s.

PLANNING FOR PERMANENCY

Planning for permanency begins at the moment a child first comes into the child care system. The first part of permanency planning is the effort to rehabilitate the child's own home as rapidly as possible. If this effort fails, the second step is the effort to locate a permanent home for the child among relatives. Only when no one in the family can care for a child permanently is adoption or permanent foster care considered – the final option in the quest for a permanent home.

It is now a legal requirement in both Great Britain and the United States that a plan must be made for all children who enter care. The plan must state clearly what the agency is going to provide for the short- or longer-term period and should outline what parents, relatives, the social worker, and others are expected to do. The natural parents have a right to participate in the planning process, unless they have disappeared or are unable to do so. Relatives, particularly grandparents and aunts and uncles, should also participate in the planning, though their legal rights are less clear. Older children, too, have a right to participate in plans about themselves. It should be noted that this planning process provides an opportunity to mobilize the natural helping networks which may be able to support the family (Children Act 1989; The Children (Scotland) Act 1995).

It is in children's best interests that all plans made on their behalf are regularly reviewed to ensure that the plans are still relevant, and that parents, social workers and others are carrying out specified tasks so that children are not lost in the system. When parents fail or are unable to carry out their responsibilities, the plan may change from reunion with the family to adoption or long-term care. Always, the prime consideration is the safeguarding and promoting of the welfare of the child throughout his childhood.

Planning needs to be done as promptly as possible. For a very young child, a year can be a large proportion of life. There is an enormous difference in the range of adoptive homes interested in adopting a 3-month-old child, or even a 3-year-old, and those interested in adopting a 6-year-old, a sibling group, or a child with a handicap or disability. Because time is so important, there is a temptation to return children to homes not yet sufficiently free of stress to care for them, or to move prematurely to adoption when a child's own home could, eventually, be rehabilitated. Farmer and Parker (1991) found from their British study that around one in five children looked after in care were unlikely to return home and long-term arrangements seemed desirable. These are some of the dilemmas of the social worker in child welfare. There are no easy answers so that each situation must be carefully evaluated.

THE RIGHTS OF NATURAL PARENTS

In the British and American legal systems, parents have obligations and responsibilities towards their children rather than rights. These responsibilities involve providing adequate care, nurture, and education to their children. Parents have a right to be involved in decision-making about their child and to have some say in choice of religion and education. They also have some right to lawfully correct their child but not to abuse the child. Finally, they have a right to administer property, and to say 'no' to adoption unless a court finds that they are 'unreasonable' (in Britain) or 'unfit' (in the United States)

Based on the protections for the 'integrity of family life' built into the legal systems of both countries, courts are in principle reluctant to terminate the rights of parents so that children can be placed in adoptive homes, a point to be discussed more extensively in Chapter 5. The court requires that it be shown, first, that the parents are unreasonable or there are other grounds and, second, that termination is in the child's best interests. Evidence must be 'clear and convincing', a higher standard than the 'preponderance of evidence required in a custody hearing' (Stein, 1991). In most jurisdictions, the social worker must convince the court that the parents have not fulfilled their responsibilities, and that reasonable efforts have been made to enable them to do so, and also that it is unlikely that they will be able satisfactorily to resume care of the child. Overall, social workers build their case on the initial care of the children and on failure to respond sufficiently once the children were in care or accommodated (Hill *et al.*, 1992). Carefully documented details of the case assist the court in the evaluation of the efforts made by the agency to reunite the family. The social worker must also address the benefit expected for the child by this termination (Ryburn, 1994).

THE RIGHTS OF CHILDREN

Children have few rights as such; the law usually says what can be done if others do certain things to children. Depending on age and understanding, the only absolute right that children have is to be consulted about their future, but that does not necessarily mean that their view will be followed. In Scotland children over 12 must give their consent in writing and this is proposed for England and Wales also. Thus older children have a right to participate in decisions about themselves, the making of plans and the review of plans.

Participation of the child and consultation does not always amount to choice, though (Triseliotis *et al.*, 1995). An implied right lies in the instruction to the social work agency to assure that caretakers fulfil their responsibilities toward children, and the instruction, when making plans, such as about adoption or foster care, to consider the child's religion, racial origin, culture and language.

The UN Convention on Children's Rights, which has been ratified by the UK, includes rights to express an opinion and to have that taken into account (Article 12); to information and freedom of expression (13); and to periodic review of placement (25). It also embraces a different set of social rights to protection and services.

Stein (1991) discusses two contradictory threads in the development of children's rights in the United States. Children are viewed as in need of the state's protection, and through this century laws have been enacted to protect them from exploitation, assure their support, protect them from abuse and neglect, and ensure their place in families and extended families. The second, more recent, trend vests children with rights such as free speech, privacy, and the right to due process when liberty is threatened. These rights apply more to older children, as do the rights stated in British law. The popular conception of the 'right' of children to a minimally adequate standard of care has been expressed in statutes that protect them from abuse and neglect.

WHEN ADOPTION IS THE PLAN

Permanency planning begins with the use of services to strengthen the child's birth family. If the child's birth family cannot resume care, the child may be freed for adoption by the court and an adoptive home sought. This may be with a relative, with the foster parent in whose home the child is living, or in a new home. As the chapter concludes, we will return again to the needs of the children, looking very briefly at these needs and how they can be met in adoption.

ADOPTION OF INFANTS

Usually when adoption is considered, it is infant adoption that first comes to mind. In both Britain and the United States there are many years of experience which demonstrate overall satisfaction of the adoptive parents and children in infant adoptions (see Chapter 2).

Though, as was noted in Chapter 1, there are now many fewer infants available for adoption than there were in the past, yet in Britain around two out of every five unrelated adoptions are still of children aged under 2 and in the United States this appears to be almost half, but a large proportion are intercountry.

The social worker's role in infant adoption

Though many who wish to adopt infants are facing problems of infertility, adoption is no longer seen by social work agencies as a solution to this problem. Rather, adoption is seen as a way to provide a home for a child. Thus, there is no longer emphasis in adoption practice on guaranteeing the 'perfection' of the infant placed in adoption. Nor does adoption practice now seek in the adopted child a biological expression of the adopters. Yet, whether we are talking of baby adoption or the adoption of special needs children, for adoption to be a viable institution, adopters themselves must also find their own satisfactions.

In the UK every adoption is preceded by a home study of the applicants and this is the case in almost every state in the United States. The dimensions of this home study vary greatly. Differing philosophies and accepted approaches for a home study are reviewed in the chapter on preparing adopting parents. When an infant, rather than an older child, is to be adopted the study may not focus as finely on the particular needs of the child, but it is nevertheless vital for the protection of the infant. In agencies which specialize in open adoptions, the social worker's role is complex indeed, as the needs of the child, the birth parents, and the adoptive parents are mediated, as described in a later chapter.

Placement of infants

The advantages to the parents and infant of very early attachment and bonding led many agencies to consider placing infants in adoptive homes at the point of discharge from the hospital. Even though a parent cannot sign a final consent to adoption until six weeks after the birth, a number of agencies started placing newborn babies with prospective adopters immediately on discharge from hospital, provided the mother's decision about the future of her baby seemed final. Many mothers themselves are happier in the knowledge that their children are going directly to the people who will rear them (Triseliotis and Hall, 1971). The open adoption of infants is usually planned on this basis. Obviously adoptive parents take a risk, as the mother could still change her mind and refuse to sign the consent form. Many adoptive parents seem prepared to take this risk as well as the risks of knowing less about the health and development of the infant, in order to have an early adoptive placement.

Temporary placement in a foster home is not good from the child's point of view, but this is sometimes inevitable to allow more time to the mother in which to make up her mind or for the father to be located and to make up his mind. A delayed adoptive placement when the child is very young is better than instability for the older child. There is now indisputable evidence about the negative impact of institutional care on young infants and children. This is hardly ever used in Britain unless there is a medical problem requiring treatment. Young babies require individualized care which, with the best will in the world, cannot usually be provided in busy hospitals or in short-staffed institutions. However, social workers involved in preparing families for intercountry adoption may have to assist them in understanding the developmental differences which an infant from an institution can manifest. As a result they can be prepared to provide the unconditional nurture which such an infant needs, and to be patient in waiting for the child's response (see also Chapter 9).

ADOPTION OF OLDER CHILDREN AND CHILDREN WITH SPECIAL NEEDS

Fewer placement difficulties are experienced with under 5-year-olds without siblings, but it gets more difficult as children get older. Adoptive families can also be found for black children, for children aged between 5 and 10, for children with disabilities and for sibling groups, but it requires effort and skill. The hardest to place children now are adolescents with serious behaviour or emotional problems, sibling groups of three or four, boys over 10 years of age, and children with multiple disabilities.

Young children with serious problems

It is easier to find adoptive homes for young children, even for many with physical and mental difficulties, than for older children. The successful placement of many of these children is a testimony to the range of difficulties adoptive families believe that they can handle and to their willingness to step off into the unknown. Some families see this as a challenge to their experience and skills. The advent of adoption subsidies in the 1970s in the United States, and of adoption allowances in Britain in the early 1980s, made it easier for families to consider taking a child with a disability, especially in the States where private medical care can be very expensive. Allowances or subsidies are meant of course to cover a range of expenses, besides medical care and associated services. In personal communications, some adoption workers have been saying that there is little difficulty in placing seriously physically challenged children, if the handicap is one about which there is a body of knowledge, and if services to accommodate that disability exist in the community. Adoption allowances can be important in enabling a family to take on the expense of a child with serious problems. (For an account of how allowances work in Britain see Hill, Lambert and Triseliotis, 1989; and for the United States Meezan and Shireman, 1985.)

Children with developmental disabilities are reported to constitute as many as half the children available for adoption in the United States (Loef, undated, reported in Glidden, 1991). These are children with a chronic disability, physical, mental, or both, which is likely to result in lifelong limitations and dependency, so that the child needs special services both as a child and as an adult (Glidden, 1991). It is not clear how many special needs children are adopted in Britain each year. Now a series of outcome studies indicate that most of these adoptions work out well, and that the extent of the difficulty is not a predictor of problems, as long as the parents have a realistic picture of the handicap prior to the adoption and feel able to cope (Nelson, 1985; Barth and Berry, 1988; Glidden, 1991). These adoptive families, if they are to function at their best, need continuing support services, including respite caring, life planning services, support groups, on-going training in care for the child, advocacy training, and information about how to access services. (These services will be further explored in Chapter 11.)

All research on the adoption of children with 'special needs' emphasizes the importance of the adopting family having a realistic sense of what they are undertaking. There is now, however, a new population of young children in the childcare system who may be available for adoption, such as the infant who has been exposed to alcohol or drugs or HIV pre-natally. Barth (1991) reports from the United States that young, drug-involved children seem to be remaining in care for long periods, in part because of attempts to rehabilitate the family and in part because of pessimism about the future of these children. This is a new phenomenon. Researchers have not yet followed these children into adulthood, and have little idea of the severity of disability or the difficulty in childrearing which will result from pre-natal drug exposure. Thus when these children are presented to adopting parents, it is not possible to tell them of the nature or extent of the child's possible disability.

However, potential adoptive parents have once again demonstrated their willingness to take risks and to parent children who need them. In a report on the first year or two of adoptive experience, Barth (1991) found that it was not possible to distinguish in measures of development or in measures of parent satisfaction between a group of 320 drug-exposed young children, and 456 not drug-exposed. These are, obviously, very preliminary data. Nevertheless, it is an indicator that the childcare system does not need to be unduly cautious about planning adoption for drug-exposed children. Rather, it needs to be open in sharing all available information with prospective adopters, and then responsible in continuing to provide supportive services as needed. One would expect that many of these findings would apply also to alcohol-exposed children.

Older children

The idea that older children could be placed in adoptive homes, and could thrive in them, represents a radical departure from the idea that children needed to be very young in order to make a successful transition to an adoptive home. Theoretical support for this shift in adoption policy and practice comes from empirical studies which were discussed in Chapter 2 (pp. 27–8). As already mentioned, until about 1970 it was widely thought that children who had experienced separations, institutionalization and other adverse emotional experiences could not recover from them. Thus older children were held back from adoption placement, in the belief that it was unfair to adoptive families to place such children with them.

Some elements of adoption may be easier for the older child. Obviously, as the child grows old enough to understand the reason for a separation, and as some sense of time is attained, separation from a primary caretaker becomes easier to tolerate. After about age 5 separations seem less devastating. This does not mean that children over this age do not experience unhappiness when separated from their carers. Far from it, but older children can understand explanations better and have a wider repertoire of coping mechanisms, and of social role identities.

Older children come into adoption with the 'baggage' of their past experiences. The adopting family needs to provide an atmosphere in which the child can express feelings, discuss past experiences, and yet feel that behaviour is safely controlled. The child who can remember a birth family, or a foster family, will need help in grieving for the loss of these relationships and sustaining any contact following the granting of the Adoption Order. Even if terrible events have happened to the child, and when the child discloses experiences that should be part of no child's life, the adopting family must support the child's sense that there were relationships here which were once of value, and their loss is important. In addition, the child's sense of his self-worth is enhanced by a belief that his birth family was inherently 'good' and tried, though unsuccessfully, to handle the problems which beset it (sadly, this is not always true). It is thought that open adoption, in which a child has some form of continuing contact with birth parents or other relatives, and with former foster carers, can be of great benefit to the child as the loss is not absolute, and some first-hand knowledge of the birth family can be maintained.

As more and more difficult children are placed in adoption, it becomes increasingly apparent that some early experiences create lasting scars. Not all trauma is reversible. We do not at this time have the assessment skills to recognize at the time of placement all of the difficulties children may have. Adoptive parents need continued support from the placing agency as they work to understand and help the complicated children they have taken into their homes, and they need support in recognizing the limits of what they can do.

There is no doubt that the process of placing older or 'special needs' children is far more complex than the placement of infants. Not only do social workers have to balance conflicting rights and wishes but also to find families that can respond to some very individual and distinct types of need. Complex decisions have to be made which require the capacity to evaluate a parent's adequacy or functioning, assess the quality of parent–child relationships, estimate the parent's future capacity, ultimately determine the best way of meeting a child's needs, select and prepare new families and, finally, help the child and family through the process of placement and then forming a family. These issues form the material of many of the subsequent chapters.

Five key points

1. To grow up into capable and confident adults, children require love, security and guidance and a secure social base from which to explore the world.
2. There are economic, social and personal factors why some families fail to look after their own children or to resume their care.
3. Adoption is only one of a number of ways the child care system tries to meet the needs of children whose families are either temporarily or permanently prevented from looking after them.
4. No child is unadoptable provided there is a suitable and willing family to offer him or her a home.
5. Though less meaningful in infant adoptions, 'matching' as a concept is of much greater importance when contemplating the adoption of older children.

CHAPTER 4
Open adoption

The idea of open or inclusive adoption is a recent development and refers to the continued maintenance of links between members of the birth family and the adopted child. It is not unusual for the child to keep links with siblings and grandparents and other important figures from the past, but not maintain links with birth parents. This can happen especially if brothers and sisters are with adoptive parents, but not placed together. It requires adopters to liaise with other families and sometimes travel long distances to facilitate contact.

These developments represent a shift away from the secrecy that has been surrounding adoption practice for many years towards a more open or semi-open arrangement. It also shifts the emphasis from adoption being a 'gift' to a more contractual kind of arrangement reminiscent of Greek and Roman times, except that now the main criterion has to be the long-term welfare of the child. All the available evidence suggests that more open forms of adoption and adoption with contact will become much more prevalent in the coming years.

THE ADVENT OF SECRECY

How secrecy came to be built into modern adoption legislation and into the adoption agencies' policy and practice is difficult to pinpoint. The practice, though, of limiting contact or cutting children and parents off from each other goes back to the Poor Law in Britain. For example, children and parents were kept separate in workhouses and until the end of World War II, and even after, parents had only limited access to their children living in children's homes. Checkland and Checkland (1974) point out that this practice was based on the Poor Law's philosophy of restricting or stopping altogether contact between children in public or voluntary care and their parents because, it was argued, the latter were a bad influence on the children. Similarly, since the start of family 'boarding out' schemes from the 1850s onwards and until about the first half of this century, children and parents were not meant to have contact with each other and often the children were boarded out as far away as possible to ensure this (Triseliotis, Sellick and Short, 1995). Dr Barnardo, for example, required foster parents to sign an undertaking not to allow personal or written communication between a foster child and his or her relatives or friends except with the written authorization of the Director (quoted by Fratter, 1995). The ultimate in the 'clean break' philosophy was the shipping of thousands of deprived children from Britain to Canada and Australia, 'not all of them orphans and not always with their parents' knowledge or consent'. Fratter (1989, p. 4) adds that 'the belief that the welfare of a deprived child was best served by his being prevented from having contact with his family – that their interests were in conflict – remained largely unchallenged' until the 1980s.

Though the keeping of parents and children who came into public care apart from each other was not new, the closed model of adoption itself apparently originated in the United States in laws designed to protect the privacy of parties to the adoption and to remove the stigma of 'illegitimacy' from the child. In Britain this closed model of adoption prevailed mainly following The Adoption of Children Act 1949 (England and Wales) (see also Fratter, 1995). This Act provided for the first time that consent to the making of an adoption order could be given without knowing the identity of the applicant for the order. Kornitzer (1968) points out that birth parents and adoptive parents could meet in court and they often did, unless the judge dispensed with their attendance. So there was the opportunity of at least meeting each other, even though further contact was unlikely. The Scottish Adoption Act (1930) provided, for reasons of inheritance, that an adopted person on reaching the age of 17 could have access to the original birth records which theoretically made it possible to identify and locate the birth parents. When the right of inheritance was abolished in the early 1960s this part of the legislation was retained and made possible the studies in origins referred to in Chapter 2. Even during this period it was not unusual for some voluntary agencies to arrange a meeting between birth parent(s) and adopters prior to placement, and a photograph and sometimes letters to be exchanged after the order was granted.

To understand the cautiousness of the early adoption Acts, adoption has to be seen in the context of the period. By all accounts, as pointed out in Chapter 1, adoption in Britain was not a popular institution and there was considerable opposition to adoption legislation. Adoption was largely unacceptable among the middle classes because of fears about heredity, bad blood and immorality. Much of the opposition was also due to resistance to the idea of the adopted child inheriting from the adoptive parents (see Triseliotis, 1995). Secrecy, it was further argued, would encourage more couples to come forward to adopt at a time when there were more children requiring new families than applicants wishing to adopt.

In its first report, the Houghton Committee on adoption in Britain (1972) reinforced the concept of secrecy by suggesting that it protected 'the adoptive parents against interference from the natural parents or the fear of this, and protection for the natural parents against any interference from the adopters or any temptation to watch the child's progress or in other ways to feel the links still in existence' (para. 29). In fact the Houghton Committee suggested that the right of adopted people in Scotland for access to their original birth records should be withdrawn to bring the legislation in line with England and Wales. However, before doing so, it commissioned research to establish what the Scottish experience had been so far. The research, when made available, not only demonstrated the immense value of this provision to adopted people in Scotland, but also argued for its extension to England and Wales (Triseliotis, 1973). The Children Act 1975 acted on this by providing for the opening up of the English and Welsh records. As stated in Chapter 2, a number of other countries followed the British example, though this still remains a hotly debated issue in the United States.

The smooth working of the Scottish legislation and the opening of birth records in England and Wales in 1977 encouraged further study and explorations with the concept of openness and with built-in contact, where appropriate, between adopted children and their birth families. In fact, the idea of openness and contact was now being re-considered in relation to all separated children. These included children in foster and residential care or children in step-parenting relationships. By the early 1980s, the impetus for further change was reinforced by studies (discussed on pp. 80–2 below and in Chapter 5) concentrating on the feelings and circumstances of mothers who parted with children for adoption and by the introduction of more open forms of baby adoption in New Zealand. As far as older children were concerned, a number of studies were now suggesting that contact tended to be a protective rather than a destabilizing factor (Fratter, 1991 and 1995; Borland, O'Hara and Triseliotis, 1991; Wedge and Mantle, 1991; Ryburn, 1994).

As an illustration of the continuing changing climate surrounding the issue of openness in childcare arrangements, including contact between separated children and members of their birth families, the UK Adoption Bill published in March 1995 gives qualified support to the trend towards greater openness and contact in adoption. It asks courts and adoption agencies to consider the value to the child of previous relationships. Subsequent rules are likely to require agencies to:

- make arrangements for voluntary contact between adopted children and their families;
- consult birth parents about whether they wish to be kept informed of the child's progress and counsel birth parents on the relative advantages and disadvantages of such arrangements;
- counsel prospective adoptive parents about the advisability or otherwise of contact between the child and birth parent(s) and ascertain their views and those of the child (see also Hughes, 1995b).

Considering the number of older children who were adopted in the United States at about the same time as in Britain, surprisingly little attention seems to have been paid to the issue of contact between them and their birth families. Research, as we shall see later, has mainly focused on openness relating to baby adoptions (see McRoy, 1991a and 1994).

OPEN ADOPTION AND ADOPTION WITH CONTACT

Open adoption is the sharing of information and, sometimes, contacts between the birth parent(s) and the adoptive parent(s) before the birth of the child, at the time of the placement, and/or throughout the child's life. It is an umbrella term used to cover a variety of patterns and scenarios. Patterns of openness range from the most minimal sharing of information to continued visits between birth and adoptive families. Not only are there possibilities for infinite variations along this continuum, the patterns may change during the life of the adoption as the needs and wishes of the two families and the child change.

In the case of infant adoptions, birth parents often exercise considerable control over the adoptions. In countries where third party adoption is not prohibited, such as some of the states in the USA, the birth parent(s) may have full control over the choice of adoptive family. In some cases, the whole process may be so packaged that the children's interests may not always be safeguarded. In situations where the agency maintains more control, 'matching' the degree of openness desired by birth and adoptive parents may be important in deciding on a placement. Research suggests that a variety of patterns tend to develop after that (McRoy, 1991a and 1994). Some arrangements are informal, but more and more it is suggested that adoptive and birth families draw up an agreement specifying the nature of contacts expected. Such contacts must, however, take into account changes which will occur over time.

'Adoption with contact', as a term, is particularly used to refer to the maintenance of links between older children moving to adoption and members of their birth families. Again similar patterns as with infant adoption tend to develop. In Britain most of the discussion on openness has focused on the placement of older children. The debate about contact between older children and members of their birth families arose mainly as a result of the 'clean break' approach which was sometimes too rigidly followed by many agencies when placing children with special needs, particularly in the late 1970s and early 1980s. Important emotional links between children and members of their original families, mostly parents, siblings and grandparents, were often disregarded in order to give the child, as it was claimed, 'a fresh start in life'.

McRoy (1991a and 1994) identified 33 categories of contact and Fratter's (1991 and 1995) study revealed an equally wide range of patterns developing. The permutations involved in arrangements for open adoption are numerous but we can identify three broad categories:

1. Indirect contact
2. Direct contact
3. No contact or closed adoption

1. Indirect contact

Indirect contact itself can be sub-divided into limited openness and semi-openness.

Limited openness

In this type of limited openness there is no face-to-face meeting but an exchange of background information and possibly photographs via the adoption agency. There is usually an agreement for 'letter-box' type arrangements, that is, updating information to be passed on to each family again via the agency. In other cases the agency does the screening of the would-be adopters and the birth parent(s) has what is called 'controlled' choice. One example of limited openness is described by Fish and Speirs (1990) arising from their work experience with an adoption agency based in Montreal.

Semi-openness

There can be early meetings between the birth and adoptive families and the sharing and updating of information as discussed under limited openness. No further meetings are usually envisaged.

2. Direct contact

There are a number of possibilities under this model of inclusiveness. It includes face-to-face meetings between the birth and adoptive families at the start, arrangements for periodic meetings in the future and the continued exchange of information and news between the two families. Again a number of patterns tend to develop under this model.

3. No contact or closed adoption

The family of origin is excluded apart from background information passed on to the adopting family to share with the child at some future date. A few details on the adoptive family are also provided to the birth parents.

Greater or full openness is argued on the grounds that it is better for all the parties involved, particularly for the child and the birth family. When it comes to the adoptive parents, the picture that emerges from the theoretical and research literature is less certain and more ambiguous. In the next few pages the arguments for and against openness and contact in relation to each of the three protagonists in adoption will be outlined and debated in the light of empirical studies.

THE CHILDREN

Not surprisingly, there are arguments both opposing and supporting greater openness and contact in adoption. The main *drawbacks* put forward against open adoption, as far as the children are concerned, could be summarized as: possible interference by the birth family preventing the child from developing attachments to the adoptive parents; the creation of a general climate of insecu.:ty; and the adoptive parents not feeling in control of the situation. Two basic questions are usually asked. The first is:

> Can children attach themselves to psychological parents whilst they also maintain contact or links with a non-custodial birth parent or relative?

The second is:

> Will the maintenance of such links confuse the child and impair his/her developing personal and social identity?

Goldstein, Freud and Solnit (1973 and 1980), whose two books had a considerable impact on social work practice over the years and particularly on the direction of the permanency movement, argued for the cessation of contact between a child and his birth parents once the child was with new long-term carers, such as in adoption or long-term foster care. Otherwise, they claimed, the child would fail to develop bonds and attachments to his/her new carers. The authors extended their warnings to children of divorce, claiming that such children would also experience great disruption in their lives if they were to live in two houses, that is, in the case of joint custody between the two former spouses. They further claimed that the growth of bonding and attachment of the child to a step-parent would be impeded because of the continued contact with a non-custodial (or non-resident) parent. As a result they went on to argue for sole custody in step-parent situations on the assumption of children having one 'psychological parent' with whom they maintain a continuous relationship and bond. In their words (Goldstein, Freud and Solnit, 1973, p. 38):

> the non-custodial parent should have no legally enforceable right to visit the child and the custodial (or psychological) parent should have the right to decide whether it is desirable for the children to have such visit.

Like the above writers, Ward (1981) also argues against open adoption, claiming that it could adversely affect the child's bonding to its new family. Other studies also would support Goldstein and his colleagues in stressing that children should have a clear idea of who their 'psychological parents' are and come to feel that they have a secure base within their adoptive family which will last for the rest of their childhood and beyond (Triseliotis, 1983; Triseliotis and Russell, 1984; Brodzinsky, 1992).

The following main *advantages* are claimed for open adoption:

Adopted children have opportunities to ask questions directly of their birth parent(s) about their background, the circumstances of their relinquishment or have a detailed family medical history. This and the periodic meetings with birth parent(s) can help to reduce the feelings of loss and rejection that studies have found to be endemic in adoption. Contacts also avoid possible fantasizing by the children about their background. They develop clearer self-images and eventually a clearer identity, including physical identity. For children adopted when older, they do not have to give up existing meaningful relationships.

The next stage is to begin to piece together the research evidence to establish the extent to which it supports or refutes the claims made for and against openness in adoption. As already pointed out, most available studies have either included very small and sometimes biased samples or were offshoots of bigger studies.

A different view from that of Goldstein and colleagues, and this time based on empirical studies, is that of Schaffer (1990). Schaffer concluded that even young children are capable of attaching themselves and loving more than one set of carers at the same time. In fact, referring to step-families, he adds that children adjust better to the step-family if they have a continuing relationship with the non-resident parent. He disclaims the fear that the relationship is in some way going to be 'diluted' by the simultaneous existence of other relationships. Kibbutzim children too are reported to have no difficulty in relating to more than one parental figure at the same time (Pringle, 1972).

When it comes to the placement of older children, Thoburn, Murdoch and O'Brien (1986) and Borgman (1981) have found that older children are not willing to move to a new family if contact with their biological families is to be severed, though of course some children, as we have found, may be unable to voice their reluctance and tend to go along with the plans. Sorich and Siebert (1982) suggest that contact can be a useful experience. Hill, Lambert and Triseliotis (1989) have found that when earlier attachments are disregarded, then the feelings do not go away but are simply driven underground. Indeed, the seriousness of the issue cannot be ignored in view of the Thoburn and Rowe (1988) findings that 20 per cent of older children in their survey, for whom adoption was planned, were said to need continued contact with a birth parent.

More recent studies from the field of adoption also claim that the stability of the placement for older children who maintained their links with members of their natural families was not threatened (Borland, O'Hara and Triseliotis, 1991; Wedge and Mantle, 1991; Fratter, 1991 and 1995). In fact, these studies suggest that breakdowns were more likely in situations where past links were ignored and contact not maintained.

None of the children in the above studies wanted to go back to their birth families, but simply to keep in contact. Both the placement workers and the adoptive parents had missed these children's feelings about important people from their past. Children in Hill, Lambert and Triseliotis' study (1989) and in Fratter's study (1991 and 1995) who maintained contact viewed the birth parents as a kind of extended family, or 'like an aunt and uncle'. Some of the evidence quoted suggests that older children who are pressurized to abandon existing meaningful relationships with members of their birth family, or any family for that matter, may find it difficult to attach themselves to a new family.

Because research on contact and openness in adoption is still too limited and imprecise, it is appropriate to have a brief look at what can be learnt from studies in divorce, remarriage and step-parenting. These situations are not exactly the same but have some parallels with adoption, especially with reference to the impact on children of visits by a non-custodial parent and are especially relevant to step-parent adoptions. We recognize that whilst there are a number of similarities between adoption and divorce/reconstitution, there are also significant differences. A major difference is that adoption replaces two genetic parents but reconstitution only one. In brief, the studies already quoted suggest that the children's adjustment following divorce is related first to consistent and ongoing relationships with both parents; and secondly, which is central to our discussion, to the parents' ability to co-operate in their respective parenting roles, that is, co-operation without rancour or conflict (see Hetherington, 1979; Keshet and Rosenthal, 1980; Wallerstein and Kelly, 1980; Mitchell, 1985).

Post-divorce relationships, as many studies show, are complex and highly variable. Possibly the most cogent lesson we can take from reconstituted families with access by a non-custodial parent is that, for access to work and to be beneficial to the child, it depends on how the

adults involved handle visits, relationships, and so on. In other words –
and this will be true also in situations of continued contact in adoption
– we must ask how far, given the unpredictability of human behaviour,
adults can co-operate. Fratter (1991) from her study of 'open adoption'
agrees that, as in step-parenting relationships, 'the attitude of the parents and parent figures to one another is crucial in freeing children
from guilt and divided loyalties'. Yet White (1993) rhetorically asks:

> If the person is a parent who is not capable of caring for the
> child, what is it that enables her to behave appropriately in
> relation to contact, especially if the case has been contested? Is
> there a danger of some parents undermining the security of
> some placements?

Kaniuk (1993) strikes another cautionary note in the case of children who may have been physically or sexually abused or who have
experienced very damaging parenting and adds (p. 22):

> it is important not to underestimate the effects of this (i.e.
> rejection, neglect or abuse by a birth parent who subsequently
> continues to profess love) and carelessly expose children to
> painful and destructive contact out of a misplaced belief that
> preserving contact is always beneficial. It is not.

The history of open adoption is too short to provide us with much
research evidence, particularly on such complex issues as those of
attachment, contact and identity development. There is possibly
more evidence emerging on the adoption of older children who
maintained contact with members of their birth families, than
studies of baby adoptions involving contact. In one of the very few
studies involving infants, Belbas (1987) concluded from a small-
scale study of infant placements in Texas that adopting parents had
no hesitation that the child loved them and that in face-to-face
contact the child turned to them for comfort rather than to the birth
parent. The children were aged 3 to 5 at the time of study.

Another study by Silber and Dorner (1990), which involved the
placement of infants with contact arrangements, concluded that the
main advantages were that the children did not have 'to be confused
by, or obsessed with, unanswered questions or fantasies. They
accept their relationship with their birth parent as extended family
members as natural and normal' (p. 66). McRoy (1994), whilst
reserving judgement about the impact of openness on the children

because those featuring in her study could not be properly assessed as they were just becoming adolescents, nevertheless makes a number of tentative observations.

First, young children seemed to derive benefit from contact with their birth parents, apparently helping them to reaffirm their love and providing the parents with opportunities to explain the circumstances of parting. Second, virtually all the children in the study, irrespective of whether they had a secret, partly open or fully open adoption, wanted to know more about their birth parents. Finally, confirming Triseliotis' study of 1973, children with less information about birth parents tended to be more curious, wondering most about their health, welfare and well-being and about what they looked like.

Looking at some cultural variations, it is claimed that black and Asian, Hispanic and Native American families are far more familiar than white communities with the idea of contact and in fact expect it, whether in short- or long-term childcare arrangements (Dutt and Sanyal, 1991), furthermore that the children are aware of who the different people in their lives are and do not feel insecure or undermined. McRoy (1991b, p. 59), whilst not referring exactly to contact with birth parental figures but with people from a similar ethnic/racial/cultural background, concluded from a review of studies in transracial adoption that:

> Adoptive families who seek and have ongoing contact with persons of the same ethnic background as their adopted child, model for the child acceptance, not only of their minority child, but of others who have the same ethnic background as their child. The child in this situation lives with others like him and no longer feels so very different from everyone. The child also learns more about and from persons of his or her own ethnic background. They find they no longer have to deny their heritage – instead they become bi-cultural and accept both worlds.

Fratter (1991 and 1995) commenting on the impact of contact concluded from her study that 'contact was not thought to have affected adversely the attachment of any of the children placed while under seven years of age, nor to have given rise to divided loyalties, even when there had been fortnightly face to face contact' (1995, p. 243). As with studies in step-parenting, her research revealed that older children were described by their adoptive parents as being more wary or taking several years to show a strong attachment.

Given the age of the children at placement the adoptive parents were satisfied with the degree of attachment and none of the children had moved to live with birth families on reaching the age of 16.

Though some young people in Fratter's study found contact at times difficult, nevertheless this was not enough to put them off the idea. One young person who felt that because of contact he was made 'to look back' instead of being able 'to put down roots' then added that the advantage of continuing contact had been that:

'I knew where I stood. I knew who was the better mother.'

Barth and Berry (1988) in their survey of older children with a high risk of disruption, whilst supporting the view that children can have multiple attachments, also sound a note of caution in the case of children whose attachments to their birth families are described as 'intense'. They go on to add (p. 171):

If those attachments are positive but not strong, children and adoptive families may be able to incorporate them with little effect on their own relationship. Open adoption provides such opportunities. If the attachment to birth or prior foster parents is more intense, then efforts to facilitate disengagement may be necessary.

These small-scale studies seem to suggest that older children, especially, are able to distinguish between different types of relationships and to have the capacity to relate to more than one set of parent figures simultaneously. It does not follow that the relationships with each of these figures is the same, as different satisfactions seem to be derived from each. The same studies also suggest that, overall, the children found contact useful because of the direct explanations they had from their birth parents about why they couldn't keep them. Comments such as 'I know my mum did her best to look after me. She has explained the circumstances' seem to assuage feelings of being unwanted and rejected. The agreement of the birth parents to the arrangement was an added source of satisfaction for the young people as well as the knowledge that 'a good relationship', or at least mutual respect, existed between the two sets of parents.

THE BIRTH FAMILY

As with the children, arguments are put forward both in favour and against openness and contact as far as the birth parents are concerned.

The main arguments *in favour* are that openness will lessen for the parents the element of loss; less guilt will accompany relinquishment because of the opportunities to explain to the child why relinquishment was necessary; there will be less worry knowing how the child is doing; mental health is less likely to suffer; and, possibly reluctance to relinquish children, especially in disputed cases, will be lessened.

The main argument *against* contact is that birth parents will be in perpetual mourning, because they cannot mourn a child that is still alive; they will be constantly reminded of a painful decision; they may interfere with the child's rearing and destroy the sense of security and belonging that is essential.

Studies discussed in Chapter 5, which demonstrate the pain and distress that many relinquishing mothers and fathers experience for years to come, would suggest a more inclusive form of adoption (Pannor and Baran, 1984; Winkler and Keppel, 1984; Bouchier, Lambert and Triseliotis, 1991; Howe, Sawbridge and Hinings, 1993). In brief, these were studies based on interviews with birth parents who parted with a child for adoption some 20 to 30 years back, but were heavily biased in their samples towards those mothers attending counselling clinics, contacting adoption agencies or responding to radio appeals. Nevertheless, all the researchers are agreed about the mother's continuing distress, grief, guilt, pain and anguish arising from the relinquishment decision. Apparently the parting decision and the loss involved was not something that these mothers could put behind them. Furthermore, Winkler and Keppel (1984) found that compared to women in the general population, the mental health of these mothers was significantly poorer. The absence of counselling and of supporting services then added to the pressure experienced at the time.

Sachdev's Canadian study (1989), using a more representative sample of birth mothers, claimed that the incidence of adverse consequences, long after the relinquishment, had been exaggerated by studies using self-selected or clinical samples. Many mothers, apparently, were unsuccessful in obtaining updated information from the placing agency. Not knowing what has been happening to the child was experienced as most distressing. No doubt knowledge can sometimes prove equally distressing, for example in the case of news about death or a life threatening illness.

The authors of the various studies urge a more open form of adoption and better counselling services before and after relinquishment to help mothers choose, or come to terms with their decision, thus preventing continuous distress and depression. Many birth mothers, seeking contact with their child when they have grown up, no doubt harbour the hope of a continuing relationship developing, but it is not always, apparently, the main impetus for the search. This seems to be linked with the wish on the part of the mother to explain to their child why they were parted from him or her, and seek a kind of reconciliation, hoping that the child will understand and forgive. In Britain, and in many states in the United States, contact registers exist for providing information on this subject and as a place where birth parents and adoptees can register an interest for contact.

Hughes and Logan (1993) who, like Sachdev (1989), used more representative samples, dispel the view that all mothers enquiring about their adopted children are seeking contact. One of the mothers' fears was that they would not cope constructively with such a degree of openness and also a concern for the children and the adoptive parents. The authors acknowledge, though, that their study dealt mainly with birth mothers who relinquished very young children many years ago and it may not be the same for those who parted with older ones or who parted with children more recently. Deykin, Pratti and Ryan (1988) claim from their American study that 96 per cent of relinquishing birth fathers who responded to their survey questionnaire said that they had considered searching and that 67 per cent had already done so. Furthermore, the search activity was highly associated with serious thoughts of taking the child back. One of them is quoted as saying:

'No one thinks of the birth fathers! I hurt every day. I can't go any place without wondering. Every 15 year old girl I see – I wonder is she my daughter? For the last 15 years I have been living in hell. I would do anything to find her.'

Are mothers though, and perhaps fathers, who maintain contact likely to be in a state of perpetual mourning? White (1993) questions the purpose of a contact arrangement made when a child is young. Maybe it reflects reluctance to come to terms with the loss of the child and may continue the pain. A couple of small-scale studies claim not to have found such evidence, as many of the mothers claimed that contact assisted them considerably in coping with and adjusting to the loss of the child (Iwanek, 1987; Keppel, 1991; Dominick, 1988). McRoy (1994) asserts that some of the birth mothers still experience grief reactions after seeing their children.

The basic argument of these studies is that open adoption empowered the birth mothers by offering them both choice and the feeling of being involved.

When it comes to contested cases in which courts terminate parental rights, tentative findings tend to suggest that birth parents, especially of older children, may not contest an adoption application if existing links with their child can be maintained (Lambert *et al.*, 1990; Fratter, 1991). Furthermore, Ryburn describes, from interviews with parents involved in contested cases, how openness can be helpful to a birth parent's self-esteem following a contested case (Ryburn, 1993). Sometimes it can be tempting to reach an agreement with birth parents, as part of a trade-off, not to contest an adoption application on the promise of built-in contact. Such an arrangement, though, should also be shown to be in the interests of the child concerned.

Hughes (1995a) wonders whether the drive for openness arises mostly from the wishes of birth parents, with less regard to whether this would also be in the children's interests. Baran and Pannor (1990), too, warn that 'open adoption can be used to institute negative, regressive practices' (p. 330). In the studies quoted earlier, some parents wanted to say good-bye and relinquish their children in a positive sense but contesting a case seemed to be the only way they could show the children that they were concerned about them. Some children were also torn by their loyalties until the court decided and some did not want further contact. More studies will be needed of contested cases before concepts to guide policy and practice can become clearer. In the meantime, policy and practice should allow for a variety of possibilities as no blanket approach can respond to diverse needs and preferences. It is important that the wishes and views of each party concerning contact are sorted out early in the process.

THE ADOPTIVE PARENTS

The main questions being asked in relation to adoptive parents and openness are:

Can they successfully parent a child and develop deep attachments to it whilst there are continued visits, contacts or even possible interference by birth parents or birth relatives?
Can adoptive parents feel 'in charge' under such circumstances, and how important is it that they do?

Can adoptive parents be found who are willing to take on this new challenge?

Overall, it could be argued that adoptive parents have nothing to gain from open adoption. In fact the advent of open adoption has exposed the adoption of babies to market forces, particularly in the States. The next question to ask is whether too much is being asked of the adoptive parents, almost to adopt the whole birth family. The appeal was made to them from the early 1970s onwards to offer their home to 'special needs' children and they responded well. Now they are being asked to accept both the challenge of 'special needs' children and the possibility of continuing contact with members of the birth family or of continued contact in infant adoptions. Adoption with contact might even be a reason for turning to the relative anonymity of intercountry adoption.

In contrast, a number of benefits are claimed for adopters:

> that it would make it easier for them to acknowledge what Kirk (1964) calls the 'difference' involved in parenting an adopted child;
> that it would make it easier to come to terms with feelings about infertility that may be present;
> that it presents the opportunity to obtain detailed information about the child from the birth parent(s);
> and, perhaps, that it enables them to experience less guilt from feeling that they deprived the birth parent(s) of their child. In other words they feel they have the permission of the birth parent(s) to parent the child.

Ryburn (1993), whose study concentrated on contested adoptions, confirms some of the advantages outlined above. He found that the most reported advantage by adopters who maintained contact with birth parents 'was in terms of fuller, more accurate and more detailed information, including medical information' about the child. The second advantage was that 'contact provided the reassurance for children, adopters and birth families in relation to each other's well-being' (p. 15). Adoptive parents with contact were also more likely to express positive views of birth parents compared to those with no contact (p. 51). (Most adoptive parents also felt that courts and agencies could do more to reduce conflict about contact in disputed situations.)

Fratter (1991 and 1995) found that around 70 per cent of adopting parents who, in a planned or unplanned arrangement, found themselves involved in adoption with contact, were positive or very positive about the effects of continuing contact for themselves and their children. The remaining families, who had adopted eight children, had reservations or had experienced difficulties regarding contact at some stage in the past or currently. The adoptive parents believed that contact had been an additional complicating factor rather than the cause of difficulties experienced after placement. Many adoptive parents described their relationship with birth parents as being like that of an extended family.

In a recent study on freeing children for adoption, in which many of the cases studied were contested ones, those who had just adopted the children said that they would not be prepared or willing to accept or consider adoption with contact (Lambert, Hill and Triseliotis, 1990). The picture that emerged was of couples predominantly against the idea of adoption with contact. A few qualified their reluctance by adding that much would depend on what kind of people the parents were, for example, disruptive or stable. Some adoptive parents who had previously acted as foster parents were more receptive to the idea of contact. The New Zealand experience suggests that those who proceed with 'open' adoption are not altogether the same as those who would have done so under the more traditional approach (Dominick, 1988).

Caplan (1990) asks whether open adoption and its success depend on the optimistic notion that people can handle unfamiliar, even unprecedented relationships. How are agreements reached at the adoption stage likely to be observed, once the pressure is off? For example, McRoy (1991a and 1994) reminds us that birth parents may send gifts and letters, but she found not all adoptive parents shared these with the children. Their explanation for holding back was that the children were too young for this information. Almost half of the adoptive families involved in sharing letters did not involve the child in the exchange and some children were unaware of the openness of the adoption. Similarly, where periodic or more regular contacts took place, in a very few cases children had been excluded from the meeting on the argument that the agreement was for meetings between birth and adoptive parents. The meetings themselves were often in neutral places, such as the adoption agency, to avoid geographical identification and sometimes identification by name.

JUDICIAL ATTITUDES TO CONTACT

Today there are two ways in which an English court can attach a contact order. First as a condition to the adoption order and, second, under Section 8 of the Children Act 1989. In the past, British judges were inconsistent in their decisions with regard to contact, especially as the current Adoption Acts did not explicitly provide for arrangements for contact. Inconsistencies in judicial decisions were meant to diminish following the House of Lords' decision in 1989 *in re* C (a minor) (Adoption: Access) 1989 AC 1. They considered the provision of the Adoption Act 1976 and confirmed that there was a power to impose a condition of access. Lord Ackner said:

> The cases rightly stress that in normal circumstances it is desirable that there should be a complete break, but that each case has to be considered on its own facts. No doubt the court will not, except in the most exceptional circumstances, impose terms or conditions as to access to members of the child's natural family to which the adopting family would not agree.

Judges seem readier now, than before, to contemplate adoption with contact. As already pointed out in the previous chapter, the Children (England and Wales) Act 1989 and Children (Scotland) Act 1995 have substituted the concept of parental responsibility for that of parental rights in order to emphasize parents' continuing duties and obligations. Recognition is given to parents' entitlement to maintain involvement in their children's lives and to give consent to plans for the children, unless this is over-ridden by a court. The England and Wales Act also gives power to courts to grant, under Section 8, a contact order in conjunction with an adoption order or any other order available to it under the Acts. Any contact order made is meant to be in the benefit of the child concerned. Those entitled to apply for a contact order, besides parents, include grandparents, a person with whom the child has lived for the last three years (such as foster carers) and those who have the consent of all those with parental responsibility for the child or the local authority where the child is in statutory care. Except for parents, all the others need the leave of the court to apply.

Judicial decisions following the enactment of the Children (England and Wales) Act 1989 have indicated that courts would be most reluctant to make a contact order which was against the wishes of the adopters. *In re* D (1992) FCR 461, Douglas Brown J approved the comments of Lord Ackner *in re* C (1989) outlined above and added:

> A condition prerequisite to open adoption is the consent and co-operation of the adopting parents. This was absent here and

the idea of open adoption had no place here ... they now have complete control as to how this child is to be brought up, and there should be no interference from outside such as that which derives from a condition of this kind.

It may be seen as highly irresponsible to impose a condition of access or contact, when it is known how infrequently access arrangements work in cases of divorce and reconstitution and how adversarial such situations become (see Eekelaar and Clive, 1982). Once a contact order is made, then there has to be provision for its enforcement. It is assumed that a step towards the enforcement of contact can only come from the members of the birth family, whilst the adopters or an older child would apply for the cessation of contact. So far, the judicial approach favours co-operation, rather than confrontation, between families. However, it is assumed that if, as an example, the adoptive parents agree to provide an annual report to the birth parents and this fails to materialize, the birth parents could go to court asking for an enforcement of the order. The court would then have the opportunity to ask the adoptive parents why they had changed their minds.

Accurate statistics are not available about the number of adoption orders with a condition of contact made by courts in Britain each year. On the whole, courts like to leave it to the parties to work out contact arrangements. Considering, though, the number of older children being adopted today, it would be unusual for an adoption not to have some form of contact with a member of the original family.

THE MANAGEMENT OF OPEN ADOPTION

The management of open adoption may present fewer problems in countries such as Britain, where only approved adoption agencies can arrange adoption. Open adoption presents different problems in those countries, such as some states in the USA, where third party adoptions are not only permissible but constitute the majority. Sometimes the profit motive factor may lie behind arrangements. The interests of children may or may not be safeguarded. For example, in a number of instances the shortlist of would-be adopters presented to the birth parent(s) is drawn up by the private firm or agency engaged by the couple and not by an accredited adoption agency. The firm's interest is in packaging and 'selling' the would-be adopters to the birth parent(s). Even in the controlled form of semi-open adoption described by Fish and Speirs (1990), which was arranged by an accredited agency, the study concluded that 'none of the participants had the child's interest as a clearly expressed priority. Many issues arise to distract the involved parties from what should be the overriding concern in placement decisions' (p. 137).

A private agency involved in open adoptions in the USA, as described by Caplan (1990), may be a firm of solicitors which attracts would-be adopters and birth parents by placing adverts in the press. The adverts are meant to appeal to the expectant mother's feelings towards childless couples' unhappiness. The 'selling' starts with the firm advising each side how to 'package' themselves to appeal to the other. Davis (1995) describes this approach to adoption as a service business, under 'a capitalistic system'. She goes on to add (p. 28) that:

> a number of for-profit agencies have emerged as it has become apparent that many people will pay a high price to adopt a child. Birth parents have learnt to shop around for agencies that will pay their living expenses and provide other benefits.

Davis also quotes Livingston (undated) noting in her report to the US Department of State that very few of the 50 states regulate the profit status of individuals or organizations involved in adoption. It is not unthinkable that at some future date, and as a result of political and business pressures, profit-making agencies might also become a feature of the British adoption scene.

The arrangement of open or semi-open adoption is presenting adoption agencies with initial problems and challenges until more guidance emerges from research and more experience is gained through practice. Apart from selecting and preparing a range of would-be adopters, including those prepared to consider adoption with contact, programmes and services will have to be developed to take account of the complexities involved and the possibility of future disputes arising. New programmes for would-be adopters and birth parents would have to consider and plan for such issues as:

- offering counselling to both parties to establish wishes; openness should not be forced on either birth parent(s) or adopter(s);
- the preparation of agreed profiles;
- establishing and matching preferences;
- establishing the child's wishes;
- identifying the best point for introductions which neither

compromises the mother's decision nor exposes would-be adopters at the child's birth;
- mediating where either party changes their mind about contact;
- preparing both parties about the handling of contact and the kind of relationships to be involved, including the handling of disputes;
- becoming involved in continued updating of records with information obtained from each side;
- the development of conciliation skills to act as mediators in future cases of disputes about contact. Much can be learnt from the use of mediation and conciliation techniques in the field of divorce.

See also Fish and Speirs (1990).

A particularly difficult area for decision-making will be that involving the placement of older children. Some of these children, even when they express a definite wish for a new family, do not wish to give up existing attachments to members of their original family. These are children with a history, memories and some attachments which cannot be dismissed. There can be different levels of contact and the following considerations could provide some guidance when considering whether contact will be in a child's best interests or not.

- Give serious consideration, particularly, to the wishes of an older child. Along with this make an evaluation of the strength of the child's attachment to the particular member of the original family, which should be reciprocated. Assessing the strength of attachments is far from easy. A distinction may have to be made sometimes between a permanent need and a temporary preference. It is not unusual, for instance, for some children to wish for contact because they feel sorry for a parent. Part of the evidence about the depth of attachment will have to come also from observations, such as the quality of interactions between the child and the visiting relative. The literature on assessing levels of attachment is now increasing (for example, see Bowlby, 1969, 1973, 1979 and 1980; Parkes, Stevenson-Hinde and Marris, 1993; Fahlberg, 1994; Howe, 1995).
- With older children there has to be evidence of meaningful contact beforehand rather than allowing for contact in a non-existent relationship. However, some adoptive parents

and children talking to Fratter (1995) supported the idea of contact even where no prior attachments existed. This was seen as desirable in relation to identity issues and in keeping them open for the future.

- There has to be strong evidence that the visiting relative does not harbour resentment towards the adoptive family and that he/she can handle the contacts in a way that is enhancing rather than disruptive to the child.
- That all parties agree to the arrangement and particularly that the child and adoptive parents can see value in the contacts.
- Parents or relatives with a history of infrequent or episodic visits usually generate rejection and uncertainty in children and the latter have to be protected.
- Be clear about the purpose of contact, that is, for whose benefit it is going to be and what the level of contact should be.
- Open adoption is likely to stretch much more the capacity of social workers to match needs, interests and preferences.

Pennie and Best (1990, p. 2), writing on black children and openness, urge less Eurocentric childcare policies and for adoption not to be regarded as a 'superior' form of permanence. Their support for more openness is based on the explanation that:

> To Black people, the meaning of bonding is very different to that which is held by society in general and social workers in particular. Bonding between Black children and parents is seen as multidimensional while in the British context, or white context, it is seen as monodimensional, i.e. the close relationship between parents and child within the nuclear family. There is little difference between biological and psychological parenting among Black families. Both are seen as symmetrical, therefore adequate parenting can be provided by the extended family without any real conflict between the natural parent and the substitute parents. This is a common historical feature of Black family life.

CONCLUDING REMARKS

From the research evidence available, it appears that provided the parties involved can handle the situation in a constructive and positive manner without acrimony and recriminations, there is no reason why contact should be harmful to the child. On the contrary, the maintenance of existing meaningful links, especially for the older adopted child, appears to be beneficial to children, to their sense of identity and self-esteem and for gaining a better understanding of their genealogical background and adoption circumstances. In effect, contact has to be seen as being of value to the child and not introduced in order to create a parent–child relationship that was not there before. It is also useful to be reminded that there can be degrees of openness. There is no indication or evidence that under such circumstances contact is confusing or leads to divided loyalties, unless the adults involved mishandle the situation.

When it comes to older children, whether the birth parents are perceived in the eyes of the adopters as stable or potentially disruptive may be decisive in any arrangement. As compared with situations in the past, most of the parents of today's children have not asked for adoption, and some of the children are reluctant to give up existing contacts. Yet the children's own families are unable or unwilling to make a home for them. Whatever the arguments, because of the kind of children now involved in adoption, issues of contact are likely to increase rather than disappear. However, openness has to be considered separately for each case, to ensure first and foremost that it is based on a child-centred approach. The research studies support a cautious move towards semi-openness until more is known. This cautious approach will also be reflected in the new English adoption legislation. The impression so far is that most contact arrangements in Britain are negotiated between the parties without resort to the courts.

Five key points

1. Secrecy was built into successive legislation at a time when it was thought that it was necessary to protect the parties involved.
2. Studies were to show that secrecy and closed adoption were not in the interests particularly of adoptees and birth parents.
3. Open adoption is an umbrella term used to cover a variety of patterns and scenarios. There can be degrees of openness.
4. The available research evidence broadly supports the idea of contact especially in the case of older children. More research is needed about the long-term impact of contact arrangements.
5. Open adoption and adoption with contact present adoption agencies with new challenges in establishing preferences, negotiating arrangements and acting as mediators where disputes arise.

CHAPTER 5
Birth parents

Traditionally, birth parents felt marginalized in the adoption process, but this is beginning to change. It is now more widely recognized that birth parents have a bigger stake in the adoption process and beyond. This is partly due to research findings on mothers who parted with children for adoption in the past. Also recent developments in relation to openness in adoption have brought birth parents much more into the adoption picture.

It was noted (p. 49) that children enter adoption either by being voluntarily released by their parents, mostly single mothers, or following a period in public care. In the latter case the parents may be unable or unwilling to resume the care of their child and either they agree to the child's adoption or the court may terminate their rights and allow the child to be placed for adoption.

Previous chapters also noted that in almost all Western-type societies the number of babies released for adoption diminished rapidly in the last quarter of the twentieth century. The majority of lone parents, mostly mothers, keep their children and many would not even contemplate adoption. This is mainly because of better social conditions, the gradual but welcome disappearance of the stigma traditionally associated with non-marital births, and possibly increased confidence of single women in their parenting skills and their right to choose.

This chapter will explore the concept of social work services to birth parents in relation to the new developments. It will focus on parents who part with babies, mostly voluntarily, and to those who contest the adoption of their children, most of whom are older. In the process, concepts of 'parenthood', 'neglect' and 'unreasonableness', which appear to influence the decision making of social workers and courts will also be explored.

VOLUNTARY SURRENDER OF A CHILD FOR ADOPTION

In considering voluntary surrender for adoption, it is important that the legal framework surrounding this be known and scrupulously adhered to. The UK and most states in the United States have statutory regulations about the length of time which must pass after the birth of a child before he or she can be legally released for adoption. The intent of these statutes is to prevent coercion of the birth mother and assure that she is giving a fully informed consent to adoption for the child. She is thus given time to recover from the birth and the effects of any drugs, and recognize, emotionally, the importance of being a parent.

Fathers also have rights, which are protected by statute. If a woman is married, her husband, as the legal father of the child, must consent to adoption. A biological father must also consent to the adoption of his child, whether or not he and the mother are married. Recently, in the United States, there have been several, very unhappy, contested adoptions in which the biological father did not give consent, and fought through the courts for the return of the child to his custody. This issue is particularly difficult for the social worker working with the birth mother. The fact that the mother claims the father is 'unknown' does not protect the adoptive parents should the father later demonstrate his paternity. In one such case in the United States a child who was adopted at birth was returned to the father at the age of 6, because the father claimed he had not known of the child's existence and so his consent to the adoption was not sought. Against all that is known about children, no account was taken by the court of the child's attachment to his adoptive parents over the six-year period and the distress this would cause him.

Older children also may become available for adoption through voluntary surrender. Ideally, this should be accomplished through skilled and sensitive social work contact with the child's parents. When parents have been treated with respect, have participated in the development of a rehabilitation plan, have received appropriate help in carrying out this plan, and have found it too difficult to accomplish, and when the relationship with the social worker has been positive, parents will often decide that planning for adoption is in the best interests of their child(ren). This, as we say elsewhere, need not always lead to the cessation of contact between the child and his original family.

INVOLUNTARY TERMINATION OF PARENTAL RIGHTS

Situations may arise where the agency has worked for some time to re-establish the child's home and, having failed, may wish to make permanent plans on behalf of a child in its care. The parents may be both unwilling or unable to resume the care of their child and also reluctant to give their consent for its adoption. At the same time the child needs a permanent family in order to receive the necessary nurturing and security. The agency may ask the court to terminate parental rights and to give it permission to place the child in an adoptive home.

In the UK, until recently, when children were identified as needing an adoptive family and the parents did not consent, either the children could be 'freed' by the court before an adoption application was made, or the court could declare the parents' refusal to consent as 'unreasonably withheld' at the point when the adoption order was heard. (For a discussion on how 'freeing children for adoption' has worked, see Lambert *et al.*, 1990.)

Courts, when contemplating such cases, have to address themselves to the needs of the child and to the degree of advantage that the child is likely to derive from having an adoptive family. The court has to satisfy itself that adoption will offer the child 'significantly' better opportunities. If so satisfied, then the court has the power to override a refusal of consent by the birth parents. The final responsibility of the agency and the court is to the child and not to the parents.

The court processes in the United States vary by state, though the overall philosophical framework is in harmony with British legislation. It is the 'best interest of the child' which is presumed to govern court decisions. However, some courts interpret this interest in a way which is more protective of the integrity of the biological family, while other courts view adoption as a more positive outcome for the child. (In the second part of this chapter we will be focusing on parents who are reluctant to sign their consent to the adoption of their child.)

SOCIAL WORK SERVICES TO BIRTH PARENTS

Social work literature supports the view that it is part of 'good' adoption practice to provide needed services to birth parents who intend to relinquish children for adoption or who eventually do so. A helpful relationship with the birth parents is essential for successfully initiating and carrying through the adoption plan. The overall aim is to develop a form of partnership between the parents and social workers to ensure that the welfare of the child and the rights and well-being of the parent(s) are safeguarded, though these may sometimes be in conflict. The legislation expects adoption agencies to provide a range of services to parents who relinquish or who are considering relinquishing their children. These services may be extended to the post-adoption period, if requested. Adoption workers are one of a number of professionals whose work brings them in touch with single or other parents considering parting with their children permanently. This can include hospital social workers, doctors, nurses, health visitors and lawyers.

The time-frame within which social work services to birth parents take place varies enormously. Arrangements for an infant to be adopted with parental consent may be completed within months, whereas the adoption of a child who has spent time in the care system and where parents oppose the decision can result in years of social work intervention. It is perhaps not surprising that a proportion of such cases give rise to acrimony between the agency and the parents and the goal of partnership ceases to be realistic. These issues will be explored more fully later in the chapter (pp. 102–12).

BIRTH PARENTS AND BABY ADOPTIONS

Initially the help is concentrated on helping mothers and, where present, fathers too, to sort out some of their feelings and thoughts in a supportive and non-judgemental atmosphere. Rowe (1966) adds that to a bewildered and confused young mother or mother-to-be (or father), everything can look complicated and overwhelming and this is where social workers can help introduce some order by partializing each problem.

Through support and the offer of real choices birth parents can come to feel in control and that the decision is theirs. Having a real choice can also help to reduce possible feelings of guilt and remorse arising from a relinquishment decision (see Winkler and Keppel, 1984; Bouchier, Lambert and Triseliotis, 1991; Howe, Sawbridge and Hinings, 1992; Wells, 1993). Whatever one thinks about the use or misuse of the concept of empowerment, it is a useful one to bear in mind by handing the responsibility, unless there are strong reasons to the contrary, back to the parent(s).

Although most of the literature on relinquishing parents addresses the situation of the single parent, each year a number of infants born to married women are placed for adoption. In some instances the child may be extra-marital, but this is not always the case. Little is known about children relinquished by married parents, although parental poverty, serious difficulties within the relationship, and mental or physical illness are known to be among the factors that can influence this decision. Some parents feel unable to raise a child born with a disability.

Because of a possible conflict of interests it is appropriate that the social worker involved in arranging adoptions should not also be responsible for helping a parent to choose between different alternatives. In other words, the birth parents need to have their own separate social worker. This can help to preserve objectivity, impartiality and continued support where needed. Smith (1984) suggests the exploration with the birth parent(s) of questions such as:

- How do I feel about the baby?
- Are these feelings related to the circumstances of conception, to the nature of the relationship with the father, to a judgement about her behaviour, or to the reactions of others?
- What are the practical constraints which will influence subsequent decisions? Is there room at home for the baby, who will look after him/her, what kinds of difficulties or tensions are likely to arise given the family's situation and attitudes?
- What is the mother's situation?
  - Does she want to leave home?
  - What are her future plans? Is she planning to continue her education? If so, what are the plans about the child and about employment?
  - Does she wonder what people will think of her if she places her child for adoption?
  - Is she concerned how they will react to her as an unmarried mother?
  - Is she worried about what kind of people will adopt her child or what her child will think of her decision?
- Does the parent understand what adoption means and especially about its finality?

EXTERNAL AND INTERNAL CONSTRAINTS

Both internal and external constraints may influence the decision of whether or not to part with the child. External constraints could be in the form of physical resources, career considerations, pressures from a partner or parents. In some cultures there could be the additional stigma associated with non-marital births. As pointed out in an earlier chapter, the external constraints are beginning to be somewhat less formidable now than in the past because of better social services and better benefits, but many difficulties still exist. There can also be internal psychological constraints such as whether a mother or father feel they can parent a child because of the limits of their personal resources or because of their general attitude towards children. Some mothers or fathers may not feel ready to care for a child.

The discussions with the parent(s) will also have to cover a range of financial and practical issues as well as the more subtle ones of uncertain feelings. Some mothers may require help to explore accommodation in the latter stages of pregnancy, especially if the extended family are unable to provide necessary space. Relatives may often make requests on behalf of single mothers, especially those who are very young, but in the end arrangements should only be made with the knowledge and approval of the mother herself. The traditional mother and baby homes have closed down in Britain but alternatives could be a lodging or foster-care arrangement. Some women may need help to organize a minimum of clothing and equipment for the child, irrespective of the eventual decision. More problematic could be situations where the pregnancy was concealed or denied and ante-natal care absent or minimal. In such circumstances there is little time for practical plans to be made or complex feelings to be explored.

It is not unusual for some single parents to have strained family relationships, which may have been created or accentuated by the pregnancy. Furthermore, stress may be increased through the attitudes and pressures of the culture and neighbourhood, especially for those mothers living at home. The mother's parents will have their own views on the matter, and they may either become over-critical or try to take over decision-making. Not surprisingly, retrospective studies (see pp. 98–100) find that a constant feeling for the mother is one of isolation and powerlessness. Social workers can use mediation and other skills to help defuse conflict and promote a better family relationship and/or create a generally more supportive environment for the mother and the expected baby, without taking the decision away from the birth parent.

Pregnancy can be a particularly stressful and anxious time for those women and their partners who are faced with a serious decision about the child's future. A start can be made towards an examination of the alternatives before the birth. Some parents are able to make a firm decision early on, thus enabling the baby to go straight to adopters, even though the consent cannot be signed until the child is a number of weeks old (six weeks in Britain). If the parent is uncertain and if unable or unwilling to parent the child, then short-term foster care can be used to give more time.

Whilst some parent(s) may need to be protected against hasty decisions, equally their decisions, when made, have to be respected. It can be assumed that a good existing relationship with a social worker, not connected with adoption, can be very supportive to the mother during the pregnancy and after the birth, especially as some may not have another person to turn to and no other meaningful relationship to rely on (see Bouchier, Lambert and Triseliotis, 1991). At the same time, the social worker needs to be aware of the immense power he/she can exercise in such a situation. Rowe (1966) also makes a strong plea for social workers in this field to try first to understand their own feelings about sexuality and parenthood to be free to examine the true facts of the situation. In some instances it will be helpful for the parent to meet others who have faced the same dilemma and to discuss the advantages and disadvantages of the various outcomes.

It would be presumptuous to think that social workers can help every parent to reach an appropriate decision concerning their child. In the first place, some parents will not need a social worker to help them make up their minds. They will do so, one way or another, and stick to it. Others may explore offers of counselling and other services but feel they are perfectly able to cope alone. Others, irrespective of how much help is offered, may still make what appears to others to be an irresponsible decision.

As already pointed out, parents need to feel that their wishes are not ignored and that decisions are not taken out of their hands. They have to be encouraged to think about their child's future and participate in making plans. This includes sharing in the thinking about the choice of adoptive parents and about whether the child should go directly to them from hospital or spend time in a pre-adoption placement.

PARENTS CHOOSING TO KEEP THEIR CHILD

The vast majority of single parents are choosing to keep their children and this pattern is unlikely to decelerate unless some drastic changes are made to existing social policies, such as that proposed by

John Redwood, contender for the Conservative Party leadership in 1995, who suggested that children of single mothers should be placed for adoption if the immediate family is unable to help, rather than become a liability on public funds. Similar ideas, centring on orphanages, have been put forward by conservatives in the United States. Pronouncements of this type are not only contrary to Article 2 of the UN Convention on the Rights of the Child, which Britain ratified in 1991, but take no account of the interests of the child. Among other provisions, Article 2 requires the State:

> to ensure that the rights of the child set out in the Convention, such as not to be separated from the parents, and the child's right to its identity, are applied without discrimination.

Many single parents are able to take care of themselves and will not need state or social work help. Others, though, may require support to obtain accommodation, income maintenance and, possibly, day care facilities. Whilst some studies suggest that non-marital children and children of single parents fare less well in educational attainment and on a range of other scores, this says more about the social conditions under which many such children have to be brought up than about their status per se. No doubt in two-parent/partner households two adults can support each other more, thus providing greater stability, but there are equally children who can benefit from being reared in a single-parent household (see also Chapter 10).

RELINQUISHING PARENTS: THE EMPIRICAL EVIDENCE

Two studies which took place at the time of or soon after birth and relinquishment, with a follow-up six months later, found that most mothers saw six weeks after birth as a reasonable time to be asked for their consents. Moreover most of them did not wish to have a second opportunity to review the wisdom of having consented to adoption. Once they gave a consent, the mothers said, they wished it to be final (Raynor, 1971; Triseliotis and Hall, 1971).

When it comes to evidence about the long-term impact of the relinquishment decision on parent(s), properly standardized studies are very hard to come by. This is mainly because of the ethical problems surrounding the topic, including having to get in touch with parent(s) many years after the event. All the studies that took this path had very low responses, whilst others got their respondents through radio or press appeals which, as would be expected, resulted in biased samples. All the studies available, with only a couple of exceptions, concentrate on mothers. These studies suggest that relinquishment is a very stressful event and that many mothers are haunted by it for years later.

Parting with a child for adoption involves a loss, which has similarities with grief response to events such as perinatal death, loss of a loved one and separation (Winkler and Keppel, 1984; Bouchier, Lambert and Triseliotis, 1991; Howe, Sawbridge and Hinings, 1992; Hughes and Logan, 1993; Wells, 1993). Besides pregnancy and relinquishment, mothers often had to change residence or move from one location to another, usually with associated loss of job or friends. The stressful nature of the event could give rise to physical and mental illness. For example, Brown and Harris (1978) argue that people who are significantly depressed are generally more likely to have experienced a stressful life-event, compared with those who are not depressed.

The studies mentioned earlier tell us that some of the lasting feelings carried by birth parents who give up children for adoption include continued guilt and anger and feelings of loss and grief. They feel responsible for giving away their child, even if at the time they had no other choice. As a result they see themselves as 'unworthy' and have a very low opinion of themselves and a poor self-image. Individuals who lack a positive sense of self-worth can feel unloved and unlovable. They expect to be rejected and criticized by others and tend to become defensive. Some relinquishing mothers' sense of loss, far from diminishing with time, seems to intensify and is particularly high at certain of the child's milestones such as birthdays or starting school. It is now recognized that many of the issues raised by birth mothers with researchers might have been resolved if they had had the support of trained and experienced professionals who were not directly involved with the adoption decision.

The variables identified as moderating the stress on mothers are associated first with the amount of available social support. Social support in this context means feeling valued, cared for and being understood by friends and family with an acknowledgement of her feelings and beliefs. Many relinquishing mothers in the studies mentioned felt that this support had been withheld from them mainly because pregnancy outside marriage was seen to bring shame to the individual and their families, so the whole subject became taboo. Not infrequently the mother experienced considerable hostility from those around her. Some mothers also felt that once the baby was taken away nobody seemed interested to hear their story and they had no opportunities of sharing or ventilating their feelings about the pregnancy and relinquishment.

In summary, a positive resolution seems to be associated with:

- experiencing understanding, care and support from all those around her (mothers who experience hostility, from social workers, hospital staff, relatives and friends, appear less likely to come to terms with the experience);
- owning the decision, that is, feeling in control through having a real choice;
- having opportunities, if desired, to select the adoptive parents and keep in touch;
- having opportunities to talk through feelings about the relinquishment, to reflect on it and to anticipate future pain and possibly remorse (such opportunities tailored to each mother's needs and not to what professionals think she needs); and
- continuing opportunities, when required, for subsequent exploration and reflection.

It can be expected that open adoption, with the birth parents having the opportunity of meeting the adopters and of maintaining some form of contact in the future, should help, among other things, to reduce the concern about the welfare of the child. The matching of expectations in this area can be crucial in how the arrangement works out in the long term. A more recent study, using less biased samples, found that the majority of mothers who relinquished children in the past would not be interested in continued contact. Apparently of greater interest to these mothers was having periodic updating about the child and how it was doing (Hughes and Logan, 1993).

One of the very few studies on birth fathers suggests that approximately half of those interviewed had some involvement with the adoption procedure and most of these said that the adoption was due to their own unreadiness for fatherhood or they felt it was in the best interests of the child. These respondents were approving of adoption. Birth fathers who were excluded from the adoption procedures and who said that adoption was arrived at because of external pressures such as family, doctors, lawyers or adoption agencies were also opposed to adoption. For this second group of fathers exclusion appeared to be long-lasting (Deykin, Pratti and Ryan, 1988). The older a birth father had been at the child's birth, the more likely he was to hold a negative view of adoption. Relatively few said that having been a birth father had an impact on their current parenting function, but apparently those who felt excluded from the adoption process were 2.5 times as likely to have fathered additional children as those who had participated in the adoption.

Almost all those featuring in the study had a desire to search for the child and two-thirds had already started a search. The researchers add that search activity was highly associated with serious thoughts of taking the child back, something that has not featured in studies of birth mothers. The mother's search activity was not related to thoughts of retrieving the child, but rather to a need 'to alleviate guilt and restore self-esteem through the assurance that the child was alive and well' (Deykin, Pratti and Ryan, 1988, p. 248).

AGENCY RESPONSIBILITY

In view of what has been said, agencies have a responsibility not only to provide appropriate counselling services to relinquishing parents but also to update their records about the child and his new family. This can enable them to convey nonidentifiable information to the birth family in later years, if this is requested. Where contact has not been maintained, a meeting in adult life between a birth parent and an adopted person may be a possibility. Agencies also need to collect detailed factual and personal data on the birth mother and father and the whole biological family, to be passed on to the adopting family and subsequently to the child (the BAAF form F provides an outline of essential information to be collected during the course of working with relinquishing birth parents). It is equally important that the reason for collecting this information is explained to the birth parent(s). The collection of similar type information is equally relevant for older adoptions. Where open adoption has been negotiated, a lot of this information is likely to be exchanged between the parties involved both at the start and subsequently, but it is not a reason for not making certain that it is available from the start.

PARENTS WHOSE CHILDREN ARE LOOKED AFTER IN PUBLIC CARE

It was pointed out at the start of this chapter that a second group of children released or freed for adoption are amongst those looked after by local authorities. It was also noted that when children are accommodated in the public care system, the primary aim is to return them to their birth families as quickly as possible. However, serious questions arise about the future of those children whose parents are unable or unwilling or are found by the courts not to be in a position to have them back and where placement with extended family members is not seen as an option. Some of these parents may come to feel that it is in the interests of their child to be adopted and some agree to it, but others do not. Following the British Children Act of 1975, and the impact of the 'permanency' movement, new interpretations were being formulated about the child's 'welfare' and on whether the agreement of a parent/parents was 'unreasonably' withheld or not. As a result the number of contested cases increased significantly from 2 per cent in 1972 to 11 per cent in 1984 (quoted by Fratter, 1995).

When parents do not agree to relinquish their child voluntarily a judicial decision is required. In this case there are currently two ways for agencies to proceed. First, they may place the child for adoption and ask the court at the adoption hearing to dispense with the parents' consent. This procedure has its hazards in that the court may not dispense with the parents' consent and the child may be removed – to the distress of the adopters and possibly of the child. The second way is for agencies either to ask the court to free the child before placing it for adoption, the procedure preferred by many adopters (Lambert *et al.*, 1990), or still place the child with prospective adopters and ask the court to free it retrospectively. (As already indicated, freeing procedures will be abolished in England and Wales and replaced with placement orders for certain children.)

Whichever approach is used to terminate parental rights, some parents and social workers are bound to become involved in disputes, making it difficult sometimes to sustain the concept of 'partnership' which is embodied in much of recent British childcare legislation. Disputes can arise from the stage when a child is accommodated or committed to the care of the local authority right through to the kind of rehabilitation plans put forward. Some disputes inevitably lead to the kind of contesting in courts described earlier. Parents who are involved in the proceedings come to feel angry and 'betrayed' by social workers (Ryburn, 1992). Services which were introduced as supportive can later feel like surveillance, especially when used as the basis of evidence against the parent.

Dispensing with parental consent or parental rights raises a number of issues about the respective powers and roles of parents and the state;

the nature of parenting; the relative rights of children and parents; and the procedures and criteria that should govern those situations when plans for children are disputed. The issues are not new, but they highlight some of the principles and dilemmas associated with making judgements about appropriate life-long parenting.

Both before and after cases reach the court stage, the various parties involved make subjective judgements about parenting and its quality. Based largely on the work of Lambert *et al.* (1990) and Hill *et al.* (1992), who looked at the process of social work and court decisions about children, we can piece together how ideas on parenting, neglect, rehabilitation and welfare are conceived by social workers and judges and how they influence adoption decisions.

IDEAS ABOUT PARENTING IN SOCIAL WORK

The question of what constitutes unsatisfactory parental care, according to current social and legal norms, lies at the heart of many decisions about accommodation in care, referrals to the juvenile justice system, and substitute care plans, including adoption. As Hill *et al.* (1992) point out:

Social science and clinical knowledge provide much guidance about aspects of parenting which may be harmful for children and associated causal factors, but less about how and where to draw the line between what is acceptable and unacceptable.

There are wide variations in the kinds of situations which different social workers regard as constituting ill-treatment or neglect. A common starting point has been to observe whether parents are meeting children's needs for physical safety and care, love, security, stimulation and so on. This, however, creates dilemmas when parents can satisfy some needs but not others. As with 'ordinary' parenting, problematic parenting is not necessarily inherent in the person concerned, but may vary according to the child, the situation, the degree of social support and so on. Child abuse inquiries have shown how difficult it may be to assess parent–child relationships which are not uniformly bad, but mixed and variable.

Account also needs to be taken of the extent to which parents are able to improve, which can be affected by environmental and personal characteristics, for example poverty, the adults' own experiences as children, and the nature of their current social relationships, all of which have significant effects on their capacity to look after children. Furthermore, testing the quality of parenting becomes more problematic when children are looked after in care. For example, once in care the continuance of the parents' role is affected by situational as well as personal factors such as visiting and remaining in close contact. Studies have highlighted the difficulties parents may face when trying to visit their children (Marsh and Triseliotis, 1993). Sometimes it appears they may be in a 'no win' situation, as early in placement they are advised not to visit in order for the child to settle, but later are criticized for letting contact lapse (Rowe *et al.*, 1984). Visiting may even be more difficult when the child is in substitute family care. Parents of children looked after in care may also be required to meet higher standards to warrant their children's return home than are employed in relation to other families in the neighbourhood. We also know from divorce that parenting from a distance can be very complex and highly variable.

CONTESTED CASES AND THE CONSIDERATIONS TAKEN INTO ACCOUNT BY SOCIAL WORKERS

It is not known how many parents contest an adoption application. The social worker will always play an important part in the court process which results in a child being freed for adoption, or when a consent is dispensed with. This is often difficult for social workers, for whom court processes and rules of evidence are unfamiliar and seem strange and intimidating. Social workers are also not accustomed to the attempt to discredit their evidence which occurs in cross-examination. They may see this as an attack on their professional integrity, rather than as the adversarial process working within its own rules to determine facts. The social worker needs also to be familiar with the rules of evidence which apply in court. Broadly speaking, testimony about first-hand knowledge of events, documents concerning events and photographs are the strongest types of evidence. This is one reason why the careful documentation of events in the case record is important. Social workers also need to recognize that, however professional they try to be, they are influenced and affected by social and political considerations. The parents' reactions, including sometimes anger and hostility, will be reflective of these. Many parents find it extremely difficult to hear an account of circumstances with which they do not agree given by a social worker whom they were formerly urged to trust and regard as a source of support.

The main factors taken into account by social workers and their departments in contested cases can be grouped according to two key phases of the children's lives:

1. initial care of children at home;
2. parental responses to the children when they have been placed in substitute care (which might include one or more spells back home).

1. Initial care of children at home

Consideration is given first to why the children came into care or were accommodated. The reasons can include any, or a combination, of the following:

- poor physical care;
- poor quality of parent–child attachment;
- cognitive failures;
- life-style factors (e.g. drink, drugs, imprisonment).

Dramatic instances of serious injury to the child and ill treatment are rather infrequent, though it is often a sudden incident that galvanizes a professional response and the removal of the child. Nevertheless, most parents who lose children through adoption do so, not because of ill-treatment or sexual abuse, but because of having failed to care adequately for their children both before and after these were looked after in care. For example, a young girl was left alone repeatedly and reported at school to be dirty and ill-cared-for; a baby had been hospitalized twice for failure to thrive and had been found at home several times 'hungry' and 'distressed' and the mother had made no attempt to feed the child.

In addition to the physical care, the quality of parent–child attachment is also referred to in all contested cases. Sometimes it may be acknowledged that there is an affectionate relationship but argued that this is outweighed by other factors. Good bonding and adequate care do not always go together. More commonly, the lack of a close bond or a distorted attachment play a part in the judgement on the quality of parenting.

Besides the absence of emotional bonding, there can be many references to cognitive failures to perceive children's needs. This is attributed to the parents' preoccupation with their own problems or to severe learning difficulties. Mental health problems and personality disorders also contribute to the parents' failure to perceive and respond to their children's needs. Life-style factors often quoted as evidence of parental failure are addictions and repeated imprisonment. Alcohol abuse is the most common.

2. Parental responses when children have been accommodated in care

The second major consideration which influences social work decisions is the parents' failure to respond satisfactorily once their children are accommodated in care.

Some of the factors pointing towards the advisability of adoption include:

- erratic and infrequent contacts with children once accommodated which do not promote or improve bonding;
- children's comparative progress and development in and out of care, highlighting problematic qualities in the original parenting;
- children's difficulties/confusion in having two sets of parental figures (though adequate evidence for this is lacking);
- failure of parent(s) to change life-style, or to use social services which might facilitate change; and
- lack of capacity/willingness on the part of parent(s) to co-operate with social workers.

THE MAIN CONSIDERATIONS AFFECTING THE JUDGES' DECISIONS

The adoption legislation sets out seven different grounds for dispensing with parental agreement but by far the most common grounds used are (a) withholding agreement unreasonably and (b) persistent failure to discharge parental duties.

(a) Withholding agreement unreasonably

A point stressed in a number of court hearings is that the legal test for this should be an 'objective' one. Several judges made reference to the words of Lord Hailsham (*in re* W 1971 AC 682 at 700): 'to be applied in the light of all the circumstances of the case'. Following a citation from Lord Simon, it was also held that to be objective judges should not simply form their own opinion of the situation, but must adopt the perspective of a reasonable parent taking an overview of the circumstances. It was also acknowledged that more than one plan may be acceptable and that it may be reasonable not to support the 'best' plan for a child. Furthermore reasonable parents can be mistaken. What matters is how seriously wrong they appear to be.

The question of how much weight should be given to the child's best interests in contested cases has also been a matter of considerable legal debate. It has been concluded that the child's welfare should be given first, but that it is not the only or even paramount, consideration. Otherwise each case would simply be determined by assessing what was best for the child without the need for separate consideration of consent.

An appeal by parents against a freeing order was upheld because the judge believed that the doubts which certainly existed about the parents' capacities to care for the child satisfactorily were within the range of risk which might be accepted by a reasonable parent. The mother had always given good care and the father (who had a history of aggression) showed some signs of reforming (see Lambert *et al.*, 1990). In a more recent case, the Court of Appeal revoked a freeing order because the mother convinced the court that she had changed since the freeing order was made and another attempt should be made at rehabilitation with the mother (*In re* W (a minor) Court of Appeal, 17/1/1995, reported in *Adoption and Fostering* 19(2), p. 45).

(b) Persistent failure in parenting

The second main ground used for requesting dispensation of parental consent, namely 'persistent failure without reasonable cause to discharge the parental duties in relation to the child', raises issues of what are the duties of parents and what might constitute 'reasonable cause' for failing to perform them. Judge McNeil (1986) spelled out parental duties as follows:

aliment (i.e. providing sustenance)
guiding the child in his or her upbringing
providing love
providing support
providing affection
providing care
providing interest

Experience from the implementation of the freeing provision suggests that in the majority (90 per cent) of cases the legal decision usually confirms the social work plan. The judgements outlining the reasons for granting an order mostly summarize key points of the social work agency evidence, so that neglect, lack of attachment and failure to respond to children's needs are again prominent. In the Lambert *et al.* (1990) study, several judges emphasized the importance of the duration and irreversibility of the problems in the family as 'the persistent failure' ground implied a 'lengthy period'. For example, a father was held to have persistently failed as a parent because :

> he served several periods of imprisonment, he frequently let the child down by not appearing as arranged, was unable to provide affection, care and interest.

Whilst judges put great stress on the quality of the original parenting which led to separation, they also take account of the extent of help offered by social work agencies to improve parenting and the nature of the parents' response to restoration attempts. Negative conclusions can be drawn if parents do not seriously attempt to change their ways or to make good use of the time since separation. Yet research consistently finds that in many cases there has been a failure on the part of social workers to attend to the family situation (Rowe *et al.*, 1984; Fisher *et al.*, 1986; Triseliotis *et al.*, 1995).

None of the decisions in contested cases is straightforward and surprising outcomes may result from contested applications. As already indicated, only around half the parents who raise objections about giving their consent to their child's adoption eventually actively contest the application. Some oppose the application up to a point and then withdraw.

FACTORS IN FAVOUR OF PARENTS

When an application is heard in court, the following factors appear to operate in parents' favour:

- *Signs of bonding, interest in child or good care.* These are seen as important, though not necessarily sufficient, in recognition of the multiple requirements of parenthood. As an example, a mother's consent was dismissed, though she was said to have a good home and to be 'brimful of love' for her daughter. She had also 'bonded herself to the child by visiting her whenever possible', in spite of a co-habitee and a violent marital relationship (Lambert *et al.*, 1990).

- An indicator of 'good' parenting, sometimes advanced by parents or their solicitors, is the *frequency of contact* with the child in care. One judgement referred approvingly to the fact that a mother had travelled over 25 miles each way to maintain twice-weekly contact with her daughter in foster care.

- The perceived shortness of the *opportunity to parent* could also be significant. One judge saw a 10-year-old's 18-month stay with foster parents (who were the prospective adopters) as too short to judge its comparative merits in relation to the original mother. In another case, two small girls had been taken into care as a result of the mother's drinking and immaturity. After they had been in care a year, restoration plans were abandoned, but the judge thought that the mother had not been given sufficient time to change, so that her withholding of consent was not unreasonable.

- *Extenuating circumstances.* A court considered that there were extenuating circumstances for the drinking of a father because his drinking had been in response to his bereavement. As a result this was not seen as enough to debar him from parenting.

- *Efforts to change.* Courts usually are favourably inclined towards a parent who makes efforts to be a better parent, even if not successfully, such as by trying to control a drug or drink problem. Other parents sometimes convince the court that they have changed since the application was lodged or that their current circumstances are quite different since the social work department has given up restoration attempts. Social workers may be unaware of such changes. An application for dispensing with consent, or for freeing or for the assumption of parental rights, can also act as a motivating factor for some parents to begin to change.

Whether birth parents simply refuse their consent to the adoption of their child or choose actively to contest it, the process can be traumatizing, generating much distress. Many of them come to feel angry and defeated, blaming social workers for misleading them, not passing on correct information, not being explicit about plans and for presenting selective evidence about them in court (Ryburn, 1992). Direct work with parents whose children have been adopted against their wishes demonstrates the extent of the bewilderment they may experience about the care system in general and the adoption process in particular. Often they are unaware of their rights, for example participation in case conferences or the availability of a complaints procedure. This does not always mean that social workers are deficient in the exercise of their duties. Many parents will have had matters explained, perhaps more than once. What is apparent is that the level of distress experienced at times of separation limits people's capacity to understand, or to request clarification.

We know almost nothing about how children who have been the subject of contested adoption fare in the long run. A study in the USA suggested that adoption placements following termination of parental rights could be particularly vulnerable to disruption, but more research is needed (Barth and Berry, 1988). Many placements of older children are contested, something which could discourage adoption.

THE REVIEW OF ADOPTION LAW

The Adoption Law Review Consultation Document (Department of Health and Welsh Office, 1992) and *Adoption: The Future* (Department of Health, 1993a) considered some of the concerns expressed to the committee in relation to the adoption of children looked after in public care, including some of the drawbacks identified with the freeing procedures. As a result, the committee suggested that freeing be abolished in England and Wales and be replaced by placement orders. In suitable cases, it was argued, adoption applications should be preceded by 'a placement application' which, when agreed by the courts, would enable the child to be placed with prospective adopters. This would mean that in cases where parents are unwilling to give their consent, they will have the opportunity to put their case before a court prior to the child being placed with potential adopters. If the court is satisfied from the social workers' and other evidence that the parents are incapable of having the child back, then it can authorize the termination of parental rights and the permanent placement of the child. If not, the court may ask for the child to be returned to its birth family. The main drawback with this proposal is the long delays that usually occur in court proceedings, during which time the child remains in limbo. The main remedy is obviously whether court proceedings can be speeded up. In Scotland, where freeing is being retained, the

Children (Scotland) Act 1995 provides that the court will draw up a timetable within which to resolve parental objections to adoption.

The Adoption Bill (England and Wales) is expected to present a modified view on the subject by providing that placement orders will only apply to those cases where the child is already subject to a care order and there is an adoption plan, or where the parents are objecting to an adoption order. In other words, where the above conditions exist, no child can be placed for adoption unless there is first a placement order. As with the revoked freeing orders, this new process is meant to provide opportunities for birth parents to defend themselves. Where also a placement order is made, adopters will not carry anxieties about possible parental withholding of consent. A judge will be able to specify a couple in a placement order, but if the arrangement breaks down, the authority will not need to go back to court to specify a new couple.

The Adoption Law Review Committee toyed also with the idea of recommending to Parliament the abolition of adoption altogether, but did not act on it. Instead, it rightly stressed that the permanent legal severance of the relationship between child and birth parents should be justified by clear and significant advantage to the child compared to the less permanent options. They went on to consider a number of alternatives to adoption providing for relative, if not full, 'permanence' for some children. Such alternatives could include 'permanent' long-term foster care, a residence order or custodianship. The committee also suggested that birth parents could retain 'parental responsibility' after adoption but not be able to exercise it.

Already the Children Act 1989 (England and Wales) and the Children (Scotland) Act 1995 impose a duty on adoption agencies to consider alternatives to adoption: for example, long-term foster care or a residence order which would provide 'permanence', but without severing legal links with the birth family. In the right circumstances and where compatible with the child's welfare, alternative orders could offer courts more disposal choices, but their indiscriminate use could prove detrimental. None of the alternatives suggested provides real security or permanence for the child and their indiscriminate use could lead to a new drift in childcare arrangements. Furthermore, hard-pressed childcare workers who find the present process of freeing and/or dispensing with consent stressful (Lambert *et al.*, 1990) may go for less conflictual orders. In a study by Hill, Lambert and Triseliotis (1989), older children who moved from what was supposed to be the 'permanence' of long-term fostering to adoption expressed their definite preference for adoption. In their view, adoption provides them with:

'legality', the knowledge that 'no one can move you', the 'right to call the adopters parents', and the fact that they now had 'a family for life'.

A SUMMARY OF SUGGESTED SERVICES TO BIRTH PARENTS AT DIFFERENT STAGES

- Enhancing birth parent(s)' feelings of self-worth by offering them opportunities to consider different options and make choices and decisions which they can feel comfortable with or own. This may involve liaison with other agencies and self-help groups.
- Information on adoption law and practice, preferably in writing. This should make particular reference to parents' legal rights, including the right of appeal. It should be translated or adapted as necessary.
- Advice on obtaining specialist legal representation for parents wishing to contest an adoption.
- Counselling to consider available options, ideally with a worker whose primary focus is the parents.
- The provision of accommodation, where needed by pregnant women, mothers and children.
- Partnership with parents in planning the child's future, including active participation in the selection of adoptive parents.
- Anticipation of continuing pain and of recurring doubts and of ways of trying to cope with this.
- Considering how to handle difficult explanations about the decision to relinquish a child for adoption, and preparing for possible hostility from friends, family and community.
- Preparation for possible meeting(s) with adoptive parents.
- Establishing preferences and wishes about further contact with child and adoptive parents.
- Explaining the need to obtain detailed background information, and mementoes such as letters, photos and possibly a video for the child's later benefit.
- Providing written, non-identifying information about the adoptive parents (unless full openness has been negotiated).
- Explaining the importance of updating information provided by each side.
- Reflecting on the kind of questions the child may be asking later in life.

- Supporting the parent(s) to mourn the loss of the child and the loss of the opportunity to bring up the child.
- Informing the parent(s) how to obtain services from this or other agencies in the future, ideally providing the name of a contact person.
- Explaining about linking registers, such as the one maintained by the Registrar General.
- Providing parents with on-going opportunities to talk about their child.
- Acknowledging that the loss of a child to adoption may affect parents' confidence in caring for other children.

Five key points

1. Birth parents considering relinquishment require unbiased counselling to help them arrive at a decision they feel they can own.
2. Birth parents vary in the way they cope with their short- and long-term feelings about parting, including those of loss and guilt. Men and women may react differently to the parting decision, depending on their participation in the process.
3. Greater openness in the practice of adoption with possible opportunities for contact seem to have made it easier for some birth parents to cope with the parting decision.
4. Social workers and courts make judgements about parenting which eventually influence their decisions in contested cases.
5. Contested cases leave many birth parents feeling angry and disaffected. The impact of contested cases on children is not yet clear.

CHAPTER 6
Direct work with children

This chapter explores some of the methods and techniques that can be used to aid communication with children and young people who have need to resolve issues of adoption. It is intended as an introduction to the subject. The ideas can be used both in preparing children for adoption and in post-adoption work.

The overall aim is to help children deal with painful and traumatic memories from the past, unravel confusion and build self-esteem. It also offers an opportunity to explore the idea of a new family and the child's wishes, expectations and possible fantasies. Helping the child to understand the reasons for the move and preparing him/her for what is to come tends to smooth the transition and settling-in period with the new family. Research outlined in Chapter 2 suggests that good preparation reduces the number of breakdowns and disruptions following the move to a new family. In some instances an educative dimension may be introduced: for example, exploring how to be a child for those children who have taken on a parental, quasi-adult role, or in relation to appropriate sexual boundaries.

A programme of direct work is likely to be particularly relevant to those children who have experienced a number of moves and changes of carer. This is partly because the 'story' of the child's heritage and life experience becomes fragmented in such circumstances, and also because of the degree of emotional damage that can occur. Such damage may result in the child becoming stuck at a particular developmental stage, or having only partial recall of people and events. However, any adopted child may need direct help in dealing with questions about birth families and about adoptive families.

It must be acknowledged that social workers are not the only professionals who work directly with children. Therapists and other practitioners from a wide range of disciplines assist children both before and after they enter placement (see West, 1992). Skilled assessment and review of a child's needs will help determine who can most appropriately offer professional help, but it should be borne in mind that work with a deeply disturbed or multi-troubled child should be undertaken by a specialist.

Although the focus of direct work is the child and it is their needs which are paramount, the worker may find himself/herself working closely with members of the child's birth family, in an effort to understand the child's past. The documentation that accrues for a child in the care system is often voluminous, but may lack the personal details that assist a child to feel complete and able to move forward. These details may only be known to close family and other past carers.

Much that has been written about direct work with children in foster and residential care is relevant for adopted children (see Triseliotis, Sellick and Short, 1995, chs 7 and 8). Indeed, many children who are adopted will have been engaged in direct work whilst they were in the care system. If this is the case it is necessary to be aware of the work that has been done. Special care is needed when trying to engage a child who has been damaged by unhelpful direct work in the past, e.g. where the pace was forced, or inappropriate methods used. Because adoption introduces a dimension of permanence, in some cases it will be appropriate to wait until a child is settled with their new family before starting the work. Once placed, the child may experience a sense of safety and security which leads to fuller discussion of past events and perhaps disclosure of previously unrecognized abuse. In this way, adoption can be a 'trigger', as well as being a significant point in a child's personal history.

Given the many dimensions of the task, direct work can be both time-consuming and professionally challenging. Consideration needs to be given to the gender and ethnic origin of the worker in relation to the child and, wherever possible, the child should be involved in the choice. Furthermore, the worker needs to be functioning in a professional and supportive climate where adequate time is available to plan, record and evaluate sessions. Skilled and regular supervision is necessary and access to consultants from a range of disciplines may prove invaluable. There are implications here for managers as well as their staff because direct work is likely to be resource-intensive, and in some cases to continue over a long period.

PLANNING THE WORK

An important part of planning work with children is to assess the stage they have reached and thus provide information for decision-making and planning. It is recognized that assessment and process work are not separate entities but usually go hand in hand. In Chapter 3 an outline was suggested of what to look for when assessing the child's circumstances and needs.

DEVELOPING COMMUNICATION

Before beginning the sessions, the worker may wish to gather information to help build a picture of the youngster and an understanding of his or her past. Studying records and summarizing change in the form of a flow chart, establishing when and why moves occurred and their impact on the child, can provide a helpful framework, and alert the worker to seasons, situations and events which may have particular associations for the child. Medical information and educational records further develop the picture of the whole person. The worker will need a thorough knowledge of child development (see Bee, 1995) and attachment theory, so links can be made between life events and the child's level of maturity (see *In Touch with Children* workbooks, BAAF, 1984). Such information, together with some early sessions devoted to establishing trust and rapport between worker and child, should enable an assessment and work plan to be made. During this stage, if not beforehand, the worker may visit key people in the child's life to explain the work that will be done with the child and to establish the contribution others can make. There cannot be a standard procedure to order the sequence but, generally speaking, the importance of preparation and establishing good relationships in the early stages of the work cannot be emphasized too strongly. A consideration throughout is the child's sense of time, and workers need to be aware of how this differs from that of an adult. For a child, waiting can be unbearable and the intervals between sessions interminable. Equally the sessions themselves can feel very long, and children should not be expected to participate for longer than their concentration span allows. The child's pace must take precedent over professional and administrative timescales.

GETTING TO KNOW THE CHILD

There are a number of techniques called 'communication facilitators' which help the worker and child get to know each other. Space precludes reference to many examples, but publications that explore the subject in greater detail include Cipola, McGown and Yanulis (1992), Corrigan and Floud (1990) and Triseliotis, Sellick and Short (1995, chs 7 and 8). Starting from the premise that the formal interview is rarely an appropriate or fruitful approach, the worker needs to devise imaginative ways of engaging the child or young person, based on knowledge of the interests and activities they enjoy.

One way of getting started is to use a game, for example, 'Getting To Know You' devised by a social work team who prepare children for adoption (Familymakers Homefinding Unit, Kent, England) (see Figure 6.1). The worker and the child each have a card marked out in squares. They then draw important people or events on the squares. By throwing a dice and moving around the board, opportunities arise to ask the other player about the drawings in the squares, or to talk in general about them.

Another game that can serve a similar purpose is the 'Needs Game' devised by The Bridge Child Care Consultancy. The idea for this originated from the staff of a family centre, who used pictures to facilitate discussion with parents about the things that were important for their child. The pictures are of everyday items, such as houses, food, television, medicine, etc., and provide a starting point for communication and an insight into family functioning. The picture cards in the 'Needs Game' are attractively presented and can be used with children from various racial and cultural backgrounds to 'trigger' memories and ideas.

For various reasons, children may be unwilling, or unable, to share information for this type of game. An alternative approach is to link into the child's fantasy world, perhaps using a theme from films or books. For example, some very productive work was undertaken with Carrie, a 7-year-old girl who was entranced by the story of *Aladdin* and used every opportunity to watch the video and acquire Aladdin merchandise. Drawings of the magic carpet were an opportunity to discuss where she would like to travel by this mode of transport and who she would most like to have on the carpet to share the journey. The idea of a lamp and an obedient genie allowed Carrie to talk about her innermost wishes and fears. This method of working can be developed in a variety of contexts and the *Anti-coloring Books* provide numerous ideas (Striker and Kimmel, 1979). The need for an approach which respects the individual child is endorsed by Redgrave: 'In my practice, and that of my colleagues, the games are being constantly adapted to the needs of the individual child. I have attempted to provide examples and to state a few prin-

Getting to know you

A game to play between worker and child to help build up a relationship

Age Range
3–14

METHOD

Design two boards sectioned off into squares.

Number each square. There should be a separate board for child and worker.

On their respective boards child and worker should do a drawing of important people or things in their lives e.g. family, toy, animal etc.

HOW TO PLAY

The worker plays on the child's board. The child on the worker's. Use a dice and markers. Move according to the number on the dice. When you land on a square you can either ask the other player specific questions about the drawing or ask the other player to talk in general about the drawing. Playing this game gives the worker the chance to begin gathering information about the child and his/her feelings. It also gives the child the opportunity to know the worker as a real person who has a life outside the social work setting.

Figure 6.1 *Source*: Familymakers (1983). © The Catholic Children's Society 1983

ciples, but each worker must draw upon his or her imagination and make up new games' (Redgrave, 1987).

For children who can express themselves by drawing, making and playing, a range of crayons, felt-tip pens, card, paper and simple craft equipment may be sufficient to sustain the session. However, some children need 'triggers' or an agreed task as a way of helping them to develop relationships and share information. A simple 'trigger' is to make a range of faces using circles of card attached to small sticks. Each face has a different expression and the child can choose the face that identifies how they feel when they think about people or events in their lives. Fahlberg (1988) and Ryan and Walker (1993) both refer to this idea, which has the advantage of being cheap, easy to make and flexible in the ways it can be used.

A task can also provide a useful focus in direct work with children. Sometimes it will feature throughout the sessions, for example, the making of a 'life story' book (see pp. 125–8), but task-based activities lasting for one or two sessions can also have a place at the introductory stage. Some children enjoy preparing a folder with sections which will eventually incorporate the information they seek about themselves. Others may like to take a large board and make a collage of photographs depicting themselves, their family and other important people and events. Sometimes children want to make a card or present for somebody else. Even if this is a way of saying that they are not personally ready to be the focus of the session, such initiatives should be respected. The worker always needs to start where the child is and to bear in mind that 'it is the process, rather than just the product, which will yield most benefits for the children and young people involved' (Ryan and Walker, 1988). Furthermore the quality of a session is not measurable by the existence of a tangible end product. Children may benefit just as much from freedom of expression using dolls and puppets, especially in the early stages of direct work. Those engaged in work with children usually ensure they have access to a range of play materials which are available in the sessions.

THEMES AND ISSUES

(a) Change and trauma

The trend towards the adoption of older children increases the likelihood that they will enter placement following change and trauma. Whereas some of this will be addressed by the chronological

People and places

Where does everybody fit into my life?

It can be confusing to a child who has had a number of
moves throughout his life to have a clear understanding
of where he belongs and with whom.

To unravel this confusion a chart can be made to illustrate who fits into his life and where, accompanied with a
'question and answer' book.

Use a large piece of card. Draw outlines of buildings relevant to child's moves and involve the child with the
drawings of the various people involved, both of the past
and present. Cut out these figures, leaving an extra strip at
the bottom to slot into card.

i.e. figures could consist of:
the child himself
birth parents
siblings
social worker
foster parents
residential social workers
adoptive parents
homefinding social worker

At each illustration of a building make slits
in the card to fit one or more of the cut-
out figures the child has drawn to
represent the relevant people.

AN EXAMPLE

a. birth parents' house
b. foster parents
c. social services department
d. hospital
e. residential establishment
f. adoptive parents

1. It is important to establish with the child the significance of each building.
2. During the preparation work done with the child, using life story work, encourage the child to slot his figures into the relevant positions in each building. The correct positioning can be pointed out to the child if he has difficulties.
3. The positioning of these figures may change periodically as new situations arise. These changes can be explained to the child verbally, but with the use of the chart it is visually clearer.
4. Questions may arise from the child's use of the chart, such as contact with previous carers, concern as to the well being of his family, etc. The use of a question and answer book becomes part of the chart where the child can write down any questions he may have that the worker cannot answer at that particular time. The answers can then be checked with the field social worker and put into the book. This is particularly valuable where the child's contact with natural family has been severed and where the local authority social worker still has the contact.

The chart also clarifies who is going to be involved with the child's future life i.e. local authority social worker, residential keyworker, adoptive parents, etc.

Figure 6.2 *Source*: Familymakers (1983). © The Catholic Children's Society 1983

approach of life story work, it may also be necessary to address some sessions to a particular aspect of a child's life, or an occurrence which holds a particular meaning, as is illustrated by the following example:

> James joined his adoptive family at the age of 2. Both his parents suffered from schizophrenia and, prior to his adoption, his mother was diagnosed with a terminal illness. Following placement, a 'farewell' visit to his mother took place at the hospice where she was spending her final weeks. James, then aged 2½, found this visit a frightening experience, as his mother's condition had drastically altered her appearance. James was later assessed as having learning difficulties and by the time he was 10, functioned at about half his chronological age. His behaviour was particularly difficult at home, where fighting and killing was a constant feature in his play and conversation. The social worker's assessment identified his mother's death as being an area for direct work, particularly as a recurrent question from James was whether she had been 'burnt or buried'. Despite protestations that he didn't care which had happened, he was most relieved when the social worker made enquiries and was able to tell James that she had been buried. At a very basic level, it was possible for the social worker to share the facts surrounding his mother's death and funeral with James, whilst his adoptive parents introduced story books on the theme of loss and dying.

Teachers were informed of this work, so they were sensitive to any questions or comments James may make at school. A visit to his mother's grave provided an opportunity to take photographs, and these were kept in a special album. Following this piece of work, James was noticeably calmer; his adoptive mother said 'it was as if an area of worry for him has been put to rest'. (Helpful material on bereavement includes Varley, 1984; Wilhelm, 1985; Nystrom, 1990; and Heegaard, 1991.)

While a child like James has one particular area of difficulty from their early years, other children may have an aspect of their lives which has been repeatedly problematic. A common example relates to the number of people and places encountered by a child as they progress through the care system. A technique for unravelling some of the confusion that can result from this continual change has been devised by Familymakers. It is called the People and Places Game and is designed for the 3 to 10 age group (see Figure 6.2).

This involves making a chart on card to illustrate who fits into a child's life and where. It is accompanied by a 'question and answer' book, where a child writes down anything that arises from discussion of the chart which cannot be answered at the time. These questions will later be discussed with other people who know the child and perhaps checked with the social work record. Once answered, they are put into the book. The advantage of such a technique is that it can be creative, flexible and visually pleasing. The child will be encouraged to draw outlines of relevant buildings and people, leaving a strip at the bottom to slot into the card. Slotting the figures and buildings into sequence gives an opportunity to talk about the changes that have occurred and clarify any confusion about where they have lived and with whom. Such work can be complemented by story books about moving and the feelings this engenders. Some of these may have spaces for the child to contribute a drawing or some written work, e.g., *Bruce's Story* (Thom and MacLiver, 1986), *Chester and Daisy Move On* (Lidster, 1995). Within mainstream children's literature, Michael Bond's numerous stories about Paddington Bear can be used with children of all ages.

(b) Identity work

Identity development is a universal process, but for the adopted person there are additional tasks as they need to explore the implications of belonging to two families (see pp. 35–42). Brodzinsky, Schechter and Henig (1992) state that, although adopted children are no different in their pattern of identity formation, when an adopted teenager asks themselves 'Who am I?', they are really asking a two-part question. Their quest is not only to discover who they are, but who they are in relation to adoption. The idea of genograms can be used to chart the birth and adoptive families and their antecedents separately, as well as the places and people that were important in a child's earlier life. (See Figure 6.3.)

The issues may become additionally complex for those black and mixed parentage children who have been adopted transracially (see Chapter 8). Direct work with black children is not well documented, although an article by Banks (1992) provides a helpful introduction. Within direct work, Banks refers to the necessity of conveying a positive image of being black, affirming the significance of black people, both historically and in contemporary society, and the importance of exploring the realities of oppression and racism as experienced by the

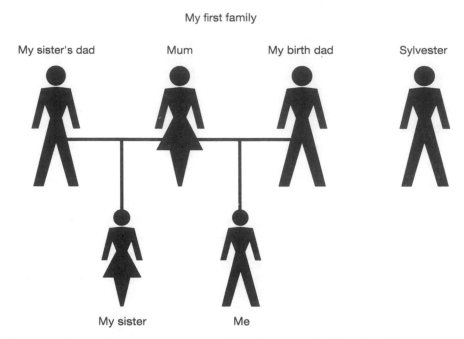

My first family

My sister's dad   Mum   My birth dad   Sylvester

My sister   Me

Figure 6.3   *Source*: Based on The Bridge Child Care Consultancy (1994)

child. The relevance of black workers is acknowledged by Banks, who says that 'adaptive reactions, coping styles and adjustment techniques cannot be adequately learned with/by white "teachers" in a white environment and passed on to black children'. Ryan and Walker (1993) also make reference to the limitations of white workers undertaking direct work with black children and stress that every effort should be made to involve a black worker.

Among the resource materials for use with black children, the *Black Like Me* workbooks (Maxime, 1992) provide valuable opportunities for discussion of race and culture. The series addresses the identity needs of mixed parentage children and includes a volume which profiles eminent black people across the centuries. In addition, there are some useful publications for children from the States, in part reflecting the prevalence of intercountry adoption within the society. *Filling in the Blanks: A Guided Look at Growing up Adopted* (Gabel, 1988) is one example. The author is the mother of four children whose family is described as 'multi-ethnic, formed through both local and international adoption'. The book addresses a range of adoption-related issues, including birth brothers and sisters, inherited traits and an introduction to the adoption process.

Religious and spiritual development is another important dimension of a person's identity. A publication commissioned by CCETSW provides a comprehensive source book on this subject (Crompton, 1996).

(c) Life story books

The life story book provides a chronological account of a child's experiences and helps make sense of the many changes that are likely to have happened prior to adoption. As the book can be adapted to the needs and circumstances of each child, the approach structures the task of direct work and provides the child with a tangible product from the sessions. Life story books can also be helpful to the child's new family, as they read about the child's past and piece together significant people, places and events. Sometimes an adopted child and his or her new family will prepare a book prior to placement, as a way of getting to know each other. Once the child is in placement, the documentation can be continued, but from a joint perspective.

Assembling information for a life story book can be a powerful and a painful experience. By highlighting change, the child may re-live feelings of loss, anger and confusion, some of which may be directed at the book itself. It is always worthwhile obtaining duplicates of photographs and other precious documents before making a start, in case some of them are altered or destroyed in the course of the work (see also Triseliotis, Sellick and Short, 1995).

There are certain core topics that life story books usually address, although the child's personal history is the final arbiter of content. The following list includes some usual themes:

Who am I?
Who are the members of my birth family?
Where are they now?
Where have I lived?
Who have I lived with?
Why did I move?
Who is in my new family?
What is adoption?

Although some children will be able to understand different family relationships, it is important not to assume a level of knowledge which the child does not have, or to use words that are unfamiliar. For example, the definition of 'step' and 'half' brothers and sisters often requires explanation. Paternity can also be problematic, especially if the child confuses an unrelated father figure who has cared for them with their biological parent, whom they may never have met. Working through these issues can be time-consuming, as they may need explaining more than once. Again the worker can use imaginative ways to help the child comprehend their situation and to describe it accurately.

The following case example describes work undertaken with Justin, an 11-year-old boy, placed for adoption shortly after his ninth birthday. Justin had a previous life story book compiled when he was living in foster-care, but this was suited to a younger child and did not answer the questions he was now asking.

Fortnightly sessions were arranged and it was estimated that the work would be completed in ten sessions. In fact, it required twelve. Among the resources and techniques used were birth, marriage and death certificates for his relatives, photographs of where Justin was born and had lived, street maps and maps of the region, which showed both where he had lived and addresses of his birth family. A map of Ireland helped identify the area in which his birth father was raised and the following year Justin visited Ireland for a holiday with his adoptive family.

Justin's life map was first of all depicted on a long roll of paper, divided into sections. The worker provided card outlines of shoe sizes typical of a child at a certain age. Justin drew around these and, inside the outline, entered brief details of each of the places he had lived and why he moved. This technique was more visually engaging for a child than the boxes used in flow charts. An alternative would have been to use house-shaped outlines.

As the work spanned two holidays from school, the adoptive parents further complemented the social work input by taking Justin to visit his maternal grandmother, a contact that was agreed at the time of the adoption. Justin had lived with his grandmother for most of his first two years and for him she had always been an important person, as well as a vital source of family information. On this occasion, Justin's 'life story' work helped him ask a number of questions and obtain a more detailed understanding of his mother's early life. The worker also contacted Justin's former foster-parents, who had subsequently moved some 400 miles away. They sent Justin an audiotape in which they talked about his placement and described the things he liked and disliked. The foster-parents' children also contributed to the tape. Quotes from this were added to the book.

The final sessions with Justin looked at what adoption means and how adoptive parents are prepared. There were pictures of his adoption, but also several blank pages in case the book was to be developed further in the future. The work concluded with the candle ritual, which symbolizes the child's ability to love their new family without relinquishing the love of their birth parents (Jewett, 1984).

There is no shortage of examples of how drawings, pictures and photographs can be used to illustrate important events in a child's life which could also be used as starters for the child's life story book. Redgrave (1987) suggests an ordinary office filing box with the child's name on the outside and using it as a collecting box for pictures and items from the child's past (see Figure 6.4).

Figure 6.4 A box file used in preparation. *Source*: Redgrave (1987). © Boys' and Girls' Welfare Society 1987

Sometimes, and depending on age, pictures can be drawn by the children themselves or jointly with a known adult, such as a social worker. Figure 6.5 is the kind of drawing that could go into a child's life story book depicting early events in a child's life.

THE USE OF GROUPS IN DIRECT WORK

Groups can be a helpful way of supplementing individual work. They may be beneficial to a wide age range of children and young people, although adolescents seem to respond particularly well in a setting which includes peer support. The planning and content of groups requires thorough preparation by the leaders and their success is largely dependent on the atmosphere that is created. It would be usual for the group leaders to be familiar with the participants and their circumstances before the sessions begin and to make a home visit (i.e. to wherever the child is living) to explain their purpose.

To date, most group work has taken place prior to placement by way of preparation, or in the early months after a child joins their new family. Although groups are easier to organize when the child is in the care system and in contact with a social worker, there is increased recognition that the group approach can be helpful at any stage in an adopted person's life. Indeed, many post-adoption services now run groups for adolescent and adult adoptees. When planning groups for children around the time of placement there is general agreement that numbers should be small. Hogan, writing in 1988 (Triseliotis, 1988), suggests three to four children in each group, whereas Ryan and Walker (1993) have incorporated six. It is usually suggested that two or three leaders be present. As well as preparing the children for the group and running the sessions, leaders will also need time to contact parents and carers. As well as eliciting their support, it will be necessary to explain that work of this kind can lead to reaction and regression, at least in the short term. Recording and evaluating the sessions are further important tasks for the leaders.

Groups which have direct work as their focus are usually structured, time-limited and have an agreed number of sessions. Membership is for the duration of the group so, although youngsters may choose to drop out, new members will not be introduced in their place. This contrasts with groups whose primary aim is support and which are more likely to be open and on-going. Group

The basic flow chart is a series of boxes, as above

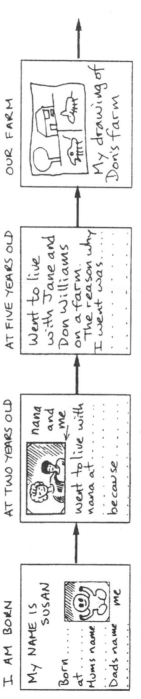

Many children like to use gummed 'Jolycraft' Squares which come in various colours, and then they can stick drawings or photographs on these squares.

Figure 6.5 Example of a flowchart. *Source:* Redgrave in Triseliotis, Sellick and Short (1995), ch. 8.

content is flexible and has to be adapted to the needs of participants. However, the writing of Violet Oaklander (1978) is often regarded as influential in this work. The first session and usually the early part of subsequent meetings is important for developing relationships and a sense of group solidarity. Games to help participants remember each other's names may be played and it is only after people feel at ease with each other that some of the tasks can begin.

Many of the themes used in individual work can be adapted to work in a group, e.g. discussion of feelings, children's questions about what has happened to them, identity work, fantasy games, making a 'life story' book. Some activities need to allow children to express angry and sad feelings, perhaps about adults who have let them down, or experiences in the care system. As well as giving the young person the opportunity to share how they feel, the group experience is valuable in lessening isolation. This is particularly relevant in the current climate when fewer children experience residential care and may find they are the only adopted or fostered child in their family or school class.

DIRECT WORK WITH CHILDREN: NEED AND DEVELOPMENT

The enthusiasm for direct work which gathered momentum in the early 1980s continues. However, the challenge presented by the task has increased and is unlikely to abate. This has happened for two main reasons.

Firstly, the financial constraints within which childcare services operate have become ever more stringent. Direct work requires time and skill and it is increasingly difficult for hardpressed local authorities to facilitate this work. It is, therefore, likely that children could enter an adoptive placement without having had sufficient opportunity to explore their past and understand significant life events. This can have implications for post-adoption services, as issues will have been deferred, rather than examined and, hopefully, resolved.

Secondly, the circumstances of the children are ever more complex. This is partly due to trends which are evident in the wider society, such as high divorce rates and families which comprise a range of relationships: full, half and step siblings, for example. Legislation underpins practice by endorsing the importance of keeping children within their family of origin but, as a result, children may enter permanent substitute families later and be more damaged. It is fortunate that some of the literature is beginning to address these issues and recognize the diversity of circumstances in which direct work is applicable, for example when children have life-threatening illnesses or learning difficulties (Ryan and Walker, 1993).

Work with sexually abused children is also increasingly documented (see for example Cattanach, 1992). Among the many challenges facing the professional is the need to see the child as a whole person. There is the danger that the abuse becomes the total focus, and the issues a child has in common with other young people who have been in the care system are overlooked. Equally there is the need to be aware of ways in which abuse, and the systems and procedures associated with it, may affect work with the child. Issues that the child brings to the sessions may be more bounded or guarded, especially if children have not disclosed abuse over many years, or have disclosed but not been believed. Developing a trusting relationship for these young people is likely to be particularly difficult, and many will bring the effects of distorted family relationships into the sessions, e.g. the conflict of parent as 'aggressor' and 'protector'. A focus for the work may include a 'remodelling' of the definition of parental care, and education about appropriate ways of looking after babies, toddlers and children. The experience of having been abused may also reinforce feelings of low self-esteem.

Caution has to be exercised in respect of the methods used in working with young people who have been sexually abused. Investigative procedures may have used play materials, and it is important not to feed into any associations. As with all direct work with children, workers need to be aware of the effect on themselves. Sessions will bring into fine focus an individual's feelings about abuse, loss and other related areas. This reinforces the importance of support and supervision mentioned earlier in the chapter.

Turning to recent techniques, progress has been made in developing new methods for direct work with children. Technological advances have benefited many processes and allowed images to be harnessed with greater diversity. Perhaps the most important development has been the use of computers in life story work, a method developed by The Bridge Child Care Consultancy. Following a feasibility study in 1988, it was concluded that:

- It was possible to use a computer creatively with a commercial graphics package to help children and young people explore painful areas of their lives.

- It could become an additional tool for childcare professionals who were computer-literate.
- It was an approach that even those adults who were not computer-literate could use with help and practice.
- Young people who were computer-literate (and most are) would be able to give technical help to those adults who were not, thus giving the relationship more equality – at least during sessions with the computer (see *My Life in Words and Pictures*, Bridge Child Care Consultancy Service, 1994).

The resource material *My Life in Words and Pictures* is multi-cultural and contains a range of themes referred to in the manual as 'ideas'. These are therapeutic work techniques and comprise traditional approaches adapted for the computer, for example figures representing family members past and present (see Figure 6.3), designed to help the child or young person sort out relationships and their place in the family, and a version of the 'Happy and Sad Faces' described on p. 119.

Making a 'life story' video is also an option for some children. As camcorders become ever more portable and easy to use, this technique offers real possibilities, especially for older children.

Five key points

- Direct work with children can encompass focused and non-directive approaches. It is used to help children understand their background, events in their lives and to prepare them for the move to an adoptive home. It may also be introduced following placement.
- It is a specialist area which requires support and supervision of the worker. Social workers, therapists and other professionals may undertake this task, using a variety of techniques, including charts, eco-maps, genograms and photographs.
- The quality of the relationship between the worker and child is of fundamental importance.
- Methods of working need to be adapted to the child's individual needs and circumstances, and to take into account the 'whole' child. Groups are a useful supplementary method of work.

- New techniques involving computer and video technology are broadening the application of direct work and creating additional opportunities to help children and young people piece together their life story.

CHAPTER 7
Recruiting, preparing and selecting adoptive parents

In the new type of adoption that has been developing, the adoption agency involved in finding adoptive families is constantly faced with the difficult task of finding, preparing and identifying couples or individuals who will provide an acceptable standard of care for children, a significant number of whom have special needs. The decision to be made will affect the child's future, the welfare of the adopting family and probably that of the birth family, as well as the standing of the agency in the community. The process of recruitment, preparation, home study, selection, matching and supervision can be long and protracted.

RECRUITING ADOPTIVE PARENTS

Reference was made in Chapter 2 to the increasing difficulties being experienced by many agencies in placing older children for adoption. Compared to the 1980s, the 1990s has been a period of retrenchment. A number of factors appear to have contributed to this, including the increasingly more difficult and 'disturbed' children requiring placement. Besides the emotional and behavioural difficulties displayed, some children have been physically or sexually abused or are HIV positive. There is a view that perhaps adopters have become less confident about their parenting skills. It is also likely that the increasing number of reconstituted families, caring for children from more than one relationship, leaves less space for non-related children. A report prepared by the Social Services Inspectorate in London (Department of Health, 1993) found that a significant number of children had been awaiting placement for over a year, and a smaller but no less significant number for over two years. The report stated that finding families for children who are over the age of 5 was becoming more difficult. Lunken (1995), reporting his survey of 144 adoptive parent co-ordinators in the USA, lists, among the reasons for the difficulties in finding adoptive families for older children, the inability of agencies to assure applicants of ongoing support and worries over openness and contact with a lot of confusion amongst adopters about the meaning of 'contact'. Finally it is thought that some of the provisions of the Children Act 1989 and the debate surrounding new adoption legislation in Britain may have been dampening the enthusiasm of adoption workers.

Following the demographic and other changes described in other chapters which resulted in the huge drop in baby adoptions, agencies now found themselves having to find ways of altering the public's image of adoption as being mainly about babies. A message had to be conveyed saying, first, that adoption was no longer about babies and, second, that there was no shortage of older children and children with 'special' needs requiring permanent adoptive or foster families.

The press, television, radio and other media were initially used to convey this new message through short articles, documentaries and talks. These were subsequently followed by advertisements, including pictures of children needing new families. It was inevitable that the first adverts were followed by heated debates on their ethical basis and particularly whether the ends justified the means. The opponents of adverts argued that this could be psychologically damaging to the children and upsetting to the birth parents. The supporters' view was that if advertisements would help publicize the needs of children, why not use them? They pointed to the apparently good results they were obtaining as the main justification for their action. As an example, at the initial stages one small agency placed 92 'special needs' children within a three-year period, through the use mainly of TV advertising.

More recently a 'softer sell' approach is being used by many agencies. Agencies avoid advertising children and instead broadcast general advertisements asking for people to become parents to children. Sometimes the adverts announce information about coming meetings for would-be adopters. The response from the public is apparently smaller but the quality is better, with fewer drop-outs. However, some agencies still maintain that to find families you need to advertise children individually, and this practice remains dominant in the United States. Another innovation has been the use of catalogues, similar to the ones circulated by mail order firms. In the UK one publication, called *Be My Parent*, is in the form of a newspaper and has photographs and information on individual children. Children also feature in quarterly journals, such as *Adoption UK*. A group of adoptive parent co-ordinators in England judged the use of television featuring specific children as the most effective method, followed by the home-finding specialist publications such as *Be My Parent* and *Adoption UK*, and then advertisements of specific children in the national press (Lunken, 1995).

The information on each child is put together by the child's social worker and by the child, when of an age to understand. A balance usually has to be struck between exaggerating or minimizing difficulties. The following are two examples taken from one such catalogue (names and other information have been changed to avoid possible identification of the child):

> *STEPHEN* Nine years old. He is angelic to look at but exhausting to live with. He has spent 5 years in children's homes and now he needs a great deal of individual loving care because he can be both restless and demanding at home and at school. At the same time he can be very affectionate and rewarding to anyone who has the time and attention that he badly needs. Stephen is desperate to find a family and loves spending time in people's houses and is making every effort to find a family for himself. He attends special school and because he has missed so much school work it is likely that he will have to remain there. There could be many rewards for the family who have the determination and patience to help Stephen to overcome his unsettled early life.

Peter, aged 10, prepared his own pen profile in the form of a shield:

Peter's shield

I like eating fries and pizzas	My favourite pop-star is ...
Some good things about me: I don't steal and I don't tell lies. I like company. I get good marks at school.	*Some bad things about me:* I lose my temper easily, and sometimes break things.
Things I help with at home: Make my own bed. Polish my shoes. Keep tidy.	*Games I like to play:* Football and going swimming.
Where I will be a year from now: I hope to find a new mum and dad.	*If I had a wish:* To find a family with other children who will all like me.

When publicity and advertisements are used, the children must be involved and their consent obtained. After all, some of their school friends, or their parents, may see their photos on TV or in the press. The parents of the children, where available, must also be consulted, unless the campaign is a very general one. (The parents' permission is not required if the agency has parental rights, but generally it is good practice to have the support of the parents.)

Agencies usually aim to prepare children thoroughly through the use of group and individual sessions before they are featured in catalogues or television and before they are placed with new families. As we say elsewhere, children have many fantasies about how families are recruited and preparation can help to clarify their minds on this and other issues. There has been no proper evaluation of the effectiveness of different advertising campaigns or of the impact of advertising on the children and their families, particularly those children for whom no families are found. For instance, does the experience leave the children damaged in any way or does the quality of preparation help to ameliorate the disappointment?

INFORMATION MEETINGS

Couples or individuals responding to a publicity campaign are usually invited to attend an information-giving meeting at the agency's premises. The room is usually decorated with children's photographs and with posters, often made by children about themselves. The object of the meeting is to give information. People at these meetings usually want to know who the children are, how they found themselves in the agency's care, details about behaviour or emotional problems, contact with birth families, and practical requirements, such as the expense involved, legal considerations, acceptability in terms of their socio-economic position and health. Other questions have to do with how long it will take, does it matter if they have children already or have been divorced or are single? Is adoption appropriate for them? What are the alternatives?

It is usual at such meetings to show a relevant video, e.g. of children in a residential unit, or of an adoptive parents' group. An adoptive parent could also be available to answer questions. Useful material could also be distributed for enquirers to consult there or take away, such as:

- a catalogue with photos and information on children;
- literature on the agency and adoption, along with brief stories on available children;

- leaflets explaining policy and procedures (including the agency complaints procedure);
- application forms for those wishing to continue. It is advisable to keep this form as brief as possible.

The information-giving meeting, which may be attended by a handful or a large group, is structured in an informal way to make people feel relaxed, and comfortable in asking questions. The first meeting usually sets the scene for the development of mutual trust and the exchange of honest communication. Agency staff have to put across with clarity and honesty the situation as they see it, including the needs of the children and their possible difficulties. This has to be done without exaggerating or underplaying the difficulties. Some agencies also provide opportunities for possible brief individual interviews. This is for those enquirers who may require the opportunity of an initial interview if their queries are not answered through the group meeting. Some agencies offer a home visit prior to an information meeting.

Following the information-giving meeting, usually a high percentage of enquirers do not return their application forms. It is thought that about a third withdraw because they think they cannot handle a child with the difficulties described, about a third require further time and perhaps a change of circumstances before proceeding, and about a third are in some way unhappy about agency or adoption procedures.

For those who return the forms, a meeting is usually arranged with them before the group preparation, to hear more from them about their wishes. This meeting provides the opportunity also of an agreement between the social worker and the applicant(s) about the process to be followed, i.e. a clear idea of what to expect, number of group and individual meetings, the shared responsibility involved, etc. Not all couples or individuals will be at the same stage of readiness, but the idea of group preparation gives everybody more time.

Agencies will take up statutory checks at this stage, and if there is a medical condition noted will seek guidance from their medical adviser. Preparing people to adopt is highly resource-intensive and costly for the agency, and the goodwill of the people is easily lost if people are told late in the process that they are unacceptable for medical reasons or due to a criminal record.

ASSESSMENT

Assessment is an imprecise process because there are no firm criteria of what qualities exactly are required to parent other people's children. Even when we know what to look for, it is not always easy to recognize the presence or absence of such qualities as maturity, stability of couple relationships, warmth and capacity for close relationships. Motivation, too, is a difficult attribute to evaluate. As an example, in the same way that good wine can be made from different types of grapes, equally people can be good parents in different ways. The task of adoptive parenting has become increasingly complex and challenging, and the tasks of assessment and preparation much more complicated, compared with arranging baby adoptions. These new challenges have also contributed to the development of new assessment and preparation methods to respond to the new requirements. The broad qualities that research suggests contribute to successful adoptive parenthood have been set out in Chapter 2.

The concept of a 'healthy' or 'normal' family is useful only in as far as it can respond to the needs of a particular child. As already noted, the recognition of these qualities is still problematic. For example, recent adoption experience, supported by research, suggests that somewhat different qualities are required of today's adopters of older children or those with physical, mental or emotional disabilities (see Thoburn, 1994; Borland, O'Hara and Triseliotis, 1991). Such adopters are sometimes older, they may already have their own children and may wish to expand rather than create a family. Others may wish to use their personal experience from caring for an own child with learning difficulties or a disability by offering a home to a similar child through adoption. Others still may have some professional expertise in caring for children with special needs and wish to use it.

When selecting adoptive parent(s), agencies have to consider the possible implications for the child of applicants who may have a history of criminality or anti-social behaviour, psychiatric disturbance, marital instability, communicable illness. disease or disability. Some of these conditions need not bar people from becoming adoptive parents, but their seriousness, extent, and the circumstances surrounding them, have to be considered in the light of the particular child's needs and circumstances.

Though adoption is not only meant for those who are well off, nevertheless it is only fair to the child that the people adopting him should have some economic security. Adoption allowances could be used where appropriate to provide some stability or to enable a family to meet the extraordinary expenses of a child with a disability.

TRADITIONAL ASSESSMENT PROCESSES

At one time the assessment/selection process was based almost solely on interviews with couples, some joint and some separate. These could be very brief or very lengthy. Even successful applicants would often express dissatisfaction with the methods of selection, because the process was seen as too slow, intrusive or investigative, and as doubting the applicants' sincerity. As a result, most of the applicants tried to create the impression they thought would be most favourable to their application. Until the early 1970s or so, three main approaches could be identified in the selection of adoptive and foster-parents:

The administrative approach

This method relied mostly on tangible criteria such as age, religion, socio-economic circumstances, personal references and statutory checks. Also on the adoption worker's estimation of the applicant's standing in the community. Overall the method aimed to satisfy explicit legal or agency requirements, and it paid less attention to motivation and psychological suitability (Triseliotis, 1970).

The diagnostic or investigative method

This method was largely based on joint and individual interviews with couples over a period of time. Applicants were interviewed, evaluated and assessed on their anticipated ability to be 'good' psychological parents. This approach had been considerably influenced by insights from psychodynamic psychology and concentrated particularly on the 'intangible' qualities of the applicants. The qualities on which it was claimed the applicants' suitability was being judged were their emotional maturity, strength of motivation, quality of the marital and other relationships, their understanding and knowledge of children and finally their total personality.

These seemed notable qualities to look for, but what generated hostility and resentment was what was seen as the inquisitorial approach of some workers and the inexplicitness about how the information was interpreted and assessed. Worst were the vague reasons offered for rejecting applicants. It was claimed, for example, that adoption workers would too frequently interpret behaviour in terms of 'unconscious' processes, thus ruling out many prospective adopters without giving them the opportunity to defend themselves. At a time when agencies were aiming to place the 'perfect' baby, it was not surprising that they were also on the quest for the 'perfect' couple. Perfection was often synonymous with 'convention' and little attention was paid to adapting methods of preparation to include black, single or inter-racial applicants.

The scientific method

This method is based on the idea of giving applicants an elaborate questionnaire and a battery of psychological tests that will separate the 'suitable' from the 'unsuitable' would-be parents. Though a number of agencies use a questionnaire in ways we shall be describing later, no agency to our knowledge has consistently used psychological tests as the main approach to selection. In the first place there are no psychological tests which can identify or predict who can be a 'good' parent. Given the variety and diverse needs of children needing families, this would be an almost impossible task. The most a test can do, as far as parenting is concerned, is to spot certain psychotic trends in some applicants. Psychotic propensities, of course, may never develop.

THE CURRENT POSITION

The emphasis in selection of adoptive parents has shifted towards preparation through the use of educative groups. Agencies are also anxious to stress the idea of 'partnership' with applicants, even if it does not always feel like that to the latter. Adoption work involves a series of decisions made by an adoption agency at different stages of the adoption procedure. Applicants also continually make decisions about their interest in continuing as they learn more and examine their own feelings more. Children in their own way are also involved in making decisions about themselves and their readiness to be adopted.

Besides looking at parenting qualities, more attention is now paid to what is called a task-centred approach which assesses and prepares people for the tasks they have to undertake. This model is usually reinforced by systemic ideas which start with the applicant(s)' strengths and take account of social and environmental factors, besides personal and family ones. An understanding and application of ideas from theories of child and general human development are central to any process of assessment and usually inform both the task-centred and systemic models (see also Triseliotis, Sellick and Short, 1993, chapter on assessment; and Davis, Morris and Thorn, 1984).

Assessment is now seen as part of a process based on group meetings and joint and separate interviews with the applicant(s) and with the whole family, where relevant. More explanation is offered to the family about the process, why information is needed and how it is viewed. Allowance is also made for the fact that people who are new to adoption cannot be expected to know all the answers to the various dilemmas and possibilities. There is a much greater tendency to look upon applicants as people offering a service to the agency, rather than as clients or those with suspect motivation. More important is the use of groups for giving information to applicants about what is involved in parenting other people's children and general preparation for the adoptive role.

THE USE OF GROUPS FOR PREPARING/SELECTING ADOPTIVE PARENTS

The main exponent of the use of groups in the preparation of adoptive parents was Kirk (1964). His ideas for an 'educative' and 'self-selection' approach through the use of groups, though published in 1964, were not more widely taken up for another ten to fifteen years. Kirk (1970) expanded his views later by explaining that adoptive parents suffered from 'role handicap' because (a) they faced a series of difficulties that are not shared by natural parents; (b) they are not prepared for these difficulties, either by guidelines in the culture generally, or by the professional groups that mean to assist in adoption; and (c) that without such preparation for their role, adopters face unnecessary strains in their relationships with the children. His position was that assessment and selection processes should be dropped in favour of an approach that prepares and educates adopters for their role. Kirk went on to suggest what he called the *group educative* approach for the preparation of would-be adopters. This method, as expounded by him, provided that once basic agency and legal eligibility criteria were satisfied, all applicants should be treated as potential adopters. From here on they would be subjected to an educational group process in which they could learn enough about themselves, their motives and needs, to bring them to the stage of deciding for themselves whether they should adopt or not.

Agencies have an enormous responsibility towards the children and their birth parents and it is appropriate that they should retain the right to say 'no', if it is felt that particular applicants are not ready or suitable to adopt. If not all biological parents can also be psychological parents, it would be naive to think that all non-biological parents can become psychological parents. Recent experience also suggests that preparation for the adoptive role does not stop at the adoption stage, but may have to continue in the form of post-adoption support and advice, especially in the light of the problems and complicated histories of children now placed for adoption. The tone of the relationship developed between adopters and social workers from the start can generate the kind of trust and confidence required for the provision of post-adoption services.

The main rationale for use of groups is the view that they provide a less formal setting for exploring ideas and feelings, that participants are more receptive to observations and suggestions made by peers, that they generate less resentment towards the social workers who hold the power, they broaden the participants' views about the kind of child they might adopt, and generally promote a better understanding about the needs of children. They are also an ideal forum for prospective adopters to meet those who have experience of the task. It is further argued that the 'preparation and social education' approach encourages prospective adopters to examine their motivation in a climate of safety and mutual support, assess their willingness or readiness to adopt, particularly 'special needs' children, and consider issues of matching and post-adoption support.

Wiehe (1976) found, from his study contrasting different approaches to selection, that would-be adopters who took part in group discussions with other applicants displayed a significant difference from others in their perception of the procedure as constituting *preparation* for adoptive parenthood. Group members were apparently able to share knowledge and ideas, and were 'able to use each other to test and expound their views'. Would-be adopters said that this had been helpful in enabling them to clarify attitudes and feelings. This, of course, still does not tell us how applicants from each group functioned with actual children, both in the short and in the long term.

Preparation groups

The use of groups for the preparation of adoptive and foster parents, with assessment not being a major component, acknowledges that many applicants are not fully aware of the tasks involved in being a substitute or psychological parent, and could benefit from information and exploration of ideas. For those adopting intercountry there will be additional issues and tasks to explore. In the early stages most groups adopted a predominantly educational model with considerable input from social workers and other 'experts' in the form of psychologists, paediatricians, and lawyers.

It was then realized that this model was simply conveying information but without much guarantee that this was assimilated or absorbed by those present. Furthermore, applicants were being made dependent on external 'experts' rather than becoming aware of their own potential to parent another person's child. This realization led to a gradual shift of emphasis from a mainly educational approach to a predominantly experiential one, or a mixture of the two. By experiential is meant the opportunity afforded to group members to explore their ideas and feelings about adoption, and to examine their motivation and readiness to parent other people's children. This approach acknowledges that much of learning is more enduring and meaningful when it is participatory.

An experiential group is not the same as a therapeutic one. It should be made clear that these groups are not meant to be therapeutic in nature. Obviously it is again difficult to deny that some form of intangible 'therapy' takes place, in as far as any meaningful interaction between people can have this kind of effect. But this is a by-product rather than a key objective.

A further conceptual issue that has not been adequately resolved is the extent to which such groups are purely preparatory without elements of assessment or both preparation and assessment. Even those who like them to be purely preparatory, and where the participants may eventually select themselves out, admit to elements of assessment being present (see Horne, 1981). On the other hand, McKay (1980) has no doubts that the group allows 'some estimation to be made of a couple's potential for adoption'. For the social worker, she adds, there is the benefit of seeing couples behaving towards other people in a more normal social setting than they do in the inevitably artificial interview. Some agencies in Britain now prepare brief profiles of each family attending the groups, share them with the adoptive applicant(s) and pass them on to the home study caseworker. The majority of agencies, though, have come to see the group method as part of both the assessment and preparation process and the two often happen at the same time to reduce delays.

Starting a group

To set up a group a number of questions have to be settled such as its purpose, composition, size and the process to be followed. The purpose of adoption groups has already been discussed. By their very nature preparatory and educational groups have to be time-limited, e.g. eight to ten sessions. The numbers may range from three to five or more couples (and possibly one or two sole applicants). If there are too many applicants they can be split into smaller groups. Other questions arising include the mixing of childless couples with those who have children, the inclusion of people from different social and educational backgrounds and racial origins, whether there should be a mix of couples wishing to adopt pre-school and those who are thinking about older children. Answers to these questions must be based on attaining a balance of support and cohesion, with opportunities for challenge and confrontation within the group. These are qualities which can help promote effective learning. It is difficult to design a group programme to suit everyone. As already said, allowance may also have to be made for the fact that some people may not enjoy groups and may require separate individual arrangements or for those who are unable to attend for other reasons. Rhodes' book (1992) alerts the reader to some of the implications arising from running racially mixed groups.

The work of the group

To promote learning, groups have to generate trust, cohesion and a supportive climate without avoiding challenge and discomfort. The role of the leader(s) is to promote these qualities, including interaction and the sharing and exploration of ideas and experiences, including their own. The leader is not expected to make interpretations about the participants' conscious or unconscious motives or behaviour. Knowledge of adoption is essential, as is knowledge about groups and their operation. It is also advisable to have an experienced adoptive parent acting as co-leader of the group or attending to share their experiences and also answer some questions. It is not 'good enough' simply to put people in a group hoping that something will happen. The leaders also have to continuously be aware of how the group is functioning, both at the group and at the individual level. Writers on group work generally suggest democratic leadership which encourages friendliness and sharing and helping to promote cohesion and a 'creative' attitude amongst participants.

It is also preferable to have a male and female worker, one black and the other white if practicable, leading a group, irrespective of the racial origins of those attending. There is also a view that with two leaders it is useful to have one who is better at promoting the 'maintenance' needs of the group and the other its 'instrumental' needs. A 'maintenance' oriented leader promotes such qualities as trust and security, whilst the 'instrumental' one focuses much more on problem-solving. To promote membership interaction, some group leaders introduce a range of games and exercises which are relevant to the task.

The following ten sessions are typical of how groups can be used to prepare adoptive parents. Variations can be introduced to take account of the particular needs and stage of the group. Some agencies use a half day or a whole day to cover one or two themes, others use more sessions but of shorter duration.

Session one

The first session can be used to introduce members to each other and consider some of the issues involved in adoption, and explore what this may mean for the members' families. Videos, slides or work sheets may then be introduced to stimulate discussion and the exchange of ideas. The aids shown have to do with adoption to enable the participants to develop a better understanding of the tasks involved.

N.B. Some agencies use the first session differently by inviting two experienced adopters to share their experiences of parenting either young or older or 'special needs' children.

Session two

'The decision to adopt' becomes the focus of this session. Participants are encouraged to discuss their decision to adopt and what has motivated them. Childlessness features a lot in such discussions, or the wish to enlarge one's own family. Group members may then go on to talk about the child they would like to adopt, and share anxieties and fears concerning behaviour, heredity and environment. Facts and fallacies about adoption can be explored. (The participants should be told that they should feel free to discuss only those matters they feel comfortable with.)

This, or another session, could find time to discuss the theme of loss as experienced by all members of the adoption triangle, so people can identify with each other. A video can be shown of a birth parent(s) talking about feelings after adoption. Applicants can then be helped to view the experience of loss as empowering in the adoption situation.

Session three

'How we have been reared and how this is likely to affect my handling of the adopted child.' This theme offers members the opportunity to share personal experiences from their own child-hood. The group leaders may in fact decide to split the group into two sub-groups (perhaps separating couples) and ask them to talk for example about the time they were adolescents or first started school, or occasions when they were separated from parents through illness or other reasons.

Another exercise is to ask members to say what it takes to be a parent. This suggestion is brainstormed, various ideas being suggested by members and listed for all to see. Then the group is asked to brainstorm the question of what additionally is required to be an adoptive parent. Apart from how personal past experiences may affect members in their adoptive role, they can be encouraged to share with each other how they think other members of their immediate family (e.g. children) are going to react, including relatives and friends. This can also lead on to a discussion of cultural perspectives on adoption. This is very important especially if participants come from different ethnic backgrounds or the adoption is transracial or intercountry.

Session four

'The child's birth family and background.' This session is used to explore the participants' views and attitudes towards biological parents and the child's racial and cultural background. In addition, how they propose to help the child understand about his adoption, his family of origin, his race, ethnic group and culture and why he was adopted. The discussion may reveal strong attitudes and views about sex, non-marital birth, neglectful or abusing parents, and about welfare benefits. Adoptive parents can be introduced to the idea of 'story books' for each child, to understand the meaning to the child of his past life and experi-ences. A useful technique, when the group is talking about the child's family, is to have one or two empty chairs to stress the importance of the birth family in the child's make-up.

This or another session will have to include the recognition of child abuse, dealing with disclosure and parenting an abused child or a child who is HIV positive.

Session five

'Openness in adoption.' Why openness and the supporting evidence. How to prepare for taking part in open forms of adoption; meeting the biological parents; presentation of self; the possibility of continued contact and how it could be managed. Providing up-dated information, e.g. using an agency 'letter box' facility.

Session six

'Child development.' This session may take a more educational form by inviting an outside speaker to talk about 'normal' child development and the various stages children go through. A way to liven this session up is to play a game. Each group member is given a number of pieces of paper which describe a developmental milestone, for example, gets excited when he sees his feeding bottle, or knows all his colours or can answer the telephone. These slips are posted into boxes clearly labelled with different ages (see Horn, 1981). Reference can also be made to the impact of separation on young children and to children's basic needs for affection, security and continuity of care.

Session seven

'Being a psychological parent.' What is similar and what is different about being a psychological but not a biological parent? What are the additional tasks involved for adoptive parents and children? Why a child needs to know about its origins. The possibility of seeking out his biological parents in adult life. The additional tasks for parents adopting inter-country and transracially. Attitudes to other races and ethnic groups. Helping a child to develop ethnic and cultural awareness and a positive racial identity. Discussion of stereotypes and role models. Sharing of the agency's Equal Opportunities Policy.

Session eight

'Managing behaviour.' As many of the children who are free for adoption are not infants but older with a history and experiences, and not infrequently displaying behaviour and emotional difficulties, the session is used to consider both the members' reactions and also handling of possible problems. After a general discussion of hypothetical situations, it may be useful to introduce one or two vignette cases. Adjustment problems, such as a child having nightmares, or a child who tells lies or steals, can be considered by the group. The leader may offer suggestions or make comments when appropriate to dispel fallacies about children, or to correct misperceptions. Attention needs to be given to helping children who cannot easily form attachments, and the feelings this can provoke in those who parent them. Case studies could be introduced to generate discussion. Some agencies arrange a visit to a residential setting for disturbed children.

Session nine

This session may be used to invite one or two adopters to share their experiences. This is usually one of the most successful sessions. There is usually a list of questions that members ask and which generate some very interesting discussions. An adult adoptee could also be introduced to share his/her experiences with the group. This can be particularly reassuring in the area of origins and backgrounds.

Every effort should be made to ensure that the birth parent perspective is also brought to life, either through a personal or video presentation from someone in this situation.

Session ten

Practical issues, such as financial and legal ones, including the conditions under which adoption allowances can be made available or benefits for children with disabilities, can be the subject for discussion at this session. This is also an opportunity to put across the kind of support adopters can expect from the agency and introduce the idea of post-adoption services provided by the agency and other adopters and organizations. (Some agencies may decide to allow for a session to talk generally about how you prepare for a child, from some very practical things such as the purchase of toys, pocket-money, clothes, to the presentation of oneself at the initial stages.)

It is impossible to cover all the subjects that one would wish to raise. On the other hand, extending the number of sessions can equally prolong the process to the frustration of the prospective adopters. Knowing also that people cannot take everything in during a preparatory stage with hypothetical situations being discussed, it may be preferable to consider some forms of preparation as going on during the individual interviews and after a child is placed. Experience and research suggest that as with many adopted children who in order to grasp the meaning of adoption need to hear about it as part of a process, so too many adoptive parents will need to go over some of these themes more than once.

Attending groups can pose major problems for people with children, shift workers, people in rural areas without cars or for those who live at a distance from the venue. Many of the group preparatory methods, though, can be adapted for use with individuals, couples and whole families. Techniques that could be used to supplement necessarily individual preparation might include visits to a children's residential unit; a visit to an adoptive family, if the applicants have not known any before; showing a video or slides or using audiotapes on adoption or fostering.

THE HOME-STUDY OR ASSESSMENT STAGE

The home-study assessment may start whilst the group preparation sessions are in progress, or after they are finished.

The individual assessment is usually structured on the following pattern:

- an interview with the applicants to explain the procedure. A good start is to ask them to comment on the group sessions and how these affected them;
- separate interviews with each partner (if a joint application) to pursue both issues of motivation and of a personal nature;
- interviews to bring together issues arising from those held earlier and to explore further preferences for a particular child, and the impact of another child on any existing children, on them and their family. This also sets the scene for the next interview;
- a family session when other members of the immediate family are invited to take part (mostly children and any grandparents living with the family).

There is no shortage of outlines detailing the kind of information the social worker should obtain for the home-study. Most agencies in Britain use what is called Form F, devised by the British Agencies for Adoption and Fostering. The form can be used both with those who wish to adopt babies and those who plan to adopt or foster children with special needs. Form F consists of main topic headings with detailed sub-questions for recording information and observations (see also Smith, 1984). Topics covered include:

Individual profiles of male and female applicants

This includes a 'pen picture' of each applicant, describing physical appearance, colouring, and impression of temperament; a description of family background, experiences of growing up, past and present family relationships, life-styles of extended family members; type of education and attitude to own experience of school and learning; occupation and feelings about work satisfaction, future plans, likely job changes; interests and leisure time and how far activities are jointly pursued; personality and philosophy of life, including attitude to religion, flexibility towards others' beliefs, approaches to problems.

Couple history and present relationship

(This area will need adaptation where the applicant is single.)

Reference has already been made to the findings of research studies connecting satisfactory outcome with the stability of the couple's relationship. The social worker will need to obtain some information about the development of the couple's relationship, what makes it stable and satisfying to both partners; the quality of communication between them, areas of strain, ways of dealing with disagreements and anger; evidence of mutual support and understanding and so on.

Equally important for assessment is not only the quality of the couple's relationship, but how far the boundaries are flexible and open to accommodate the new child. Some applicants may have been married before and experienced feelings which can be relevant to how the contemplated adoption may affect their lives. In situations of childlessness, it is useful to obtain information about the reasons and how the couple have coped with this loss. To what extent have they accepted this before viewing adoption as a desirable alternative? What effect is this likely to have on their ability and readiness to explain to a child about his origins? What meaning should be attached to a couple's reluctance to find out the reasons for their childlessness? Is this a cultural phenomenon or are there other emotional factors? Attitudes to children with a different racial and ethnic background and an understanding of raising children in a multi-cultural society?

Parenting capacity of applicants

Most research into baby adoptions suggests that satisfactory adoption outcome has more to do with the qualities of the adopters than the characteristics of the child. With older adoptions the variables refer both to the child and to the adopters.

A way to understand the couple's parenting capacity or potential is by reflecting on their own childhood experiences and how these are likely to influence them in the rearing of an adopted child. Would they be repeating these experiences? If not, what would they change?

This topic also gives opportunities to discuss children's needs, ideas about child development, attitudes to children, to adolescent behaviour, coping with children's growing independence and sexual development and relationships. If they are considering children with 'special needs', or intercountry, the extent to which they considered particular challenges and how they might respond. It is somewhat easier with applicants who already have children to review their experiences, joys and frustrations in bringing them up.

Other children. Pen pictures of each child already in the household can be constructed. They should cover the children's physical characteristics, personality, intelligence, interests, any special needs, feelings and level of understanding about adoption and how far they have been involved in discussions about the contemplated adoption. At some point the worker should talk directly with the children. In spite of all the emphasis in the literature about the importance of involving particularly the adopters' children, experience and research suggest that the children appear to be mostly taken by surprise (see London, 1992). Though children of adopting and fostering families on the whole enjoy the company and friendship of the new children coming, nevertheless sometimes there can also be problems. Those with work experience with families who separate and reconstitute themselves will know how one of the main issues faced by the partners in reconstitution is managing the relationships between the two sets of children. The children themselves may resent their territory being invaded or having to share a parent. (The video *Children Who Foster* can help to introduce the subject to a group.)

The extended family. Extended families can be supportive or not. Adopted children usually start adoptive life with a narrower circle of relatives and, if not accepted by the wider family, can find themselves isolated. This can be even more difficult for children adopted intercountry (see Chapter 9). The social worker tries to assess the quality of the couple's relationship and contact with the extended family and with neighbours and friends. A child may develop psychological bonds or attachments to his new parents, but it does not follow automatically that such bonds will also develop with relatives.

Family life-style

This topic is meant to give a picture of how the family works and operates. The quality of interactions taking place within the family and those between the family and the outside world. In other words, what kind of a family is the child likely to join? What is its philosophy of life, its value system, its emotional climate, the rules and regulations operating (how strict or flexible)? Are family members open or controlled in expressing feelings? Are they 'cuddlers' or 'touch-me-nots'? Do they do things as a family group or have separate lives and activities? How much are they involved with neighbours, friends, religious activities, clubs? (As we will be saying later, this can be particularly important for those adopting inter-country.) What kind of interests and hobbies do they have and how much fun do they have as a family? What are their attitudes to money, food, play and school achievements? How is another child going to fit into this household? Will they make space for him?

By using ideas from systems theory, the social worker can engage the family in mapping their own family system. This exercise reduces the amount of questioning on the part of the social worker, and involves the family in a joint activity. Existing children can join in and enjoy a lot of fun. The main aim of the exercise is for the family to map out its relationships, boundaries, resource systems (including physical, emotional and recreational resources). The map can demonstrate in a concrete way how the family system is in constant exchange and interaction with itself and also with its environment on which it depends for resources and information. Hartman (1979) calls this an 'Ecomap' and adds that 'an ecological view not only recognizes that stress and conflict are always a part of any living system, but also that some sort of balance must be achieved between stress and support, between demands and resources, for a system to survive and grow'. The map can give a quick look at the total family set-up with its strengths and networks. It offers the additional advantage of highlighting possible weaknesses, such as neighbourhood isolation, or strained relationships with relatives. Knowledge of these before the placement of a child enables the agency to provide or link the family to supportive services to make up for certain deficits, e.g. absence of play space or of someone to child-mind for the parents to give them occasional relief. There may be existing resources in the community which the family are unaware of, or unsure how to access. A link may be arranged with a local club or religious centre or an activity group.

Genograms. Genograms resemble the mapping demonstrated and their main aim is again to involve family members in drawing their family tree and talking about it. Genograms can be used to help a family become more aware of their origins and to reflect on the kind of people their ancestors were. The adopting family, by being helped to draw their own family tree, can later on help an adopted child to do the same. The adopted child can have his adoption family tree and his biological one side by side.

Motivation to adopt

The applicants are invited to comment about their motivation to adopt. Applicants may express a range of different motives which are not necessarily suspect. More important is their capacity to adapt and respond to the needs of another person. In the end, whatever the motives, the child must be wanted for himself. Some common motives related by prospective adopters aiming to adopt pre-school children include:

- unable to have own children;
- unable to have more children;
- unwilling to bear any children or another child;
- to have a companion for a child of their own;
- to balance their family by sexes or numbers;
- to replace a child who died.

Other motives could be a companion for their old age; somebody to inherit from them.

Those adopting children with special needs may express any of the above motives, but more often emphasis is placed on enlarging a family; offering a home or a service to a child with special needs because the applicant(s) feel they have the skills and experience for this, perhaps seeing it as a challenge.

Other areas to be explored include the possibility of adoption with contact, or a contested application, willingness to work with the agency, and parenting an abused child or a child who is HIV positive.

Attitude to the family of origin and the child's background

We have outlined in Chapter 2 the importance of the family of origin to the child's self-concept and identity. Here the social worker aims to explore with the family their attitudes and feelings towards parents who relinquish their children. Also how they intend to explain to the child the circumstances of his adoption and his origins, and particularly how to help him feel positive about his heritage, which contributes to a positive self-image (see also Chapters 8 and 9).

This topic also affords opportunities to consider issues connected with heredity, the transmission of aspects of behaviour from parents to children and the impact of environmental factors. How realistic or unrealistic are they about expressed fears or anxieties? The social worker's familiarity with research studies can be of help in both explaining to applicants and also in evaluating their capacity to change views and ideas.

Expectations of child to be placed

Applicants should be encouraged to talk about the hopes and ideas they have about the child who may be placed with them. Do they have specific expectations about the child's appearance, educational achievements, behaviour, medical problems, etc.? Another very important area to explore is their approach to discipline. What methods of control would they use? Are these appropriate for a child who has been abused and neglected? What alternatives exist? It is recognized that applicants may find it difficult to consider some of these issues in the abstract. If they have no children already, encouraging them to relate their experiences and knowledge of other people's children could go some way to help to clarify and identify attitudes.

Managing openness

Exploring feelings and attitudes about open forms of adoption (see Chapter 4).

Factual information

This factual form of information should preferably be collected in advance by asking the applicants to fill in a form giving basic information.

MATCHING PARENTS AND CHILDREN

At the end of the assessment and preparation process, the applicants are ready to meet a child and, hopefully, accept him or her into their home. Sometimes interest in a specific child begins early in the preparation process, particularly when applicants are urged to 'select' particular children of interest from a catalogue. If an agency is recruiting for a specific child it usually makes available videos of the children in play or other activities to would-be adopters to get a view and feeling of the child without the necessity of a meeting. More often, however, it is as the preparation process continues that both the agency and the applicants begin to get a clear picture of the most suitable child for their home.

In the years of infant adoptions, agencies spent much effort in matching infants and families in terms of appearance, ethnic background, religion, intellectual achievements (and infant potential), and background. Eventually adopting families convinced agencies that they could take more risks and adopt a wider range of children. Theorists such as Kirk (1964) also began to suggest that recognition of 'difference' was a healthy factor in adoptive families. And, finally, the children available for adoption became older children, with more experience with their own families, with more difficulties, and with more memories. Matching took on a different character.

Current matching takes more the form of discussion with potential adoptive parents about their ability to tolerate specific behaviours, and their ability and interest in helping children toward specific developmental goals. Preferences of applicants concerning age, gender and general characteristics of the child need to be respected, but at the same time it is possible to introduce the idea of somewhat older or somewhat more difficult children and evaluate the response.

Besides professional staff, final placement decisions are made by panels, which in Britain are required by law. In the United States, similar adoption committees are often used. The panel must have before it all available information, including medical and legal advice, in order to make the best possible decision. New regulations circulated by the Department of Health provide for the setting up by adoption agencies of 'complaints procedures' to which applicants could have recourse, such as challenging the panel's decision.

The final step in matching is the meeting of the applicants and the child. Prior to the meeting, there will have been complete sharing of information with the applicants and with the child. Pictures or videotapes of the child are used prior to the meeting. to supplement the information given. Videotapes of the would-be adopters in their homes or work could equally be made available to children, especially older ones, to enable them to get a feeling of the family. The goal is to arrange a meeting only when there is reasonable probability that the match is a good one.

The meetings can sometimes turn out to be disappointing for either the child, the would-be parents, or both. It is crucial to meet individually with both child and applicants after the first (and subsequent) meetings, and to listen carefully and respect any doubts or hesitations. These hesitations can sometimes be worked through, but the placement should proceed at a very slow pace until they are resolved. And if hesitation remains, both child and applicants should be helped to see that a different match may work better. There is no substantive research about matching of children and families, and there are many different opinions about what is important.

THE PLACEMENT PROCESS

The meeting of child and parents is the beginning of a placement process, which should be deliberately paced and proceed at a speed which is comfortable for both applicants and child. Except with infant adoptions, it is often the child who needs additional time to accept the move to a new home and the loss of the home in which he has been living.

Usually placements are effected through a series of visits, often first a day-time visit, followed by an overnight visit, and then one or more weekend visits. If this is to be an open adoption with contact, those members of the child's family who will remain in contact with the child need to be introduced to the adopting parents during this time. Sometimes these visits seem very difficult to accomplish, particularly if long distances are involved. They are, however, extremely important. If things are going well, the impulse of parents, worker, and sometimes child is to complete the move as rapidly as possible. The need for time to work through this major life change should, however, always be remembered.

FOSTER PARENT ADOPTIONS

Sometimes an older child is to be adopted by the family which has fostered him. Obviously, in this situation, issues of matching are not applicable, for the bond has already formed between parents and child and has led to the request to adopt. Nor are pre-placement visits necessary.

With the foster parents, the decision to adopt must be carefully considered. Foster parents report that they are sometimes 'pressured' into adopting a child in their care by social workers searching for a permanent home for the child (Meezan and Shireman, 1985). If there is to be continued contact with the child's original family, an agreement about the nature and extent of this contact must be made. Finally, foster parents must be warned that the child's behaviour may change after the adoption. Seldom does it immediately improve, as is always hoped. More often, difficult behaviour increases temporarily as the child tests the new permanency.

The transition to adoption must also be carefully considered with the child. This is the point at which the child must have opportunity to review his feelings about his birth family. He needs to evaluate his loyalty to that family and the meaning of accepting a new family, of changing his name, of giving up hope of returning to his original home. Techniques for working with children (reviewed in Chapter 6) will be useful in this work.

FINAL COMMENT

More recently the recruitment of adoptive families to parent special needs children has been going through difficulties which are attributed to:

- the increasingly more difficult and 'disturbed' condition of children requiring placement;
- the lack of assurance to adopters about continuing support (Lunken, 1995);
- lack of confidence on the part of adopters, compared with the apparent confidence displayed in the 1980s, about their parenting skills;
- concerns over contact between the children and members of their birth families;
- increasing reconstitution, with many households already rearing children from more than one family.

Selection methods have been considerably adapted in the last twenty or so years, mainly to counter criticisms about the predominantly investigative approaches used in the past. The methods have also changed as a response to the needs of the children and families who are now involved in adoption. The emphasis has decidedly shifted from selection to preparation and from individualized to group methods. Agencies now aim to develop a climate of partnership with adopters that will last well beyond the placement to the post-placement stage and beyond.

Five key points

1. Compared with the situation in the previous decade, the recruitment of families for older children has become much more difficult in the 1990s.
2. Advertising specific children on television and in the national press still appears to be the most successful way of recruiting adoptive families for children with special needs.
3. During the last twenty or so years adoption agencies have moved away from 'idealized' images of adoptive parenting to matching what adopters have to offer with specific children's needs.
4. Most adoption agencies now view preparation and selection as a partnership between themselves and applicants.
5. The process through which specific applicants and children become acquainted is a crucial process, and needs to be facilitated with sensitivity and with adequate time and opportunity for the expression and working through of feelings.

CHAPTER 8
Transracial adoption

Transracial adoption is the adoption of a child of one race by parents of another. In our world, because of unequal distribution of social and economic resources, this has almost always meant the adoption of a black, Asian, Native American, or Hispanic child by a white family. Children are transracially adopted from wartorn countries, from poor countries and from a Western country's own population. Chapter 9 explores the issues which arise when a child from one culture is brought into another through adoption. In this chapter the focus is on the adoption of children born in-country and adopted by families within the same country. So far this has meant the adoption of 'black' children (or children of 'colour', see below) by white families; there are no significant examples of adoption being practised the other way round.

The word 'black' children itself is an umbrella term that leaves out many other races, such as Asian, Native American, or Hispanic children. In the United States, the term 'children of color' is preferred as a descriptive, all-inclusive term. In this book the authors have used the descriptive term 'black', which is familiar to British social workers.

Much of this chapter draws from the perspective of adoption in the United States, as this is where most of the research has taken place. It is recognized that there are many historical differences between the States and Britain as far as ethnic minorities are concerned. The United States has a sad and difficult history of race relations, including much overt coercion and oppression of non-white minorities. The resulting deep feelings and tensions sharpen the issues of transracial adoption. These may be less manifest in Great Britain, but many of the issues identified and explored in considering transracial adoption will be the same throughout Western countries.

Regardless of the perspective from which transracial adoption is examined, it raises strong passions with positions being taken either for or against. Empirical arguments of what is good for children and how it seems to work out in practice are helpful, but they cannot be considered in isolation from the social, economic, political and moral context within which transracial adoption takes place. Whilst recognizing that people's views on transracial adoption do not fit into neat categories, three broad groupings are possible:

- Those who look toward a single society in which the uniqueness of the individual is prized, and in which persons can move among cultures without being discriminated against but, on the contrary, are valued. They acknowledge the links between poverty and adoption and of the impact of racism on black people and the injustices that follow from this. The emphasis is on fighting racism and on recognizing the structural traps in which all disadvantaged groups are caught, irrespective of colour. They could be called internationalists/integrationists (see Ratansi, 1992; Macey, 1995).
- Others who are more pragmatic and are concerned about the plight of the individual child for whom the alternatives may be continued fostering or transracial adoption. These could be described as 'child rescuers'. Their major concerns are not the social and racial injustices that contribute to the rise of much of childcare need, including adoption. They point to the empirical evidence concerning the well-being of transracially adopted children to support their position. Pragmatists/rescuers/assimilationists (Tizard and Phoenix, 1989; Bagley, Young and Scully, 1993; Gaber and Aldridge, 1994).
- Finally there are those who oppose transracial adoption on racial, ethnic and cultural grounds. They see identity as rooted in culture. They view transracial adoption as psychologically damaging to the child placed with white parents. They question the basis and validity of much of the research, or question its interpretation, especially where it refers to racial identity and ethnicity. They look toward a society in which each individual is a part of his or her own culture and expect adoption to be an institution which promotes a society within which distinct cultures interact but are kept separate (see Chestang, 1972; Small, 1986; Maxime, 1993).

Reflecting these differences in the community, the three authors of this book take different positions on the subject. Whilst the details and some of the overlaps of the above positions cannot be examined here, account will be taken of them in the discussion that follows. In this chapter, an attempt is made to help the reader understand the context of transracial adoption, the empirical work which has been done, and the theoretical perspectives through which this work can be viewed. Armed with this knowledge and understanding, the reader will determine his or her own position.

A BRIEF HISTORY OF FOUR DECADES OF TRANSRACIAL ADOPTION

Same-race adoption is a form of 'matching', an attempt to create a family as 'like' a biological family as possible. For a long time, adoption workers thought that a family would be better able to guide a child and to facilitate optimum development if child and parents were alike in race, temperament, intelligence, culture and appearance.

Four factors interrupted this generally accepted policy:

- adoptive parents began to insist that they could handle more risk and more differences and wanted to care for children as early as possible; this led to the placement of infants soon after birth;
- the work of Bowlby (1951) and others (discussed in Chapter 2) sparked the recognition of the difficulty that even very young children had with separation and change of caretakers and therefore it was no longer thought good practice for a child to wait until a 'match' was arranged;
- writers such as Kirk (1964) began to suggest that the attempt to create a family which resembled a biological family was in fact a handicap in adoption, making it more difficult for a family to acknowledge and handle the differences between adopted and biological children; and
- there was growing awareness of the number of black children in public care identified by research (Maas and Engler, 1959; Finch and Fanshel, 1985; Rowe and Lambert, 1973).

Adoption of black children by white families began cautiously in the 1960s both in the States and in Britain. It was a 'fit' with the civil rights movement in the United States and the spirit of a society moving toward racial integration, and a 'fit' with a world in which adoption agencies were experimenting with the placement of older children, and were more and more willing to create families different from a biological family. This move was accelerated by decreasing numbers of white infants available for adoption, increasing numbers of black children, and a new commitment to finding an adoptive home for every child who was in need of one. Numbers of placements of black children in white homes increased until 1971, a year in which 2474 black/white transracial adoptions occurred in the United States. The exact number in Britain is unknown.

Ignored in these increasing numbers of transracial placements was the fact that non-white communities, particularly in the States, have a long history of being denied equal access to the resources which support family life, and at the same time of having their children 'rescued' by the mainstream, white community. The latter has been particularly well documented for the Native American population, with its history of Indian Bureau boarding schools with curricula designed to teach children 'white' values and skills, while depriving them of their own culture, and later in the shocking statistics of loss of children to white families through adoption.

A reaction to these placements came in the 1970s, and was in part a response to a changing community perception of race relations. Integration was no longer seen as a solution to the racism, oppression and racial inequalities of the United States or of Britain. Merging into the traditional 'melting pot' was not the goal. The black and native communities in countries such as the United States, Canada, Australia and New Zealand, instead, began to cherish and rediscover culturally traditional ways of life and it became increasingly important to them that their children be exposed to this culture.

For years the Native American community had been protesting against the placement of its children in white adoptive homes. But it was the black community that finally caught the attention of the adoption agencies in the United States. In 1972 a pivotal statement of the National Association of Black Social Workers in the States, strongly rejecting the practice of transracial adoption, shook the child welfare world. Similar objections were later raised in Britain by the Association of Black Social Workers and Allied Professions (1983) and others.

The opposition of the black community is based on the premise that black children who have grown up in white families suffer severe identity problems. The white community does not fully accept them; however, they have no significant contact with black people and do not know how to act in ways acceptable in that community. In addition, black children adopted transracially do not develop the coping mechanisms necessary to function in a society that is inherently racist (Chestang, 1972; Small, 1986).

A major step towards ensuring that children grew up in their own ethnic communities in the United States was the Indian Child Welfare Act of 1978. This Act created tribal control over the adoption of Native American children and, now no Native American child can be placed for adoption without the consent of his/her tribe. Similar approaches have been adopted in Canada, Australia and New Zealand with regard to their native populations.

These barriers, both of law and of community pressure, have resulted in an enormous decrease in the numbers of transracial adoptions. Most adoption agencies now have policies discouraging transracial adoption (Bartholet, 1991, provides extensive documentation about the States and Bagley, Young and Scully, 1993, criticize local authorities in Britain for their reluctance to place black children transracially).

CHILDREN WHO NEED HOMES

Reliable statistics about the number of black children in out-of-home care and of those available or free for adoption do not exist. In Britain it is asserted that black children looked after in the care system return home at a much slower pace, and wait longer for adoptive placement than do white children (Barn, 1993; Chambers, 1989). The same situation prevails in the United States; the American Public Welfare Association estimates that, in 1987, around 37 per cent of the children in out-of-home placement were black. Of children legally free for adoption, 34 per cent were black, yet in the States black people represent only 12.3 per cent of the general population (reported in Bartholet, 1991). It is assumed that black children are disproportionately represented due to the poverty, educational limitations and lack of opportunity which too often afflict their families, as well as to the actions of a predominantly white child welfare system more prone to 'rescue' them than to understand their strengths and develop the resources to rebuild their families.

There is evidence that black children wait longer for adoptive homes than do white children (Fein and Maluccio, 1992; Barth *et al.*, 1994; Chambers, 1989). In the child welfare systems of many states in the United States, it can take up to two years, after it has been determined that a child cannot return to the biological family, before he is freed for adoption. Once free for adoption, unwritten agency policy often specifies that a transracial placement cannot be considered until extensive efforts, over a period of time, to find a same-race home can be documented (Bartholet, 1991). Whether the situation will be greatly changed by the passage of the Federal Multiethnic Placement Act of 1994 remains to be seen. This act makes it illegal for any agency receiving federal funds to delay an adoptive placement while a search is made for a same-race home. However, agencies are permitted on an individualized basis to consider 'cultural, ethnic, and racial background' and the capacity of adoptive parents to meet the needs of the child.

The policy direction in Britain is ambiguous. First the Children Act (England and Wales) 1989 stresses the need 'to give due consideration ... 'to the child's religious persuasion, racial origin and cultural and linguistic background' (section 22) and suggests that this usually requires 'placement with a family of the same race, religion and culture' (vol. 3, para. 4.4). A circular letter issued by the Department of Health (1992) to local authorities sets out the principles which should inform the practice of social services departments in the family placement of children and refers to the provision of services which will reach all members of the community. The letter calls for the development within social services departments of 'awareness, sensitivity and understanding of the different cultures or groups in the local community; and an understanding of the effects of racial discrimination on these groups'. It then goes on to say that:

> where placements are needed or likely to be needed for children from minority ethnic groups or for children of particular religious affiliation, sustained efforts may be needed to recruit sufficient number and range of foster parents and prospective adopters from those groups and that religion.

Unlike foster care where the statutory Boarding-Out of Children (Foster Placement) Regulations of 1988 require agencies to be satisfied that a child's needs arising from his racial origin and cultural background are met in a foster placement, 'so far as practicable', these requirements do not extend to adoption. The 1992 circular, though, advises social services departments to apply similar considerations also in adoption. Later on, the circular adds that a child's ethnic origin, cultural background and religion are important factors, but only to be taken as a guiding principle of good practice and of other things being equal.

A decisive change of mood is detected in the Department of Health's White Paper on adoption (1993a). This warns against 'reliance on ideology' (section 4.27.20) and affording ethnicity and culture 'an unjustifiably decisive influence' (section 4.31-4-34). In another part the same paper warns adoption agencies to ensure that their decisions are based on 'objective professional assessments and avoid reliance on ideology' (section 4.27-29) (see also discussion by Macey, 1995).

This shift in tone may well have been precipitated by the evidence that black children were waiting for long periods of time in foster care, and moving slowly into adoptive homes. When a child's move to permanent arrangements is seriously delayed, normal child developmental progression is interrupted, often with lasting damage to the child's future.

In the United States families of similar racial background are available to adopt some of these waiting children. In 1988, 23 per cent of finalized adoptions were of black children, almost all placed with black families (Stolley, 1993). Sullivan (1994) reports that healthy infants and pre-schoolers do not, at this time, have to wait for same-race adoptive homes and that there are, in some areas, black families waiting for long periods of time to adopt. But data from the adoption exchanges, where the most difficult to place children are listed, make it clear that there are not enough non-white families to adopt all the older and/or special needs waiting children. It appears from the materials of adoptive groups, from the inquiries received by adoption agencies, and from the press, that there are waiting white families. Again no accurate picture is available from Britain of who adopts black children or who is waiting to be adopted.

THE EMPIRICAL EVIDENCE

There is an extensive literature on the outcome of transracial adoption, mainly from the United States. Children of colour placed transracially in the 1960s and 1970s have now been followed in longitudinal studies through adolescence (Simon and Altstein, 1977, 1981, 1987, 1992; Shireman and Johnson, 1976, 1985, 1986; Shireman, Johnson and Watson, 1987; Shireman, 1988; Vroegh, 1991) and have been studied during childhood (Falk, 1970; Fanshel, 1972; Grow and Shapiro, 1972; Ladner, 1977; Zastrow, 1977;

Feigelman and Silverman, 1983) and adolescence (McRoy and Zurcher, 1983; McRoy *et al.*, 1984). The great majority of children featuring in the main British study on the subject were of mixed parentage placed transracially in the 1960s (Gill and Jackson, 1983). A new study is under way monitoring in-country own-race and transracial placements of black children placed in the early and mid 1980s. The study is being carried out by Thoburn and Rashid at the University of East Anglia. Studies by Fanshel (1972) and Bagley, Young and Scully (1993) of Native North American transracial placements are the only ones to focus on this group. Other studies have provided information primarily about black children and black, Asian and Latin American children adopted inter-country (see Chapter 8).

The findings of these studies have been broadly similar. Repeatedly they find 20 to 25 per cent of transracially adopted children who experience moderate to severe problems in adjustment to family, school or community. This proportion is about the same as the proportion of adopted children in same-race homes who experience problems of the same intensity. Most families have raised their children in predominantly white neighbourhoods, and as the children have grown older they have paid progressively less attention to the child's cultural heritage. In spite of this, and of the measures used, the transracially adopted children appear similar to adopted children in same-race homes on measures of self-esteem. Measures of racial identity elicit expressions of pride in their racial heritage. They appear comfortable in the white world and in the world of their ethnic origin.

Given the concerns about the development of racial identity, studies which investigate the adjustment of transracially adopted children at adolescence are particularly interesting. There are some major studies which have assessed family integration, self-esteem, school performance, racial identity and overall adjustment, and which provide comparison groups. McRoy and Zurcher (1983) compared 30 white families who had adopted black children with 30 black families who had adopted black children. At the time of the study, the children were 10 years of age or older and most had been placed as infants or very young children. Parents and children were interviewed separately, and standardized instruments were used to measure self-concept and family integration. Transracially adopted children were usually attending predominantly white schools and had limited opportunity for interaction with black peers or adults. However, both groups of parents reported satisfactory school progress. Both groups reported strong family bonds, with great satisfaction with the adoption. No differences between groups were found in self-concept scores. However, only 30 per cent of the trans-racially adopted group identified themselves as black, and the identification of the others as 'mixed' or 'human race' seemed to mirror the identification their parents encouraged. The authors expressed concern about this finding, and suggested that the parents were failing to respond to 'the necessity of equipping the child to become bi-cultural and to realistically perceive the historical and cultural black–white relations in American society' (p. 140).

Two longitudinal studies of transracial adoptions are particularly interesting in their picture of children's adjustment over time. Shireman and colleagues have followed 35 transracial adoptions and 20 same-race adoptions of black and mixed-race children, with interviews and selected standardized measurements with both parents and children every four years for sixteen years (Shireman and Johnson, 1975, 1986; Shireman, Johnson and Watson, 1987; Shireman, 1988; Vroegh, 1991). Simon and Altstein (1981, 1987 and 1992) have followed 157 transracially adopted children, of whom 76 per cent were black and the remainder mostly Asian, over 12 years, comparing them with birth children or same-race adoptions in the same families. Fourteen of these children were over 3 years at adoption, making them 15 or older at the last follow-up. Both studies used interviews with parents and children to assess overall adjustment and a variety of age-appropriate projective materials and standardized measurements to assess self-concept and racial identity.

As in the McRoy and Zurcher study (1983), transracially adopting families tended to move to white suburban neighbourhoods as the children's school years began. Both longitudinal studies found the overall adjustment in school, community, peer and family relationships to be, for about three-quarters of the youngsters, free of serious problem, in both groups, at every phase. The transracially adopted children looked much like children in comparison groups, except with regard to school performance. At no time, in either of the studies, have there been significant differences in self-esteem or self-concept measures between the transracially adopted and other children. In both studies, in early years the transracially adopted children expressed greater pride in blackness than did the children being raised in black homes. In later years the two groups have been similar. However, racial identification differs. Vroegh (1991) reports that at age 17, 83 per cent of same-race adopted children identified themselves as black, while only 33 per cent of transracially adopted children identified themselves as black, and 53 per cent as 'mixed'. In contrast, Simon and Altstein (1987) focused more on racial preference, and found 66 per cent of the transracial adoptees stating they were proud to be black or brown, with only 6 per cent expressing pride in 'mixed background' and 11 per cent expressing white preference. The difference between studies on preferences and self-definition highlights the complexity of measures of racial identity, of which preference and self-definition may be two distinct components.

Bagley and Young (1979) followed 31 black children in Britain, mostly of mixed parentage, adopted by white families (no comparison group was available). The children were aged 7–14 at the time of the study. The researchers found that about half of the children identified themselves as white and there was a positive relationship between racial awareness and self-image. The main and most recent British study (Gill and Jackson, 1983) confirmed the findings of most American studies, i.e. of generally favourable outcomes. Many of the 36 children involved had one or two Asian biological parents and were aged 12 to 16 at the time of the study. They were brought up with no contact with their ethnic community. The researchers noted that the children 'saw themselves as "white" in all but skin colour'. In spite of how the children described themselves, the study claims that their self-esteem, as assessed by an inventory, appeared to be high. Few showed evidence of confusion about their origins. The study is not specific about the extent to which these children experienced racism and how they coped with it. The authors, though, expressed some concern about this in the future.

Though the data reported in these studies are positive, the conclusions drawn by the researchers vary. McRoy has expressed doubts about the wisdom of transracial adoption, as it has become evident that children tend to grow up in white communities. Simon and Altstein suggest that, despite their findings, same-race adoption is probably preferable. Tizard and Phoenix (1989) too, in a review of the research literature, added that it is possible 'at a later stage the difficulties in terms of the children's inability to relate to their own race or to cope with racism, as many black writers suggest, may emerge'.

Most children adopted intercountry are also adopted transracially. Almost all the studies, which have reported 'good' family and school adjustments for most children adopted intercountry, also raise some concerns. These have to do mainly with racism and discrimination experienced by some children, along with a poorer sense of racial and ethnic identification. Alstein and Simon (1991), whose studies suggest overall good adjustments, also report examples of racism and discrimination. In one of their studies almost a third of the children said that 'the fact that they looked different from their parents and siblings had caused them some problems' (p. 43). In another study, reported by the same authors, over a third of the children 'recalled problems during the preceding three years involving children calling them names and making fun of them because of their racial backgrounds' (p. 37).

Bagley, Young and Scully (1993), in one of their studies, contrasted native Canadian Indians adopted by white families with inter-country adoptees and with non-adopted native Canadian Indian children. They found that the majority of native children adopted by white parents had experienced difficulties, including profound identity problems which did not feature in the other two groups. They attributed these problems to racism and discrimination. The white adoptive parents' efforts to give their children 'a sense of identity' as a native Canadian person were cancelled by the adverse effects of racism. In contrast, native children brought up by their birth parents did not display similar difficulties and identity problems to those who were adopted by white families. Why native Canadians seem better able to protect their children against such negative influences, compared to white families adopting native children, raises wider issues about survival skills in black children requiring further study. Broadly similar observations have been made by Butler (1989) about aboriginal children adopted by white Australian families. Butler comments that aboriginal children were brought up with 'a consciousness of themselves as white' only to find that they experienced rejection and discrimination in the majority white culture.

In considering the needs of children, it is apparent that it is older black children, with special needs stemming from difficult early experiences, who are particularly in need of adoptive homes today. There is, at this time, only one study which investigates the adjustment of transracially placed, special needs adopted children (Rosenthal and Groze, 1992). The study focused on levels of parental satisfaction, and measures of family cohesion, in a survey which included 63 transracial and 230 in-racial placements of black children and 460 placements of white children in white families. Family cohesion scores were significantly lower for the transracially placed group. However, a higher proportion of the transracially placed children were disabled, had been in group homes or psychiatric placements prior to adoption, or had been sexually abused. When these factors were allowed for, the difference disappeared.

Charles, Parvez and Thoburn (1992) report an early phase of a projected qualitative research study of children who were older when placed transracially. Their outcome measure was whether the child was still in the adoptive home two to seven years after placement. Though numbers and differences are small, their data suggest that, when risk and protective factors are held constant, black children of mixed parentage (most of whom were placed transracially in their sample) and transracially adopted children were found more likely to experience breakdown of the adoption. (The identification of continued contact with the birth family as protective factors is a particularly interesting facet of this research.)

It has been noted by those who work with post-adoption counselling (see Chapter 11) that it is when transracially adopted young people leave home that difficulties begin. Adults in this situation talk about how safe and sheltered they were at home. Certainly there is anecdotal evidence of difficulties in adolescence and young adulthood. However, the studies which continue through adolescence do not document these difficulties.

Overall, the studies which have assessed the outcome of trans-racial adoption report that most of these children and adolescents are doing well in their families and the 'mainstream' society in which they live through their adolescent years. They exhibit overall good adjustment at home and school, and families report satisfaction with the adoptions. Mixed findings are reported on issues of race preference and self-definition. Nonetheless, on the measures used, self-concept scores are identical to those of in-race adoptees and birth children. Just as it was thought for many years that difficulties not apparent would emerge in adolescence, it is now thought by some that young adult years, when the shelter of home is left behind, will be the difficult ones. Empirical work informs us most about transracially adopted children, somewhat about transracially adopted adolescents, and as yet very little about transracially adopted young adults.

THE INTERPRETATION OF THESE FINDINGS

These findings have, in some ways, been puzzling. Adoption is complicated and so are families. When the factor of racial difference is added, one would expect to find additional difficulties. This logic is behind the recommendation of virtually all workers in adoption that, when a good same-race home can be found, it is advantageous for the child. Yet the empirical work on transracial placements shows that children and adolescents seem to do well, suggesting that the quality of parenting may be the paramount factor, rather than racial matching. There are two distinct theoretical lenses through which these findings can be viewed. Both attempt to explain the puzzle.

Apparent good adjustment masks incomplete identity formation

Young children conform to the environment of their family. For many transracially adopted children, difficulties begin in school, with the ascription to them, by teachers and by peers, of stereotypical characteristics attributed by mainstream society to their race. At that time the children gradually recognize dissonance and begin to wonder 'Who am I?' and 'What does the world say about me?' As powers of abstract reasoning grow, the children begin to deal with this dissonance. In the third stage, attempting to deal with this dissonance, children first resist their own culture, minimizing the differences between it and that of the dominant culture. This posture sends them back into conformity, and the cycle repeats itself as dissonance again emerges and must be handled (Atkinson, Morten and Sue, 1989). The apparently successful outcomes of transracial adoptions may well be manifestations of incomplete identity formation, with the young persons 'stuck', resisting and minimizing dissonance and exhibiting behaviour in conformity with 'mainstream' expectations.

If the process of identity formation proceeds beyond this, immersion in their own ethnic culture takes place (Atkinson, Morten and Sue, 1989). This immersion is often in a negative aspect of the culture, and serves additional functions of adolescent demonstration of independence from parents. For the transracially adopted child, this is a frightening and difficult experience, for he/she has only the adaptive skills of the white culture, except perhaps in those cases where their adoptive families have actively tried to link them with persons of their own ethnic group. We have no research to tell us whether those young people who become involved with negative aspects of their own cultures indeed do, in the end, succeed in establishing their racial identity, or whether their lives are destroyed by drugs, by the prison system, or by suicide. Anecdotal evidence from Australia on aboriginal children adopted by white families tends to support this finding (Butler, 1989).

The perspective taken by the above researchers views racial identity as part of the core identity of a person, with Tizard and Phoenix

(1989) pointing out that racial identity is one of a number of identities. Little work has been done in probing the underlying processes of the development of self-esteem and the closely linked concept of group esteem. Thus the measures may be misleading. If they are accurate, the good adjustment of transracially adopted children is only apparent, and represents incomplete identity development.

Racial identity as reference group orientation

From another perspective, Cross (1987), writing on the same topic, has been curious about the positive findings concerning transracial adoption, and suggests that they can be explained through a distinction between the development of personal identity, a mental health function, and the development of a reference group orientation. He suggests that the transracial adoptive homes which have been studied have been good and nurturing homes, and that the 'self esteem and general personality' of the children is well provided for. Cross adds (p. 133):

> Black children raised by White parents are no more or less likely to be psychologically healthy than children raised by Blacks, but the evolving frame of reference of the two groups of children may well differ.

Both proponents and critics of transracial adoption have accepted the assumption that it is 'healthy' to have a single reference group orientation, as white children do, and that transracially adopted children should choose their own racial community as their reference group orientation. However, Tizard and Phoenix's (1993) study of mixed parentage children, though biased in terms of its sample, suggests that many of these children had developed a bicultural orientation, suggesting that the transracially adopted child too could develop a dual culture group orientation and be comfortable with it.

Racism

Racism is another risk factor for transracially adopted children which has been identified, but not well studied. Though the presence of racism in our society can differ depending on the area and locality, black children must have the skills to cope with it and to protect their self-esteem. These skills have not been systematically studied or delineated, so that it is difficult to evaluate the statement that they can be taught only by a black family. Chestang (1972) writes that the 'social inconsistency, social injustice, and personal impotence' of racism generate 'loss of autonomy, diminished sense of self-worth, and low self-esteem'. Yet the empirical work that has followed transracially adopted children through adolescence has not found that they have displayed the frustration and anger that racism generates, nor the predicted low self-esteem. No doubt questions could still be asked about why this is so. Responses to racism are notoriously difficult to study. It is probable that qualitative research is needed to focus the definition and measurement of self-esteem, as well as to track the defence measures against racism actually used by transracially adopted children.

Almost all of the empirical work on transracial adoption is based on studies of families in which the adopted child was placed as an infant. What we know about the experiences of families who adopt older black children, from the Rosenthal and Groze study (1992), is that these adoptions also seem to be working satisfactorily. These authors promise a follow-up study containing longitudinal data soon. It is reasonable to suggest that the family adopting an older child transracially must be ready to engage in the experiences of racially integrated living, and at this point we have no evidence that white families are willing, or able, to effect this shift in culture.

SERVICE DELIVERY TO BLACK COMMUNITIES

It is important to consider the context in which so many black children are identified as needing new homes. One does not have to look far for an answer. On all indices of deprivation, the ethnic minorities in the United States and Britain come out worse. Additionally, the childcare system itself may create the need for adoptive homes. Studies consistently document that black children, both in the States and Britain, are over-represented in the care system and/or stay there longer (Fanshel and Shinn, 1978; Stolley, 1993; Barn, 1993; Barth et al., 1994). In the States, where figures are available, they are also over-represented in those children legally free and awaiting adoption placement (Stolley, 1993). These same children are under-represented in the intensive family services or preventive type work designed to prevent placement away from home (Close, 1983; Barn, 1993).

Those who view transracial adoption mostly in pragmatic terms, divorcing it from the economic, social and political realities within which it is taking place, may add to the divisions between the affluent and the deprived communities. (See for example contributions to Gaber and Aldridge, 1994.) Clearly, the provision of greater resources to the black community, and the creation of opportunity for education and training in those skills which will enable a decent level of earning and advancement in the wider world, will have an impact on the numbers of children whose families are unable to care for them. After all, economic improvement has been one of the most decisive factors that has led to a reduction in white babies being released for adoption in Western Europe and North America. This denial of resources and opportunities has created a bleak underclass of society, where poverty and violence are so pervasive, especially in the States, that families are hard-pressed to raise children.

This is a world which is familiar to many social workers. Many agencies have failed to adapt their structures to the multi-ethnic world in which they work. There is little theoretical development concerning work with these 'at risk' families. Often there is little training in cultural understanding, and few resources provided, when social workers are asked to work with these families. When social workers and child welfare workers are not very successful in supporting these families in attempts to raise children, they resort to 'rescue' solutions through the care system, and then try to find them new permanent homes through adoption.

Enhanced training and service delivery to black families might substantially reduce the number of children entering the public care system or requiring new homes. A great deal is known about how to improve life for these children in their own homes but the commitment of the necessary resources is not there (Schorr, 1988).

FINDING FAMILIES FOR BLACK CHILDREN

The same factors that increase the numbers of black children needing permanent homes impact also on the availability of racially matched homes for these youngsters. When these families are sought through the usual methods of the social services and child welfare agencies and assessed and supervised by these methods, there are indeed few. But demonstration projects and agency-sponsored efforts have shown that with intensive recruitment by persons of the same ethnic group, with study through the customs acceptable to that group, and with supervision and support in a manner which is meaningful to the family, black families can be located and maintained. Such efforts are not successful if they remain policy statements or are superficially implemented.

For departments accustomed to delivering services to the white majority community, major cultural and organizational adaptations are required. Such changes and adaptations do not come about easily. Those who are comfortable with current service delivery patterns will have to change, and those who have the power of being 'experts' in these patterns of service delivery will find their knowledge no longer relevant. Giving up this comfort and power is necessary if black children are to be served in their own homes, and if black families are to be found to adopt them when necessary.

It is some twenty years after the Soul Kids (1977) campaign in Britain, which demonstrated how black families can be found, yet it is still most unclear what kind of concerted efforts are being made in this direction, apart from those of some individual agencies. As an example, the Commission for Racial Equality (1990) found from its 1988 survey that 'social services departments had not been taking appropriate steps actively to recruit ethnic minority adoptive and foster carers'.

No national system of monitoring is available to establish how much or how little is being done. Often overworked practitioners, when faced with a child that needs a new home, opt for what is available. Changes are not impossible, but they will not come about by wait and see approaches. The black and Asian communities need to be convinced that a real commitment exists to set up systematic programmes, with black and Asian social workers spearheading the recruitment of black adopters and foster carers. At the moment this still depends on a small number of agencies. Pennie (1995) has commented that adoption is a service primarily for children and that they have rights which must include 'taking into account their race, religion, language and culture'. On the same topic of demonstrating a determined effort to find black families, Kaniuk (1991, p. 40) comments that:

> Despite the apparent consensus in social work circles about the importance of recruiting black adopters this does not seem to be reflected in much current practice.

Sullivan (1994) suggests that sound adoption practice for the recruitment of black families includes at least these seven key traits:

1. An ongoing recruitment programme that educates the public about the availability of children.

2. Child-specific recruitment for individual waiting children.
3. Staff and board members who represent the ethnic mix of the communities to be served, and have vital connections to these communities.
4. Flexible hours, including evenings and weekends.
5. Accessible office locations.
6. Realistic eligibility requirements for adopters in terms of age, income, length of marriage, and other factors; and
7. Service available without fees, or sliding scale fees based on the service provided, not the type of child sought.

Even within the limitations outlined above, significant numbers of non-white families do adopt. Practitioners in the East Midlands in Britain suggest that there is a growing interest from Asian families in having placed with them a suitably matched child (Asian Families Adopt, 1995). Many of them stretch minimal resources in order to take in additional children. Changes which would provide a better financial resource base for adoptive families would increase the number of adoptive homes. Good adoptive homes cannot be created without a resource base, otherwise a family is continually coping with crisis. One way is through more generous subsidies/adoption allowances or children's allowances, which would doubtless increase the numbers of black families able to adopt. This, and other measures discussed earlier, would be of help to children.

SOME PRACTICE CONSIDERATIONS

There is agreement that adoption is complicated, and transracial adoption adds another complication. Therefore, everything else being equal, it is preferable to find a racially and ethnically matched family to foster or adopt a black child. However, at least in the immediate future, it is evident that individual children will continue to need adoptive placement, and that some practitioners think that this can only be achieved, without undue delay, with a transracial placement. Besides everything else that has been specified about the assessment, preparation and post-placement support of adopters and the preparation and follow-up of children, there are a number of additional tasks for those adopting transracially. These include:

- how to foster their child's racial and ethnic identity within white structures, leading to a positive self-image;

- what is meant by a particular ethnic perspective and how it can be achieved – cultural, heritage, ethnic pride, positive knowledge of people and positive role models within the child's racial and ethnic heritage;
- the development of racial awareness;
- acceptable ways transmitted to the child for dealing with racism and discrimination and the fostering of coping skills;
- preparation for and commitment to living in integrated neighbourhoods and involvement in a multi-ethnic community and its institutions;
- recognizing the history, cultural traditions and ethnic celebrations of their child's heritage;
- the use of black and ethnic literature, including such things as multi-cultural books, cards, arts and toys.
(See also Small, 1991.)

Social workers and adoption workers will also be faced with families who have already adopted transracially or children who have been likewise adopted without the kind of preparation suggested above. Mullender (1988) gives a good account of how groups can be used to assist both parents and children featuring in transracial arrangements. The same methods/approaches can be adapted for use on an individual basis.

THE AUTHORS' DEBATE

Transracial adoption evokes strong passions. A review of the empirical literature does not settle the debate, for there remains the question of the theoretical lens through which the evidence should be viewed. Not only are there differences in theory, there are differences in world view which shape the definition of a successful adoption. And from these differences, follow differing practice implications.

The pragmatist

The dilemma is whether black children are going to continue to reside in residential or foster homes until social services departments put much more effort into finding black families. As children wait for permanent black homes, they become older and may experience unnecessary moves and consequent disruptions in relationships. We know the terrible damage to a child's capacity to trust and to form attachments which such disruptions can cause. Transracial placement can be a good alternative for these children.

In spite of methodological reservations about the way notions of 'self-esteem' and 'identity' are defined, on the basis of the currently available research tools, transracial adoption does no empirically discoverable harm, if success is measured through ability to adjust and achieve in the white/black world which transracially adopted children inhabit.

The integrationist

One theoretical lens through which the relevant empirical findings may be viewed is that self-esteem and group identity are conceptually separate domains. All black children grow up in a dual world and are so extensively exposed to white culture that a mixed black–white preference pattern may be indicative of health. A person need not have a single culture as a reference group in order to avoid identity confusion. Those who grow up transracially adopted seem to do well in 'mainstream' culture. They seem to move with some comfort within their own racial cultures. They evidence good self-esteem. They date and have friends in both worlds. Perhaps these young people will become for our society needed bridges between worlds. Transracial adoption may be an institution that promotes a society in which the individual can be a real part of more than one culture.

The separatist

In terms of the cultures the children come from, transracial adoptions are failures, for most of the children so adopted are lost to the original culture. The loss of a culture's children is indeed serious for that society, and will weaken the vision of a society in which separate, strong cultures interact. The goal of adoption work must be to give every child access to his or her community of origin. If racial identity is an integral part of mental health, then the surface adjustment of transracially adopted children disguises incomplete identity formation. If this is the case, one can anticipate that, unless the adoptive parents have been most atypical and have brought the child up in an integrated neighbourhood, the adoptee will in young adulthood experience extensive problems related to racial identity.

THE AUTHORS' CONCLUSIONS

Choice of a theoretical framework for the interpretation of the quite extensive research data makes a difference and so also does the reference point from which success is defined. So, in the end, does the vision of the society which we are trying to build. In the long term, of course, we need to commit resources so that all groups in our society, and world, have an equal capacity to raise their children. Equality of opportunity is the cornerstone.

As is always the case, the adoption worker who is planning for a black child is left with the necessity of exercising his/her own professional judgement. Knowledge, experience, and understanding of the issues inform this judgement. The particular situation will have its unique elements. The issues are complex, the decisions are not easy.

Five key points

1. Perhaps more than any other aspect of adoption, transracial adoption practice is shaped by social attitudes and changes as those attitudes change.
2. Reflecting unequal economic structure and opportunity, almost all transracial adoption involves non-white children being adopted by white parents.
3. Empirical studies which have followed transracially adopted children, placed as young children, through adolescent years indicate that outcomes appear to be favourable for the children. There is, as yet, very little research concerning older, special needs transracial placements. The research concerning adults has not yet been done.
4. Transracial adoption offers the opportunity of a permanent home to some black children currently in the foster care system. However, it is possible that more aggressive and culturally sensitive recruitment could provide same-race homes for these children.
5. Adoption is complicated, and transracial adoption is an additional complication. Most of those involved in adoption think that, all other things being equal, same-race adoptions are preferable.

CHAPTER 9
Intercountry adoption

Intercountry adoption is not new and some would quote the adoption of Moses as having been both intercountry and transracial and that of Oedipus as interstate, which was the equivalent of intercountry in present day terms. The shipping also of thousands of children from Britain to the Commonwealth, from the last quarter of the nineteenth century until the 1960s, was a mass exercise in a kind of intercountry foster care and *de facto* adoption. However, intercountry adoption as understood today became much more prominent following the end of World War II and has remained so ever since for reasons that will be discussed later. In contrast to the experience of some other Western countries, intercountry adoption had a low profile in Britain until the aftermath of the Romanian revolution in 1989.

Irrespective of the circumstances under which intercountry adoption takes place, it poses political, moral, empirical, policy and practice issues. From the policy and moral perspectives its practice gives rise to many similar questions to own-country adoption. In-country adoption in the West too has often come under criticism for involving the move of children mainly from poor to better-off families. The legitimacy of in-country or intercountry adoption will continue to be questioned until such time as adequate income maintenance schemes and preventive type services are developed to provide real choice for all birth parents.

An examination of the adoption statistics of some European countries strongly suggests that it was mainly new social policies affecting single parents, such as improved benefits and services in countries such as Scandinavia, Germany, Holland and Britain, that have been one of the major factors contributing to the drastic reduction in the number of young children surrendered for adoption. No doubt the lessening of the stigma associated with non-marital births was also of great importance, but it waits to be seen which was the most decisive. Even in countries such as Korea, which was a major sending country, intercountry adoption started to decline in numbers with increased prosperity after the early 1980s. Other factors, besides social policy and improved standards of living, are involved in whether or not a country becomes a sending country for adoption purposes. It is not surprising, therefore, that much inter-country adoption is not from the most absolutely poverty-stricken countries. The factors can include acute stigma for women giving birth to a non-marital child, giving them little choice but to relin-quish the child, wars and conflict, religious factors (which, for example, would mean that children from most Muslim countries would not be available for adoption to a non-Muslim culture) or the child's colour.

Political factors also play a part. China's policy of allowing only 'one child' per family, and the undervaluing of female children there, lead some couples, keen to have a male descendant, either to abandon or to dispose of female children. Whilst many of the abandoned find their way to 'orphanages', which are bursting to the seams, a few more fortu-nate ones find homes with adoptive parents in the West. In Romania it was Ceauşescu's policy that each woman should have a minimum of four children that led to many children entering institutions because their parents could not support them. The numbers entering institu-tions did not decline after the revolution because of the continued extensive poverty and hardship in that country (Triseliotis, 1994).

BACKGROUND ISSUES

Initially intercountry adoption was seen as a humanitarian response to wars, destruction and other calamities, before it became a much more organized activity, sometimes involving trafficking in children for profit. There were many examples in the past of United States army personnel stationed in Germany and Japan adopting children from 'orphanages' at the end of World War II. The Greek civil war, between about 1945 and 1952, also led to thousands of children being adopted by Greek expatriates and others in the United States.

The next movement of great numbers of children to be adopted intercountry, mainly in the United States, was from Korea, which was ravaged by the war of the early 1950s. Some fifteen to twenty years later, this was followed by children from Vietnam going both to the United States and to countries of northern and western Europe. This initial response appeared to be motivated by humanitarian concerns for mostly older, abandoned, destitute or orphaned children.

In more recent years, Vietnam, Bangladesh, Korea, India and other Asian countries have either banned altogether or begun to exercise stricter controls on intercountry adoption. Romania too, at least officially, has almost stopped the sending of children abroad for the purposes of adoption. Most of the attention of the receiving countries centres now on the Philippines and Latin America, including El Salvador, Guatemala, Honduras and Brazil.

As the number of infants released for adoption in Western countries continued to fall dramatically during the 1970s, there was a shift from war 'orphans' to any children now that could be had from the developing world. So few, in fact, own-country adoptions now take place in some European countries that adoption in these countries is synonymous with intercountry. As an example, recently in Sweden there have been only one or two own-country adoptions each year and in Holland about ten. Because of such demographic changes, it has been argued that much of recent intercountry adoption came about, not because of humanitarian concerns, but as a result of the acute shortage of babies for adoption in the Western world. In contrast to the early pattern, involuntarily childless couples now constitute almost nine out of every ten intercountry adopters keen to adopt infants, irrespective of whether they are abandoned, orphaned or homeless (Hoksbergen, Juffer and Waardenburg, 1987). Carstens and Jullia (1995) quote Pahl, who claims that intercountry adoption takes the most desirable children in terms of age, health and racial heritage and leaves hard-to-place children in their countries of origin.

It is estimated that something like 10,000 overseas children are adopted annually in the USA and a similar number in western and northern Europe, but this is likely to be an underestimate. Holland and Sweden have been receiving about 2000 intercountry adoptions each year for a number of years and so has Germany, with about 600 annually in Denmark. There have been many examples of buying and selling children and of bribery. There has also been evidence on the existence of fattening farms in countries such as Honduras and Guatemala to make the children more presentable and to fetch higher prices (Ngabonziza, 1991). Textor (1991) adds that in Germany there has been considerable disquiet because of 'the use of bribery, forgery and money' in intercountry adoption. But examples of the sale of children are not confined to the developing world. There are examples of this happening also within the United States, Italy and Romania (see Triseliotis, 1991a and 1993b). A more recent ugly side to intercountry adoption was revealed in the Ukraine and involved 'the illegal sale of babies by corrupt doctors and officials to the West, and the wholesale deception of their impoverished mothers, who were told that their newborns had died, or would have a better life being brought up by the State' (*The Times*, 9 February 1996, p. 4). Some children were sold for as much as $40,000.

Though both sending and receiving countries have a responsibility eventually to co-ordinate intercountry adoption in the interests of the children, nevertheless some of the abuses referred to could be seen as a consequence of the failure of a number of the receiving countries to regulate their incountry adoption. Too many arrangements in some of the receiving countries are left in the hands of third parties and sometimes of private or independent non-regulated and possibly profit-making agencies. Davis (1995) quotes Livingston, who noted in her 1994 report to the US Department of State that very few of the 50 states regulate the profit status of individuals or organizations involved in adoption. She goes on to add that 'as adoption has become a business, a sense of competition has developed. Professional co-operation and efforts towards internal monitoring are hard to find' (p. 27). Commenting on this, Carstens and Jullia (1995, p. 29) add that 'trafficking and sale of infants is more likely to occur when independent adoption agents are involved because there is opportunity for improper financial gain at each stage of the adoption process'. Results from Hoksbergen's (1991b) study showed that a high percentage of intercountry adoptees in residential care had been adopted privately.

The UK, Norway and Finland restrict adoptions to those arranged by agencies, but not Sweden and many other European countries. Even so, Britain largely sidestepped this restriction in the case of a number of Romanian children brought into the country. Equally flouted is the requirement of the United States Congress that only 'orphan' children could be brought into the country for adoption purposes, that is, both parents must have died, or have abandoned the child, or the 'sole or surviving' parent must be unable to care for the child.

During the early phase of intercountry adoption, a fair proportion of children adopted were older and some were handicapped or both. However, because of adaptation, behavioural, health, educational and other difficulties posed by the older children, especially in the early stages, adopters from about the 1980s onwards turned their attention to babies who were neither orphaned nor abandoned. For example, approximately two-thirds of the children coming in now are less than 1 year old and only 16 per cent are 3 and over. (Germany: Bach, 1988, quoted by Textor, 1991; Netherlands: Hoksbergen, 1991a; and Britain: Ahlijah, 1990). By 1984, 70 per cent of the children brought into Sweden for adoption were less than 1 year old (Zaar, 1984). Greenfield (1995) found that 50 per cent of the children featuring in her study covering intercountry adoption in France were less than 6 months old. The International Social Service, which deals with thousands of intercountry adoptions each year, has noted that in the majority of cases adopters bring back with them 'new-born, healthy and smiling babies provided by intermediaries in the countries of origin, at unreasonable prices' (Ngabonziza, 1991). A survey by the British Agencies for Adoption and Fostering (1991) found that almost nine out of ten children brought into Britain were under 6 years old when joining their new families, with 55 per cent being 1 year old and under.

THE BRITISH RESPONSE TO INTERCOUNTRY ADOPTION

Nobody is certain how many children from other countries have been adopted in Britain but the numbers cannot be high. Accurate statistics are missing. Until about 1989, apart from occasional individual arrangements, intercountry adoption had a very low profile in Britain, though it varied by area. The only organized effort had been the bringing into the country of around 100 children from Vietnam in the 1970s. A survey carried out by the Children's Legal Centre (1989), just before the Romanian revolution, found that the 57 of the 177 social services departments that responded indicated they had dealt with just over 300 cases of intercountry adoptions in the previous four years. The small response rate to the questionnaire provided no realistic picture of the extent of intercountry adoption, but it is doubtful whether they exceeded 200 each year.

Following the Romanian revolution, some 300 children are known officially to have been brought into the country during the first couple of years, and possibly a further 300 unofficially. In comparison with other European countries and with North America, the number of children adopted intercountry in Britain has been very small. In fact, after about 1993, when Britain and the Romanian government signed a bilateral agreement setting down certain rules about adoption between the two countries, hardly any children have been brought into the country. More recently a few children have been brought in from China, for reasons explained earlier. What the Romanian situation did was to expose the lack of British policy on intercountry adoption and to raise its profile in Britain.

There are a number of reasons why, until recently, intercountry adoption featured very little in Britain. The main ones are:

- concentration on own-country special needs children;
- the prohibition of third party placements and the strict immigration controls;
- the absence of intercountry legislation governing adoption practice;
- lack of clarity of procedures ;
- lack of overall national policy among local authorities; and
- an ideological stance by many agencies and professionals against intercountry adoption.

Following the drastic drop in baby adoptions, adoption societies and social services in Britain, unlike those on the continent of Europe, made a determined effort to place children with special needs from within the country. With resources being finite, perhaps the needs of the intercountry adopter and adoptee were seen to be of a lower priority. In the United States, because of the demand, attention was paid both to special needs children and to intercountry adoption. Another key factor in both countries was the opposition by many adoption and social services agencies and by social workers to both intercountry and transracial adoption.

Recently the British government has taken exception to the apparent opposition of many social services departments to intercountry adoption and has asked them to provide home studies for applicants in advance of a child being identified in the 'sending' country and also to speed up such assessments. At the same time it maintained, in the person of the then Secretary of State at the Department of Health, that it had no wish to promote intercountry adoption. However, because of public pressure, it financed a Helpline hosted by The Bridge Child Care Consultancy Service, based in London, to provide advice and information to those wishing to adopt intercountry and to professionals working in intercountry adoption (Bottomley, 1991). The Helpline has received around 9000 enquiries since it began operation in May 1992 (Haworth, 1995). It is thought that many of those enquiring do not proceed with an application, while a number of enquirers are seeking the Helpline's assistance after they have the child. A small number of those who adopt intercountry have also been approved to adopt in-country, whilst others proceed to adopt one or more children in the UK after they have adopted intercountry.

THE RESEARCH EVIDENCE

Much of the research evidence on intercountry adoption comes from the United States, Scandinavia, Holland and Germany where intercountry adoption has been extensively practised. There is one British study under way at the moment. This is directed by Rutter at the Maudsley Hospital and is concentrating on the recent adoption of Romanian children, with the focus on their development and progress.

The methodological problems that beset outcome studies (outlined in Chapter 2) apply to research on intercountry adoption, with the added factors of colour, culture and ethnicity, especially for the older child. Apart from some of the theoretical research issues (see Triseliotis, 1991c), the available studies have been conducted in different countries with different systems in operation, applying varying definitions of health and adjustment, studying the children at different stages following placement, often with no controls, and with large sample losses.

Another big drawback in intercountry adoption research has been the absence of reliable information about the children's experiences before arrival and the difficulty, as a result, of establishing reliable baselines for comparison purposes. Much of the background information has been speculative or based on observations of the children's state on arrival. These and other methodological and definition problems make comparisons between studies difficult.

In spite of methodological and definition problems, and despite a number of contradictions in the research findings, there is an interesting degree of consensus, suggesting on the whole favourable outcomes. Studies focusing on intercountry adoption divide into (1) studies on how children are functioning on a range of dimensions within the adoptive family and at school and (2) studies that focus on issues of the children's racial, cultural and ethnic identity.

1. THE CHILDREN'S FUNCTIONING AND ADJUSTMENT

Studies of the first kind have chosen health, language, schooling and general behaviour as relevant areas in which to evaluate children's functioning and adjustment.

(a) Medical and health issues

The main studies carried out are agreed that on arrival in their new countries older children, especially, exhibit a range of health problems in the form of malnutrition, skin diseases, intestinal parasites, hearing impairment and physical disabilities. As one Swedish study put it, barely one-third of the 207 children were free from physical symptoms on arrival but most of their symptoms were rapidly cured. The adoptive parents described the children as physically strong and only infrequently ill (Gardell, 1980). The same study also found that there was no relationship between any of these symptoms on arrival, including malnutrition, and current adjustment problems.

A Dutch study involving 1000 children (72 per cent under a year on arrival) found similar initial health problems as identified in the Swedish study, but again after two years most children were judged to have made a continuous improvement (Sorgedragen, quoted by Hoksbergen, 1991b). Similar findings were reported from another study of children from Thailand arriving in Holland (Hoksbergen, Juffer and Waardenburg, 1987).

(b) Schooling and linguistic development

Leaving aside non-verbal forms of communication that can differ from one culture to another, children over about 1 year old on arrival are bound to experience communication difficulties. They not only have to learn an unfamiliar language, but also to interpret and understand the new sounds they hear and the body language they see. In addition, and possibly more important, they have to interpret and understand the mood of their carers and of those around them. As with verbal and non-verbal forms of communication, mood and the expression of feeling are all culturally bound and misunderstandings can easily arise about meaning and intentions. Cederblad (1982) describes how the adoptive parents in her study mainly used sign language at the start supplemented by some words in the child's initial language that they had learnt. Research cannot throw much light on the intangibles of behaviour such as non-verbal forms of communication and the expression of mood and feeling. Not surprisingly, it has concentrated largely on the measurement of observable language attributes and behaviours.

Whether the linguistic skills and language development of inter-country adopted children suffer in the long run as a result of the change from a first to a second language is still not agreed upon. Two Swedish studies express some concern about the children's linguistic development, associated mostly with the children being over about 18 months on arrival (Gardell, 1980; Hene, 1988). On the basis of her Norwegian study Dalen (1988) supports the Swedish findings with regard to language skills. She claims to have discovered a general lack of language skills and particularly of basic and everyday words and concepts.

However, three Dutch studies failed to confirm the above findings. On the contrary, the authors were surprised that neither in their longitudinal, nor in a cross-sectional, study could they find any alarming problems in the acquisition of the Dutch language (De Vries, 1988; Schaerlakens and Dondeyne, 1985). Similar findings were reported in Cederblad's Swedish study (1982). She found that the children had adjusted well at school and that specific reading, writing and numbering disabilities were no more problematic among them than among the Danish reference children. Other studies too claimed to have found that intercountry adopted children eventually managed to cope well with the academic side of school (Cederblad, 1982; Hene, 1988). These studies also suggest that during the initial stages after arrival, some children repress their first language and refuse to converse in it. Haworth (1995) reports that adoption practitioners have noted other contexts in which the child's original language has importance, particularly in communicating pre-adoption abusive and traumatic experiences. Apparently, where there has been a change in language, it can significantly inhibit or delay disclosure, as the child no longer has access to the actual words in use at the time the events took place.

(c) Emotional adjustment

It would be surprising if full agreement were to be found among the different studies on such a complex subject as that of emotional adjustment and the display of problematic behaviour. Many of the intercountry adoptees would perhaps be expected to display significantly problematic behaviour in view of their previous experience of institutional living, separation and loss. Nevertheless, and in spite of some conflicting evidence provided by studies, it does appear that the great majority of these children eventually overcome initial emotional and behavioural problems, which are either significantly reduced or disappear altogether. Furthermore, overall, intercountry adoptees do not appear to display higher levels of difficulties than other children, adopted or not. Lingering difficulties are usually associated with children who are older on arrival (Holfvander *et al.*, 1978; Gardell, 1980; Gunnarby *et al.*, 1982; Alstein and Simon, 1991; Bagley, Young and Scully, 1993).

The adoptive parents who responded to Ahlijah's (1990) British study expressed considerable satisfaction with the children's adjustment and the way adoption was working for them. The author herself, though, queries her own findings, suggesting that only families who had a 'good adoption' kept in touch with agencies which were facilitating intercountry adoption and responded to her questionnaire.

In the United States Feigelman and Silverman (1983), relying on the perceptions of adoptive parents, contrasted the long-term adjustments of Colombian, Korean and African-American trans-racial adoptees with those of own-country racially adopted whites. After adoptees had been in their adoptive homes for at least six years, the results showed that the adolescent and school-aged inter-country adoptees were no less well adjusted than their inter-racially adopted counterparts. In fact, Korean adoptees were better adapted than white adolescents. Only with regard to their appearance, Koreans showed more of a negative response than white adolescent adoptees. Kim (1976) also reported good adaptation achieved by Korean children, including the observation that their self-concept was 'remarkably similar' to that of other American teenagers.

A German study compared a random sample of 145 children adopted from Korea, Vietnam and Latin America, aged 13 to 18 at the time of the study, with non-adopted teenagers and own-country adoptees in the same areas. The intercountry adoptees were placed when on average 6 years old, with 22 per cent being under 2 years and 38 per cent between 6 and 10 years. Postal questionnaires to parents and the children were the main method used for data collection. The researcher concluded that no difference could be found on any of the measures such as making friendships, positive or negative feelings about themselves, educational achievements and self-concept when compared with own-country adopted and the non-adopted group (Kuhl, 1985). Equally similar positive findings were reported by Kvist, Viemero and Forsten (1989) on children in Finland who had been adopted from Asia. Cederblad (1982) referred to a study in Denmark by Pruzan, who studied 168 children who had been in Denmark for at least two years and who were aged between 8 and 12 years old at interview. They were found to be as well adjusted as a similar group of Danish-born children.

Another study with positive findings was reported by Hoksbergen, Juffer and Waardenburg (1987). They studied 116 children from Thailand who were on average 10 months on arrival in Holland with just over 10 per cent being over 2 years. The children were 8 years old when the study took place. The researchers found that the parent–child relationships were good and the children's behaviour at school and their attitude to school work was said to be better than that of their non-adopted classmates. Children who were older on arrival were apparently lower achievers and initial settling-in problems were greater for these children.

Poorer subsequent adjustments have been mainly noted with those children who were older on arrival and at adoption placement (Holfvander *et al.*, 1978; Gunnarby *et al.*, 1982; Hoksbergen, 1991b; Alstein and Simon, 1991). As an example, Gardell (1980), who studied 207 youngsters adopted in Sweden, reported that only 4 per cent of the children who were aged less than 18 months on arrival, as compared to 64 per cent of those who were 6 years or older, had 'serious adjustment problems'. A Dutch survey of 2148 children aged 10-15 who were placed for adoption between a few days old and 10 years showed that the adopted group had a somewhat higher rate of behaviour problems than non-adopted children of the same age. However, the authors go on to add that the difference was mainly due to a minority of 12- to 15-year-old boys (23 per cent compared to 10 per cent of the controls) who had particularly high problem scores above the 90th percentile. The major problems were lying, stealing, truanting and hyperactivity. The older the child at placement, the greater the likelihood that problem behaviour would be reported (Verhulst, Althaus and Beinman, 1990).

One Dutch study claimed that almost 6 per cent of children adopted intercountry needed residential care at some time, three times the number of own-country adopted children in such need. Adoptive parents, according to the same study, were six times more likely to ask for psychiatric help on behalf of the children compared with non-adoptive families (Hoksbergen, 1991b).

The conflicting results of the studies outlined above mirror those evaluating the outcome of in-country special needs children adoption. For reasons outlined earlier, some of the findings and inconsistencies should not be surprising. What is equally important is the high percentage of children who appear to do well. We could in fact conclude that studies in intercountry adoption lend support to those in-country studies of adoptees which suggest that children who experience adversities, separations and loss in early childhood are able, given a nurturing and stimulating environment, to overcome many of their difficulties. With some the difficulties can be more persistent. Older age at placement again emerges as a decisive factor, with more persistent difficulties being experienced with children placed when over about the age of 6 or 7.

2. RACIAL, CULTURAL AND ETHNIC IDENTIFICATION

Almost all the studies referred to earlier and which have reported 'good' family and school adjustments for most children adopted intercountry also raise some concerns. These have to do mainly with racism and discrimination experienced by some children, along with a poorer sense of racial and ethnic identification. Alstein and Simon (1991), whose studies suggest overall good adjustments, also report examples of racism and discrimination. In one of their studies almost a third of the children said that 'the fact that they looked different from their parents and siblings had caused them some problems' (p. 43). In another study, reported by the same authors (1991, p. 37), over a third of the children 'recalled problems during the preceding three years involving children calling them names and making fun of them because of their racial backgrounds' (see also Chapter 8).

Feigelman and Silverman (1984), whilst noting discomfort expressed by Korean adolescents adopted in the States about their appearance, found that this apparently had not affected their overall adjustment or self-esteem. Saetersdal (1989), who studied 41 Vietnamese children brought to Norway when aged between 2 and 5, remarked that in follow-up studies 'none of them mentioned their ethnic background when asked to describe themselves'. In the researcher's view, the adoptees seemed 'to deny or minimize their feelings of differences and dismiss the importance of ethnic identity'. It is not clear how far the children's denial of difference was an attempt to be accepted by Norwegian society.

A Danish study of 455 young adoptees aged 18–25 at interview, who had been adopted mainly from Asia, two-thirds of them at the age of 3 or over, found, not surprisingly, that hardly any of them could remember their native language (Rorbech,1991). However, one-third could remember people and incidents, often violent, from life before they came to Denmark. Almost all felt themselves to be mostly Danish and two-thirds did not feel that they were a 'kind of immigrant'. Similarly two-thirds felt no emotional attachment to their country of origin and the same proportion did not want information about their family of origin. Furthermore only 7 per cent wished they had stayed in their country of origin, whilst a few gave no clear replies to the question.

Somewhat different results were obtained from similar questions asked of 202 Korean children adopted in Germany (Kuhl, 1985). At interview three-quarters were aged 13–18 and the rest over 18. In this study one-third said they were somewhat or very interested in their country of origin and two-thirds said they would like to visit it. The majority, however, said they felt themselves to be German. At a weekend seminar organized by the researcher, some of the adopted people interviewed said how their national identity evolved over a period of time and it was mainly with older age that they began to see themselves also as partially Korean. One of them is quoted as saying:

'I've only now managed to see myself partially as Korean. When I was small, I always wanted to be German.'

In contrast a younger boy demonstrated with his comment the attempt of some to express the reality of their adoption and of its bi-cultural and bi-racial nature, saying:

'I feel myself to be wholly German, but I look Korean, and that's something I don't like ... because internally I'm German, and externally Korean.'

Like first-generation immigrants who see newcomers as a threat to their own apparently insecure situation, there is some evidence that intercountry adoptees, too, shun refugees or immigrants from their original country, urging stricter immigration controls to keep them out (Rorbech, 1991).

Tizard and Phoenix (1989 and 1993), whilst acknowledging that racism impinges on the identity of all children who are perceived as black, argue that racial identity is only one factor contributing to their identity formation and is not sufficient by itself to influence psychological adjustment in a negative way. They then assert that the paramount factor is the quality of parenting the children experience. Triseliotis (1973) and Triseliotis and Russell (1984) would confirm this from their studies of white children adopted by white families. However, where racism and discrimination are widespread, it is possible that the attributes of racial and social identity may assume greater importance in the hierarchy of factors contributing to a social and personality identity.

On the evidence so far, we could accept that during early childhood the quality of parenting is probably the most important factor in the building of self-esteem and of a positive self-concept. However, as the intercountry or transracially adopted person grows up and away from parental protectiveness, then community attitudes assume much greater importance and, if hostile and rejecting,

they can prove devastating to the self. Evidence for the latter asser-
tion comes mainly from some studies of adult intercountry adopted
people which are discussed below.

First, on a positive note, Bagley, Young and Scully (1993) studied 44
women aged 22 to 28 adopted in Britain from Hong Kong in the early
1960s when they were infants or young girls. Their overall conclusion
was that these women had not experienced racism or discrimination,
had few problems of identity and the only negative feature found was
'some degree of anxiety and over-protection in about 10 per cent of
parents'. On a range of measures there was 'no statistically significant
difference between the adoptees and the controls' who were white and
of British, Irish or other European 'ethnic origin'. Almost all of the
women in the sample made 'excellent' adjustment and in the authors'
words, 'these adoptions have been highly successful'.

A different picture, however, is painted by two Norwegian
researchers who followed up intercountry adoptees in their late teens
and young adulthood. The 41 intercountry adoptees featuring in their
study were dispersed in different parts of Norway (Dalen and
Saetersdal, 1987; Saetersdal, 1989). They found that whereas most of
the adoptees adjusted well 'both psychologically and socially during
childhood', when they reached adulthood they felt themselves driven
into a more 'marginal position' as they faced more direct situations of
discrimination. The researchers describe the adoptees as being in a no-
man's land because they at the same time both belonged and did not
belong to that society. In their words, they were not fully accepted citi-
zens and they tended to avoid making contact with unknown people or
placing themselves in situations that might invite rejection, discrimination or being patronized. The adoptees generally tried to surround
themselves with 'secure friends'.

As in the case of the Norwegian study, Rorbech's (1991) update of
his Danish study indicated that between the ages of 8 and 12 years
old the intercountry adoptees experienced little negative discrimination, but ten years later the situation changed significantly for them
because of 'increased intolerance to foreigners'. In the German
study, quoted earlier, half the teenagers said they had been teased
because of their appearance (Kuhl, 1985). An anecdotal study of
sixteen adult adoptees in Sweden (Zaar, 1984) who were adopted
mainly when older, and who on the whole claimed to have experienced no unusual hostility, nevertheless has some of them making
comments such as: 'I've almost always felt like two people' or 'My
passport says I am a Swede, but I'm nothing'.

It is relevant at this point to be reminded of Goffman's (1963) pioneering work which highlights how the images people develop of themselves are considerably influenced by the way others see them. He developed the concept of 'spoiled identity' to signify the impact of stigma and labelling on individuals and minority groups who are seen to be different or perceived as out groups. In his view and that of Mead (1934), a sense of spoiled identity usually develops from the receipt of consistently negative messages. Haworth (1995) reports how 'trans-ethnic' placements frequently result in the child and family being the object of a degree of public interest, scrutiny and curiosity from which there may be little escape, something which children of mixed parentage seem to perceive as a negative experience. Even where such curiosity may be well meant, the family becomes involved in a continuing process of explaining, or indeed justifying to others, their family relationships.

On the basis of the above studies and of Bagley's study of native Canadian children referred to earlier, we can conclude that the impact of racism on identity has to be considered within the context of the specific country, and even area within the same country, where the children happen to grow up. Furthermore, that racism and discrimination are relative to the degree of pigmentation and physical difference displayed by the children. It is for this reason that studies about racial and ethnic identity carried out in one country, with a different population mix and different attitudes to race and culture, cannot be totally transferred to explain the identities of adoptees in other countries or even areas of a country. In conclusion, the 'marginalization' and rejection of any ethnic group is a poor predictive factor in either intercountry or own-country transracial adoption. Many of these environmental forces are obviously outside the control of adoptive parents, though they have some choice. Stone (1981) and McRoy (1991b) suggest that by choosing to live in more integrated communities with different population mix, some but not all of these aspects may be addressed.

POLICY AND PRACTICE RESPONSES

Intercountry adoption has exposed the limitations and often inadequacies of legislative provision not only in the sending but even more so in the receiving countries. It is perhaps too much to expect sending countries emerging from wars, dictatorships or colonialism to have had time and resources, amongst all their other pressing problems, to give priority to the regulation of adoption policy and practice. As an example, because of its rather archaic legislation, it was much more difficult, and partly still is, for Romanian families to adopt Romanian children than for foreigners going to the country. This is also the case in a number of other sending countries where adoption and fostering within the same countries have hardly been explored yet (Tolfree, 1995).

Sending countries are increasingly regulating intercountry adoption; Bangladesh and Peru have banned it altogether. Peru will now only allow adoptions on the basis of bilateral agreements. Others, such as Korea and more recently Romania and India, have developed laws to regulate it. For some countries it has become a matter of national pride not to send children out of the country, but it is too early to know whether this translates also into policies and programmes for in-country arrangements for the children.

As already said, a certain amount of intercountry adoption has its place and banning it altogether does not seem to be a realistic option. It is also doubtful whether a ban could be enforced. Other developments taking place now also make moves in this direction unhelpful. For example, and in spite of the re-emergence of extremes of nationalism, the movement of populations across countries has 'aggravated' two situations. First, thousands, if not millions, of people emigrate to new countries but still have their roots in their original ones. Adoption and other childcare arrangements between the 'immigrants' and their parent country will continue to be needed for very good reasons. Second, the same movement of populations also leads to more mixed marriages and partnerships. Within a few decades distinctions between races are likely to become more blurred, particularly in the predominantly white populated countries of western Europe and North America. With so many families having biracial, binational and bicultural roots, issues of race and of transracial placements, which intercountry adoptions most often are, will likely recede in importance.

Having said that, there is an urgent need for an international legal framework based on what is known to be best for children, to strictly regulate a limited form of intercountry adoption. So far, much of intercountry adoption has been adult-centred and recent developments, particularly in the United States outlined in Chapter 1, are moving adoption much more in that direction. For intercountry adoption to gain the legitimacy it badly needs, it has to be demonstrated that any arrangement:

- is in the children's best interests;
- follows closely standards of good practice set by accredited agencies;

- strictly adheres to the laws of the sending and receiving countries;
- is freely entered upon by all parties;
- involves no profit; and
- is covered by a comprehensive range of after-care services in the receiving country.

To achieve a child-centred approach to intercountry adoption, close co-operation will be needed between sending and receiving countries, with the latter shouldering the main responsibility because they have the resources and organizational structures to make this possible. At the moment, and unlike some other European countries, there is no systematic co-operation and partnership between UK adoption agencies and adoption organizations in other countries. Haworth (1995) sees the need for a structure which facilitates agency-to-agency communication and co-operation between sending and receiving countries, among other things, to develop:

- an understanding of the routes children follow to intercountry adoption and the characteristics of children for whom intercountry adoption is sought;
- an integrated and mutually informed approach to counselling birth families, assessment and preparation of children, assessment and preparation of adopters and post-adoption services to all parties;
- services which ensure that the fullest information possible is provided about the child's background and that continuing links between both countries enable a two-way flow of information, if this is desired, and is in accordance with the respective countries' laws; and
- services which ensure that post-placement experiences are open to review by both countries to inform future policy and practice.

There is as yet no international law regulating adoption. Much of what happens today is dependent on bilateral agreements between countries. For example, Britain has such agreements with a number of countries, a recent addition being Romania. Because of the absence of international law and co-ordination either some families experience untold difficulties or, worse still, great numbers of children are treated as commodities and are protected by far fewer safeguards than apply to in-country adopted children.

A first step towards bringing some order to the intercountry placement of children has been taken by the United Nations. It has rightly recognized that there is a place for intercountry adoption, but not in the largely commercial and unrestricted form that has been taking place over the last thirty or so years. In any arrangements, the central test that should be guiding both policy and practice is the welfare of the child, which is implicitly recognized in the declaration of the Convention on the Rights of the Child (November 1989, Article 21):

> The primary aim of adoption is to provide the child who cannot be cared for by his or her own parents, with a permanent family. If that child cannot be placed in a foster or adoptive family *and cannot in any suitable manner be cared for in the country of origin*, intercountry adoption may be considered as an alternative means of child care.

The next stage towards the implementation of the UN declaration has been the initiatives taken by the Hague Convention for the Protection of Children. The Hague Conference on Private International Law brought together over 65 sending and receiving countries, including Britain and the United States. They have participated in a number of Special Commission Sessions and signed a declaration on processes to be observed in intercountry adoptions. The published Convention consists of a number of parts, each part dealing with one aspect of intercountry adoption. Its basic approach, though, is to leave the responsibility for decisions relating to children available for adoption in the hands of the sending countries and to make receiving countries responsible for assessing and preparing would-be adopters.

Part II of the Convention requirements are set down outlining the respective responsibilities of sending and receiving countries. For example, the state of origin has to ensure that the child is 'adoptable', that an intercountry adoption is in the child's interests and so on (Article 4). The receiving state must ensure that the prospective adopters are eligible and suitable to adopt, that they have been appropriately counselled and that the child will be authorized to enter and reside permanently in the country (Article 5) (see Duncan, 1993). Sadly, the Convention has failed to reach agreement on the banning of third party arrangements and both approved adoption agencies and private individuals will continue to be involved in arrangements.

Chapter IV of the Convention sets out procedures to be adopted by the central authorities (or accredited bodies) in relation to the preparation of reports and the screening of prospective adopters, the placement process, the obtaining of consents, receiving permission for the child to enter the receiving country and the measures to be taken in the event of the arrangement breaking down.

As with other declarations by Conventions and UN bodies, states may or may not implement the requirements, or may be selective, even after they sign them. Events have shown that, even in sending countries that are determined to regulate arrangements, an unofficial route seems to exist side by side with the official one. In spite of these limitations, the Convention holds the best hope for the future.

THE EUROPEAN RESPONSE

Reference has already been made to the fact that outside the UK, over 10,000 children are adopted intercountry in northern and western Europe each year. Although independent and third party adoptions are allowed in countries such as Sweden, Germany, the Netherlands and France, there are also official or officially recognized routes which can be used. As an example, Sweden has an accredited National Board for Intercountry Adoptions which is under the Ministry of Health and Social Affairs, which has the total responsibility for the regulation and overseeing of overseas adoptions, even though independent arrangements are also allowed. A Swedish couple wishing to adopt intercountry have to be approved and have the same 'home study' made of them by social workers as for a Swedish adoption (Anderson, 1988, quoted by Tizard, 1991). Would-be adopters are also advised to attend a preparatory course and apparently around 70 per cent do so. Furthermore, the Swedish source to whom the couple are applying for a child must also be approved as 'reputable and competent', able to ensure that the child is free for adoption and that the laws and regulation of the donor country are followed. After placement, the child is supervised by Swedish social workers until the adoption decree is issued.

Broadly similar arrangements exist in France but there most families adopting intercountry seem to take the independent rather than the agency route (Greenfield, 1995).

In the Netherlands there is an Act on Intercountry Adoption and anyone wishing to adopt a foreign child must first contact the Ministry of Justice. There are certain eligibility requirements, such as the age of adopters and children, that have to be met first. Once approved, the applicants must first undertake an information and preparation programme and then have a home study prepared by a local authority council. Applicants can then register with an agency approved by the ministry for the mediation of overseas adoptions, or can act independently (see Selman, 1993). Accredited agencies put would-be adopters in touch with specific organizations in donor countries, which can then suggest individual children.

There are a number of problems associated with accredited agencies set up by governments to manage intercountry adoption outside the mainstream childcare systems. It is in the nature of all types of organizations, and intercountry ones are no exception, to want to expand, to promote and prolong their operations rather than stick to their initial remit. Etzioni (1964) makes the point that once formed, organizations acquire their own needs and these sometimes become the masters of the organization. Because those who usually adopt intercountry are better-off, middle-class families, able to exercise political and other pressures to secure their aims, 'the demand somehow generates a market which in turn takes every effort to generate the supplies when the existing stock can no longer satisfy the demand' (Ngabonziza, 1991, p. 76).

The setting up of separate agencies also takes intercountry adoption outside the mainstream of own-country adoption and of family and childcare services, where it belongs. Even though countries that have gone down this route, such as Sweden and the Netherlands, would deny it, nevertheless, this circumstance does reinforce the adult-centredness of much intercountry adoption (Duncan, 1993). It has already been said that Britain has no official policy on intercountry adoption, but it is expected that a policy will be outlined in the new Adoption Bill. Events such as the Romanian situation exposed the low-key approach and made it necessary, if not inevitable, to move towards new legislative arrangements regulating, rather than promoting, intercountry adoption. The new Bill will largely reflect the Hague Convention.

THE ORGANIZATIONAL STRUCTURE

Organizationally intercountry adoption cannot and should not be separated from own-country adoption work and from the wider childcare field where it belongs. To be practised efficiently and effectively, and with the child's interests remaining central, it requires a range of knowledge, expertise and resources to be available for use at the different stages as indicated earlier. As an example, preparation of those wishing to adopt intercountry has to build on the knowledge and skills developed when preparing those wishing to adopt in-country. Similarly, post-placement services (described in Chapter 11) have to be available for *all* children, whether adopted in-country or intercountry. Here, we concentrate on what are seen as key *additional* agency tasks that have to be taken on board in intercountry adoption.

THE PREPARATION STAGE AND HOME STUDY

Preparing applicant(s) to adopt is a complex task made more so when it involves adopting intercountry. A number of social services departments in Britain have drafted policy and procedures documents for intercountry adoption which are made available to would be intercountry adopters. They usually describe the respective departments' philosophy and policy on the matter; the legal basis of adoption; the immigration procedures; steps to be taken by applicant(s); procedures; home study reports; welfare supervision; the court application; and emigration for the purpose of adoption (Humphreys, 1992).

Additional preparation for would-be intercountry adopters, given either individually or in groups, would usually include:

- preparation for coping with the uncertainties implicit in intercountry adoption at every level, including the legal and financial requirements and likely timescales;
- preparation for coping with any health, linguistic and behavioural problems that some of the older children especially may display, and provision of information on sources of support;
- information on the kind of background and genealogical information that adoptive parents should seek from the country of origins and/or birth parents, why this is necessary and how it can be used;
- advice on the importance of obtaining, where possible, a detailed medical history, and a developmental history, especially for the older child; also of obtaining details about attachments to parents or carers and how an older child can keep in touch, where desirable;

- guidance on establishing why the parents parted with the child and how it came to be available for adoption; who and how to get in touch with for up-dated information. (The reality is that often there will be little information to pass on to the child and it is a question of supporting the child in coping with its absence and the unknown.)

The following apply also to own-country adoption but because of their centrality they are included here:

- guidance on how adoptive parents can foster their child's racial, ethnic and cultural awareness and heritage within predominantly white structures, contributing eventually towards a more positive self-image for the intercountry adopted person;
- guidance on how to become involved with their child's ethnic community, its institutions and literature;
- consideration of the possibility that some children will want to visit their country of origin and perhaps meet parents and relatives, if available, and recognition that this need not pose a threat to the adoptive parent–child relationship;
- advice on how adopters can help their child to find acceptable ways of dealing with possible experiences of racism and discrimination; and
- information on how to help the child answer questions about his or her adoption, appearance and background.

As with own-country adoption, would-be intercountry adopters can benefit immensely from being put in touch with others who have adopted in this way. It is also important that intercountry adopters are made aware how and where they can obtain services after they have a child placed with them. It is thought that possibly because of the apparent mixed feelings among professionals and others towards intercountry adoption, adopters may be even more reluctant than in-country ones to seek services and help if needed.

In Chapter 7 we described the preparation of adoptive parents through the use of individual and group meetings to ensure that would-be adopters have sufficient knowledge to make an informed decision about whether they will finally proceed to adopt. Here, Humphreys (1992), of Bury Social Services Department, describes how she used six group sessions to convey additional information on issues relevant to intercountry adoption, in this case the adoption of children from Romania. No doubt the sessions can be adapted to suit the adoption of children from other countries:

> **Week 1.** A paediatrician who had worked in the developing world and who had a special interest in the long-term effects of institutionalization spoke about AIDS, Hepatitis B and other possible conditions.
>
> **Week 2.** Talk by a dietician and a speech therapist, who, amongst other things, explained the reasons for lack of speech in some Romanian children, usually arising from palates not forming properly because the children are fed with bottles until they are about 3.
>
> **Week 3.** Additional input on attachment and separation.
>
> **Week 4.** The health visitor and the panel medical adviser who had offered to follow the children up talked about child development and what services are available to children and families.
>
> **Week 5.** A session on the child's cultural and ethnic background.
>
> **Week 6.** Discussion about telling about adoption, life story books, the importance of gathering as much information as possible from the sending country.

THE CHILD'S ADDITIONAL TASKS

In Chapter 2 we outlined the additional psychological tasks faced by adopted children, particularly in acknowledging and assimilating the concept of a separate psychological and a biological parent, and in resolving the element of loss and rejection which adoption implies. The intercountry adopted child faces the same tasks and some additional ones. The main additional task is the acknowledgement of the duality of his heritage, including ethnic, cultural and, where present, racial characteristics. Adoptive parents again have a key role in helping their child reach this acknowledgement in a positive way.

As with mainstream adoption, children adopted intercountry will vary in the stage at which they will begin to acknowledge the difference between their psychological and biological parenting and the idea of two families. Some may not do so until adolescence and beyond (Craig, 1991). Like some in-country adopted children, some intercountry ones too may want to deny that they have another heritage, have roots in another culture or that they are different in appearance or colour from their adoptive parents. In fact some of them may actively reject their black or Asian or Latin American identity, insisting it is nothing to do with them. The reasons for this are unclear, but they could be related to a number of factors such as:

- some insecurity about their position within the family;
- the way they are perceived by the surrounding community and peers;
- resentment at what happened, finding it difficult to resolve the element of loss and rejection involved; or
- responding perhaps to some unspoken parental wish.

There is no shortage of examples of pre-adolescent transracially placed children denying they were black or Asian, refusing to associate with other children from a similar background or declining to visit eating places or places of worship associated with their original roots and ethnic community. Some even use racialist language against other children from a similar background. Such denial is also equivalent to non-acknowledgement of one's adoption. This denial is likely to begin to crumble with adolescence, which marks the onset of a search for self. It is unlikely that a positive resolution can be reached without gradually acknowledging the difference and the children beginning to construct their identity on the duality of their parentage and heritage, if they are to face the future. As Taylor (1989, quoted by Giddens, 1992) writes:

In order to have a sense of who we are, we have to have a notion of how we have become and of where we are going.

Tizard (1991, p. 753) comments:

it is clear that the task of combining and integrating their dual inheritance, without denying either, is a difficult one that proceeds over many years, and into adulthood.

In her subsequent study (with Phoenix, 1993) Tizard provides evidence to show that children of mixed parentage can develop a positive bicultural identity, without having to reject either.

More worrying is the possibility of breakdown in the adoption with intercountry children having to enter local authority care. As pointed out elsewhere, unlike in-country adoption, where an older child can theoretically turn to members of the original family, the intercountry adolescent or adult has nowhere else to turn and can become rootless. Already at least two to three of the Romanian children are in local

authority care. These concerns are more real in countries where intercountry adoption runs into thousands each year.

THE BIRTH PARENTS

We have already referred to evidence showing that many intercountry adopted children are neither orphaned nor abandoned. The
reason that many of them are given up is their parents' extreme
poverty which makes the lure of money irresistible. What is later
said to the children about their original families and countries of
origin can be as crucial almost as the quality of care they receive. We
have already discussed extensively, in Chapter 2 , why the positive
inclusion of the family of origin, including ethnicity and race, in the
child's concept are important.

There is a view that with in-country adoption becoming much
more open, maybe involving continuing contact between the original and adopting family, some of the attraction of intercountry
adoption may be in its almost total guarantee of secrecy. In many
countries the transactions are carried out by intermediaries, and
adopters and birth parents do not set eyes on each other. Even in
cases where the adopting and birth parents meet at the parting stage,
further contact is usually highly unlikely. Greenfield (1995) cites
Thailand and India as examples where contact is not allowed at all.
She also adds that most of the French agencies which bring children
to France would not accept such a meeting.

Some sending countries do not allow any contact between birth
and adopting parents. Where meetings take place, these are often
unplanned and unprepared. Apparently over half the families
Greenfield interviewed, in France and England, expressed disappointment at the amount of information given to them about the
child's background. She quotes one French couple, amongst others,
who said that they found it difficult to ask questions because of the
fear of jeopardizing the arrangement.

Regulating intercountry adoption through properly accredited
agencies should, in the first instance, guarantee the collection of
detailed background information, photos, medical records, letters
etc. – all very necessary, for reasons explained in Chapter 2. The
existence also of proper channels of communication should make it
possible for updated information to be provided periodically by both
sides, so that birth parents and children do not constantly worry
about what may have happened to each other. The possibility of

future visits and meetings can only help in strengthening the child's identity and self-concept, for reasons discussed in Chapter 4.

We recognize that these are optimum expectations. In reality there are many impediments and reasons why they may not be fulfilled, including the fact that in some countries (e.g. Bulgaria) birth records are destroyed when the adoption order is made. Sometimes adopted children lose contact with birth parents because of the expense involved in maintaining records. Additional problems arise from illiteracy and huge physical distances.

CONCLUDING REMARKS

Irrespective of the political, moral and empirical issues, a certain amount of intercountry adoption is inevitable for reasons outlined earlier. The empirical evidence with regard to the children's adjustment is on the whole positive. The experience of racism and discrimination, as the children move on to adulthood, seems to depend largely on the areas where they happen to grow up and its population mix, though the alerting of adoptive families about how to prepare children can help. The Hague Convention for the protection of children has made a start by bringing together over 65 countries to agree to regulate adoption arrangements in both the sending and receiving countries so that the various countries' policies and practices become child-centred. New envisaged legislation in Britain is very likely to move in this direction. There are more problems with the United States where many adoption arrangements, both own-country and intercountry, are in the hands of private agencies.

Five key points

1. Intercountry adoption dates mainly from the end of World War II in 1945, but its extensive practice in western Europe and North America coincided with the rapidly diminishing number of own-country babies for adoption.
2. Though there have been many notable exceptions, nevertheless, intercountry adoption came to be associated in many people's minds with the sale of children, bribery, forgery and child abduction.

3. Unlike its early stages, most intercountry adoption now involves very young children or babies and a middle-class families.

4. Empirical evidence suggests that children adopted inter-country, especially when young, do as well as those adopted own-country. Less is known of how they are perceived in their new countries when they grow up.

5. The Hague Convention for the protection of children has been encouraging sending and receiving countries to regulate and control intercountry adoption, eventually turning it into a more child-centred activity. It is expected that new British legislation will reflect this view.

CHAPTER 10
Single-parent adoption

It is difficult to estimate the number of single-parent *non-related* adoptions, as national adoption statistics are not kept either in Britain or the States. In the States it is estimated that the number has grown rapidly from about 3 per cent of all adoptions in 1975 to about 15 per cent today. We have no knowledge what percentage such adoptions constitute in Britain but it is unlikely that they number more than a few. Impressionistic evidence suggests that the vast majority of existing single adoptive parents are women, a significant number of them black.

The possibility of single-parent adoption by non-relatives existed from the very beginning of British adoption legislation. The legislators, though, were very cautious about such adoptions. The legislation conveyed the view that two people were better than one, and only exceptionally a single man could adopt, such as a stepfather following the death of the child's mother. It also seems that most agencies are reluctant to place children with single parents, except when it is almost impossible to secure a couple. Rarely is a single person the first choice and, when they are considered, it is more often for older children, usually with special needs.

In 1965, when single-parent placements began to be made, child-care was heavily influenced by psychoanalytic theory, which postulated that both a mother and a father figure were necessary for a child's intrapsychic development. It was not until the pressing needs of older children for adoptive homes were coupled with a general willingness to look beyond the traditional home which wished to rear an infant, that single parents were considered as adopting parents. Most people have known someone who, for some period of time, was raised by a single parent, or was a parent raising a child alone. Observation suggests that this form of family 'works' for a child. The placement of children with single parents began, and has continued, to be based on these commonsense observations.

There is, however, a newly articulated discomfort with the assumption that single-parent families are an acceptable alternative for children. Concern now centres on the ability of the single parent to meet the economic and social needs of the growing child. There is also developing, in some quarters, an almost moralistic concern about the 'rightness' of single persons as parents. 'It is difficult, but not impossible, for a single person to become a single parent', a recent handbook for single adoptive parents begins (Marindin, 1992, p. 1).

THE SINGLE-PARENT FAMILY

Earlier chapters have noted the rapid change in social customs and values in Western society. The commonsense experiences of the past, and the research literature of earlier years, may have little relevance to the experiences of single-parent families today. Thus, the material reviewed here focuses on recent years. However, data about single parents refer to the experiences of a much more disparate group than that small number who become single parents through adoption. Though always present, and relatively common today, the single-parent family is not the normative family of our society. Nor is it a family structure which is encouraged by the public policy of Western countries.

The experiences of single parents, and of their children, may vary greatly, depending in part on the reasons they are single. In 1992 in the United States, approximately 40 per cent of single mother-headed households were the result of divorce, while another 20 per cent were the result of separations. Six per cent were widowed (Bianchi, 1995). For all of these households, disruption and loss were part of the experience of the children. Thirty per cent of single mothers had never married. A disproportionate number of these were black and a disproportionate number of these mothers were very young at the time of their first child's birth (Bianchi, 1995). These are the families whose earning potential is most compromised. However, these are not the families likely to decide to adopt a child.

Those who discourage the formation of families with a single parent cite a line of research which has documented the difficulties of single parents. Foremost among these difficulties is income. In Western countries, with the changes in the economy, real wages for the lower paid have fallen in recent years. Two-parent families compensate for this with the addition of a second earner. For single parents this is not an option. Not surprisingly, at all educational levels, single-parent families have about half the income of two-parent families. In addition a single parent with a college degree has household income slightly less than a two-parent family with less than a high school education (McLanahan and Sandefur, 1994). More than a quarter of single-parent families have incomes below the poverty level.

Poor outcomes of childrearing are also associated with single-parent status. Recently McLanahan and Sandefur (1994) have published a review which documents that adolescents and young adults who have been in single-parent homes for some part of their childhood are twice as likely to drop out of school, to have a child before age 20, and one and a half times as likely to be out of school and not working. The reason for single status seemed to make little difference. It may be comfortable to believe that children thrive in single-parent homes, but there is evidence that this is not so.

On the other hand, writers concerned with the mores of our changing society write of the increasing economic and social independence of women, which make the economic contribution of a father unnecessary for the formation of a family. The woman who chooses to have children, who is able to support them, and who has never married has achieved a 'legitimate' status in this new society (Donati, 1995). Horowitz (1995) identifies the tasks of parenting, and suggests that single parents are competent to accomplish them. However, she notes the need for public policy to eliminate the poverty which makes the carrying out of these roles unnecessarily difficult.

Every adoption results in the creation of a newly defined family. Those involved with the policy of adoption, and those who daily facilitate adoptions, are closely concerned in the shaping of the forms of family which we, in this society, will view as acceptable. In adoption, tendencies to be protective of children can result in caution. Often policies favour the replication of the two-parent biological family insofar as possible. The married applicant, of an age to bear children, with the resources to raise a child, is accorded most favourable status in adoption, and is most likely to receive a same-race, healthy, infant. Furthermore, single people have to demonstrate more to agencies how they will cope with work and childcare, especially when the child is ill. Yet such detail is not always demanded of those who are married.

The evidence suggests that more marginal applicants, such as single parents, and even more so, single men, are unable to obtain healthy young children and they usually receive children who are more difficult to place. This is also documented by Groze and Rosenthal (1991), who discovered that single parents adopting in the United States are more likely than couples to adopt older children, non-white children, and children with learning difficulties.

Some single-parent adopters are gay or lesbian, probably many more than has been admitted by adoption agencies, though there are no data available. Agency reluctance to place with a gay or lesbian parent is even greater than with other single parents. Because of the reluctance of agencies (particularly those with certain religious affiliations) and of courts to make adoptive placements with gay or lesbian families, many such adoptions are completed by one parent as a single-parent adoption. Under British law, where two people live together but are not married, only one can make the application to adopt. These adoptions will be explored in a separate section of this chapter.

Single persons who wish to adopt an infant or young child without serious problems have increasingly, in the United States, turned to adoption of a foreign-born child. Not all countries accept applications from single women (Altstein and Simon, 1991). Independent adoptions are not legal in Britain, but in the United States where they are, many single parents, faced with the reluctance of agencies to place children with them, turn to independent adoptions. Though there is evidence that a growing number of public and private agencies are making placements with openly gay and lesbian couples, independent adoptions are often recommended as the most sensible course for gay or lesbian parents wishing to adopt (Ricketts and Achtenberg, 1987). These adoptions carry more risk and are generally more expensive than adoptions arranged by agencies (Marindin, 1992).

THE RESEARCH

Almost all of the studies of single-parent adoption have focused on the experiences of parents who have adopted young children from agencies. Two approaches have been used. One has been to recruit samples from adoptive parent support groups and use a mailed survey (Feigelman and Silverman, 1983; Dougherty, 1978). The other has been to follow agency placements with a longitudinal research design (Branham, 1970; Shireman and Johnson, 1975, 1976, 1985, 1986; Shireman, 1988). The former approach has produced larger numbers for study, the latter perhaps a more typical cross-section of adoptions and more qualitative data. There are some data about how single-parent adoptive families fare over time. Feigelman and Silverman re-contacted adoptive parents six years after the original survey, while the longitudinal study of Shireman and Johnson continued over fourteen years.

Though older children with emotional difficulties are part of the sample of the Feigelman and Silverman (1983) study, the first study to focus on single-parent adoptions of special needs children appeared in 1991 with a large sample of agency placements (Groze and Rosenthal, 1991). Other studies of special needs adoption contain a percentage of single-parent adoptions (Nelson, 1985; Kagan and Reid, 1986; Partridge *et al.*, 1986; Barth and Berry, 1988). Additionally, descriptive data have been collected by the Committee for Single Parent Adoptions since its founding in 1973; the data include some material on patterns of adoption, including adoption from foreign countries (Marindin, 1992). One English study has just been completed but not yet published (Morag Owen and Roy Parker, Bristol University).

CHARACTERISTICS OF SINGLE-PARENT ADOPTIONS

Most single-parent adopters are women and most single parents adopt a child of the same sex (Shireman and Johnson, 1976; Feigelman and Silverman, 1983; Groze and Rosenthal, 1991). About one in seven people who contact the National Committee for Single Adoptive Parents in the States is a man, but probably a considerably smaller proportion of men succeed in adopting (Marindin, 1992). The frustrated efforts of men to adopt have received even less attention than adoption by single women.

There has been no systematic exploration of the motivation for single-parent adoption and particularly for single-parent fatherhood through adoption. Neither do we know whether motives differ between single women and single men. Information about the characteristics of single-parent adopters comes mostly from data gathered from those who are members of single-parent adoptive organizations and are therefore biased. These data indicate that most single adoptive parents are in their mid to late thirties at the time of adoption, that a majority have graduate education, and that they hold stable jobs, usually in the helping professions (Dougherty, 1978; Feigelman and Silverman, 1983; Marindin, 1992). The incomes of single parents tend to be lower than those of couples who adopt (Feigelman and Silverman, 1983), although 40 per cent of men adopters earn over $40,000 a year (Marindin, 1992).

In reviewing research on the adoption of special needs children, Groze found a range of single-parent placements from 5 per cent in a 1970 study to 34 per cent in a 1984 study (Groze, 1991). The best current estimate available is that 25 per cent of special needs children may be adopted by single men and women (National Adoption Centre, reported in Harrison, 1991). It is highly unlikely that such high numbers adopt in Britain. It is also not clear whether the US percentages include adoptions by relatives. The high percentages could equally be explained by the fact that single parents who adopt special needs children there are more likely to be black, compared to couples who are more likely to be white (Groze and Rosenthal, 1991).

ISSUES FOR SINGLE ADOPTIVE PARENTS

Single adoptive parents have a more complex task than do other single parents or other adoptive parents. They must handle issues of economic stress, social isolation and role strain, which have been identified as problems for all single parents (Worell, 1988). Additionally, they must handle the special issues of adoption, as do all other adoptive families – issues of grief and loss due to separation from the birth family; loss of continuity of care; obvious physical and temperamental differences which impair the child's identification with the adoptive family; a possible lack of self-worth, stemming from the perception that he/she was bad or unworthy, and hence was 'given away'; and a need for information and, perhaps, a chance to get to know the biological family (Bourguignon and Watson, 1987). If a child is from another country, issues of ethnicity and cultural identity must be considered, and if of another race, racial identity.

Economic stress

All single-parent families have, by definition, one income. Family income is thus markedly lower when comparisons are made with couples who adopt (Groze and Rosenthal, 1991; Feigelman and Silverman, 1983). The income data are further skewed by the fact that most single-parent adopters are women, whose incomes tend to lag behind those of men. In a longitudinal study, low income was a major problem for half of the sample, though, as the children grew older and needed less expensive childcare, the problem became somewhat less acute (Shireman and Johnson, 1976, 1985; Shireman, 1988). However, the expenses of late adolescence and education after college were yet to be met for this sample.

Social isolation

Data on the relationship with the extended family are unclear. In the research of Feigelman and Silverman (1983), 55 per cent of single adoptive parents saw extended family members frequently. The extended family was often used for childcare (Shireman and Johnson, 1975). However, two-parent adoptive families also have close family contact, with Feigelman and Silverman (1983) reporting this for 68 per cent.

Children in single-parent families may not have the opportunity to interact with a single, important adult of the opposite sex over an extended period of time. Very few of the women in Shireman and Johnson's longitudinal study (Shireman, 1988) made permanent partnerships. Male friends 'disappeared', grandfathers and uncles died. The community in which a child is raised can also be important to the success of the adoption. Feigelman and Silverman (1983) found that though families generally responded positively to single-parent adoptions, friends of singles were not always as enthusiastic as were the friends of couples.

Role strain

It would be expected that the energy needed for meeting all the demands of childcare and employment without the support of a partner would engender greater role strain among single adopters than among couples. However, direct comparison seems to indicate that this is not so. Managing childcare while maintaining employment has not been noted as a problem. Additionally, the single adopters have shown capacity beyond that demonstrated by many parents in ability to cope with changes in family structure and with family crises, being able to recognize their own feelings, make necessary arrangements, and be sensitive to the feelings and needs of the children (Shireman and Johnson, 1985; Shireman, 1988).

Accounts by single adoptive parents of their experiences with special needs children are perhaps more revealing. Themes that run through them are the continual stress of dealing with difficult behaviour without the support of a partner, and without the respite that a partner can provide. The need to care for oneself, and to use the respite provided by community resources such as schools, summer camp, and friends, is stressed. The emotional support and help in evaluating difficulties and decisions in parenting that can be obtained from parent support groups is repeatedly noted. When an organized support group does not exist, single adoptive parents sometimes develop them for themselves (Ludden, 1992).

Issues of adoption

Indicators of success in accomplishing the tasks of handling adoption are found in the openness with which parents and children discuss adoption, the handling of issues of loss, and the building of trust and a shared value system. These are subtle behaviours.

There is little data on the degree to which single adoptive parents have been able to discuss adoption with their children. At each interview time during the longitudinal study reported by Shireman (1988), single parents have had more difficulty discussing adoption with their children, and have told them less and at a later age than have two-parent adopters. The questions of children concerning their birth parents seemed to be similar in one- and two-parent homes. The capacity of single adoptive parents to build homes in which there is a shared value system and sense of trust can perhaps best be gauged by research on the outcomes of single-parent adoptions.

Data from the longitudinal study are consistent with other studies in showing that the self-concept and overall adjustment of children adopted by single parents is similar to that of children adopted in two-parent families, and, indeed, similar to that of children who have grown up in birth families (Shireman, 1988). When the children were in early adolescence, identity was carefully examined using the behavioural referents of (1) family relatedness, (2) peer relations, (3) gender identity, (4) school performance, and (5) self-esteem. Both parents and children were interviewed, together and separately, and a number of standardized paper-and-pencil assessment instruments were administered to the youngsters. In all of these measures, about two-thirds of the children adopted by single parents were without problems, which was similar to the proportion among children adopted by same-race couples (Shireman, 1988).

Whether these results can be generalized to the adoption of older, more troubled children has just begun to be answered. In a mailed survey, Feigelman and Silverman (1983) found a statistically significant relationship between single parenting and poorer emotional adjustment. This was not true for children under 6, but 'persisted in children six years or older. It is our belief that these trends reflect existing placement realities', the authors conclude. The authors add that 'single parents, as the agencies' adoptive placements of last resort, are more often obliged to accept children whose earlier experiences of deprivation, instability, and abuse have led to substantially more emotional adjustment problems. In addition, the professional experiences of these parents may lead them to recognize such problems more readily than other parents' (Feigelman and Silverman, 1983, p. 185).

In a follow-up study six years later, these differences remained, but were no longer statistically significant. The authors report (1983, p. 191):

> When controlling for the age of the children adopted, both direct and indirect assessments of children's overall adjustments show fundamentally corresponding patterns among single parents and adoptive couples.

If, indeed, more disturbed children are placed with single parents, the tendency of single-parent adoptions to look like other adoptions over time would indicate strength in the single-parent homes.

Groze and Rosenthal's (1991) follow-up of special needs placements showed the same strength in single-parent placements. Using standardized measures of behaviour, completed by responding adoptive parents, they found that adopted children did, indeed, exhibit serious behavioural problems. At all ages, however, children adopted by single parents had the lowest percentage of scores in the problematic range (Groze and Rosenthal, 1991).

The literature on adoptions which disrupt provides additional evidence. In those studies in which data concerning single parents were reported, single- and two-parent families were equally represented among those adoptions in trouble. Other factors (such as age of child at placement or the child's prior experiences) were associated with problems in the adoption (Barth and Berry, 1988; Kagan and Reid, 1986). A more indirect measure of handling of serious behaviour problems by single parents is found in the work on problematic and disrupted adoptions, in which single-parent homes are not identified as a risk factor (Groze, 1991).

STRENGTHS

There has been little writing or inquiry from the perspective of the strengths of the single-parent adoptive home. Rather, under the assumption that two-parent homes were best, single-parent homes have been examined to discover the extent to which they 'look like' more traditional families. However, it seems reasonable to think that single adoptive homes may have a unique contribution to make for particular children. As an example, in some cases a single carer is the placement of choice by the social workers and is also the preference of the child. Similarly children who have been severely abused, both physically and sexually, by male carers may thrive in a single-female household.

One quality which emerges in the literature on single-parent adoptions is the close relationship which these parents have with their children. Shireman and Johnson (1985) report worry about the exclusiveness and intensity of this relationship, even though its expression was in appropriate nurturing activities. As the children entered school, the expression of nurture turned to involvement in school activities, in the parent–teacher association, as teacher's helpers or as advocates for their children, and seemed to remain wholesome and supportive for the children. This close bond may have made it more difficult to be open about adoption. However, these adopted children experienced a constant affection, focused on their interests.

A second notable attribute has been the strength of these parents in adversity, and their capacity to cope with crisis. Shireman and Johnson (1985) report that the adoptive parents' task as single parents was in many cases more difficult than they had expected. They were resourceful, sought help when it was needed, and continued to cope with whatever difficulties arose. Childcare has not been reported to be a problem. Even during periods of illness or family crisis these parents kept the child's developmental needs in sight.

The simplicity of relationships in a single-parent home has been noted as a potential strength for some children who come from complicated and disrupted backgrounds. With one adoptive parent, affection comes without competition. It is not possible to recreate family situations in which two parents are manipulated into conflict, disagreement over childrearing principles, or even physical abuse. There is a security in the simplicity, which can be healing.

Among the other strengths of the single-parent home, one should list the ability to develop and use networks for support. A potential adoptive parent has written:

I become part of the network of adoptive parents and potential adopters and learn how essential this network is as a source of information, assistance, and support. (Bartholet, 1993a, p. 64)

As older and more difficult children have increasingly been placed in adoptive homes, it has become apparent that continuing support services are needed by many of these families to help in management of the complex issues of adoption. In their study, Groze and Rosenthal (1991) found approximately one-third of the single parents and one-fourth of the two-parent families working with a family therapist. In addition, one-fourth of the single parents and one-fourth of the couples were in contact with other families who had adopted a special needs child. Contact with parent support groups was evaluated as being more helpful than contact with therapists.

What, then, are the strengths of single-parent adoptive families?

- commitment to the child and the adoption;
- strength and capacity to handle crisis;
- a relatively simple family structure; and
- self-confidence, independence, and ability to develop and use supportive networks.

Surely these are qualities to be valued in an adoptive home.

GAY AND LESBIAN ADOPTIONS

It is difficult to estimate the number of children being raised by gay or lesbian parents. Numbers are built from estimates that 10 per cent of the population is gay or lesbian, and the recognition that many of these persons are parents, either from former heterosexual marriages, from planned families using donor insemination or coparenting, or because they have adopted children. The reluctance of gay and lesbian families to identify themselves as such has probably increased their opportunities to adopt, even while it makes it difficult to estimate numbers or to evaluate these adoptions. Though agencies address the sexuality of applicants in their assessment work, the extent to which those who are gay or lesbian are willing to disclose this probably varies according to their own trust in the philosophy and policy of the agency with which they are working. Additionally, it is complex to include a section on gay and lesbian adoptions in a chapter on single-parent adoptions, for many of these adoptions are in the context of a committed relationship, and the child is actually going to a two-parent family.

Sullivan (1995) in a review of policy issues identifies three 'myths' which lead to public reluctance to place children in gay or lesbian adoptive homes. The first is the fear that children might be molested, a fear which stems from the failure to distinguish homosexuality and paedophilia. The suspicion that a man who wishes to adopt is gay, and that a homosexual may be sexually attracted to children, has made it very difficult for single men to adopt. In fact, most paedophiles are heterosexual males (Finkellor, 1986).

The second fear is that children will become homosexual, or be pressured to become homosexual, if they are placed in homosexual adoptive families. In fact, sexual orientation does not seem to be determined by family of origin. Most gay and lesbian adults grew up in heterosexual families. The third concern is that children adopted by homosexuals will be growing up in an 'immoral' environment. Morality, Sullivan (1995) points out, is a very personal issue, and whether one is more morally outraged by children growing up without families, or in homosexual families, is personal. However, the persistence of these myths, and their effect on public policy, frustrates the attempts of many gay and lesbian persons who seek to adopt as single parents.

If the above listed fears are unfounded, then one must ask whether the gay or lesbian adoptive applicant has the capacity to perform the functions of an adoptive parent, and what particular strengths and difficulties may be present in these homes.

The tension produced in a home by the need to select one partner as the primary parent for legal purposes, when partners view themselves as co-equal, may be significant (Rohrbaugh, 1989). It is important that the child's rights of inheritance from the non-legal parent, as well as the non-legal parent's rights to custody should anything happen to the legal parent, be established. Changes in public policy to recognize the right of non-married parents to co-parent will probably be slow in coming.

There is no research on gay and lesbian adoptive (or foster) parents. What is known comes from research on gay and lesbian parenting. Most available research concerns lesbian mothers; our knowledge of gay fathers comes from smaller studies and is more anecdotal in nature (Hutchins and Kirkpatrick, 1985). Overall, the research suggests homosexual parents carry out parenting roles much as do heterosexual parents (Hutchins and Kirkpatrick, 1985) and that the overall adjustment of their children resembles that of all children (Gottman, 1990; Hutchins and Kirkpatrick, 1985; Golombok, Spencer and Rutter, 1983). Like heterosexual households, they differ greatly. Gender identity does not seem to be affected by upbringing in a lesbian household (Gottman, 1990).

Nor, though the studies are more limited, do the children of gay fathers seem disadvantaged. Golombok, Spencer and Rutter (1983) add from their British study that:

> We should cease regarding lesbian households as all the same ... Some, although lesbian, have generally good relationships with men (this was true of most of those in our sample) whereas others denigrated men. Perhaps it is the quality of family relationships and the patterns of upbringing that matters for psychosexual development, and not the sexual orientation of the mother.

The impact on a child of feeling 'different', and fearing ostracism from belonging to a different household, has received considerable attention. There seems to be agreement that children have to learn to be discreet in selecting those friends to whom they will explain the true nature of their household (Flaks, 1995). There is also agreement that this differentness, like all differentness, is a problem, particularly in adolescence. However, the issue does not seem to overwhelm children, and it must be noted that being a foster child, without a permanent home, is also a different status which must be explained. Golombok, Spencer and Rutter (1983), relying on data obtained solely from mothers (both lesbian and heterosexual), concluded that the children were able in adolescence to maintain relationships with people of their own age without significant difficulty.

Turning to dangers to the child from caregivers, Richardson (1981, pp. 149–58) suggests from her review of statistical evidence that children are in fact safer in lesbian than heterosexual households, as not only are the majority of crimes against children committed by men but often these crimes are by adults who are members of the same household. Again, there is no comparable data regarding gay households, but it must be repeated that most paedophiles are heterosexual men. With regard to the stability of households, again it is suggested that although male homosexual relationships are apparently characterized by greater instability than heterosexuals, the same does not hold true for lesbian relationships (Kenyon, 1970).

Despite these relatively positive findings about the outcome of childrearing in a homosexual household, it remains very difficult for gay or lesbian applicants to adopt a child. Two states (New Hampshire and Florida) explicitly prohibit the adoption of children by gay or lesbian parents. In other states, and in Britain, the general prejudice against gay and lesbian adoptions leads most to adopt as single parents, making no mention of sexual orientation. The Canadian Royal Commission on New Reproductive Technologies (1993) concluded that the evidence did not show different outcomes in children born to or raised by lesbians, when compared to outcomes in children born to heterosexual women and couples. Thus, the Commission went on to say, 'the best interests of the child cannot be used as a reason to deny access simply because a woman is a lesbian' (p. 456).

Adoption must be seen as a changing area of social work practice. Today children are placed in adoption who would not have been considered adoptable ten years ago, and the families who adopt them are diverse in background, income and interests. What they have in common is a capacity to parent the children who need homes. Within this context, the move toward placement of children in gay and lesbian homes is not surprising. Sullivan (1995) points out the need for adoption agencies to take a definite position on permitting adoption by gay and lesbian persons, in order to use all available resources for children, and also to avoid both legal challenges of discrimination and a continued move toward independent adoption with its risks. What is needed is more information about whether there are particular characteristics of these homes which make them positively suitable for children with specific needs. The research to answer this question is yet to be done. We also need to provide satisfactory answers to those parents who would have concerns if they knew that their child was to be adopted into a gay or lesbian household. There have been cases in both Britain and the United States where parents forced a local authority to change its decision on such placements.

SOME UNANSWERED QUESTIONS

The primary question about single-parent adoptive homes is the way in which these homes meet the challenge of providing role models of both genders to the growing child. The extended family may seem to provide both men and women as role models, but these relationships can become more distant with family moves and deaths.

The impact on the child can be assessed in part through looking at gender identity. Shireman and Johnson report that at age 4, children of single parents were clear in gender attribution (Shireman and Johnson, 1975). At age 8, the grade school age children's strong overt identification with children and activities of their own sex was evident (Shireman and Johnson, 1985). At age 14, gender identity was measured using a standardized scale. Responses were found to be similar to the distribution in same-race, two-parent adoptive homes (Shireman, 1988). Thus, the evidence we have suggests that, up to early adolescence, children are having opportunities to develop appropriate gender identity. However, the impact of growing up in a unique family cannot be fully assessed until these young people are followed into their own marriages and family-building years.

Boys may have more difficulty with adoption than girls. Adopted girls tend to have fewer adjustment problems than adopted boys, among both single parents and couples (Shireman, 1988). Placement with a single parent may make adoption even more difficult for a boy. A study of 73 adoptions of older, emotionally disturbed children found that of the six boys placed with single women in the sample, five of the adoptions did not succeed, with the children leaving the adoptive home. No other significant differences between single-parent and two-parent adoption were found (Kagan and Reid, 1986).

There are no systematically collected data on outcomes for boys placed with single men and there is very little information on single adoptive fathers. A 1985 unpublished survey, done by Timothy Gage, of 80 single men who had adopted or who wanted to adopt 'convincingly demonstrated the value of these fathers as a resource for parenting special-needs children' (Marindin, 1992, p. 32). Most of the children adopted by the men in this survey were boys; 90 per cent were school age, and 62 per cent were identified by their fathers as having 'special needs'. Two respondents declared to the anonymous survey that they were gay (Marindin, 1992). When single fathers are identified in the single-parent adoption research, they have usually adopted boys, and usually older, troubled boys. There is no evidence that the experiences of fathers differ from those of women who adopt, except that incomes are more adequate. Otherwise, they apparently face the same stresses and cope with the same skill. It would be helpful to know what their particular strengths are, and which children they are particularly gifted at raising.

Little is known also about lesbian women and gay men who adopt. Again, these data are hidden in the studies of single parents, for surely some of them at least are lesbian or gay. Many of these adoptions are only nominally or legally single-parent adoptions, for there is often a partner forming a two-parent family. Whether these households have special strengths in helping adopted children with particular problems is not known, nor is the impact of a lesbian or gay orientation on the capacity to seek adoption support groups or other help when there are difficulties known.

There are absolutely no data on how single parents will respond to the newer models of adoption, in which the adoptive parent is asked to incorporate into the family the biological grandparents, aunts and uncles, and perhaps even parents, who maintain a continuing interest in the child. The close relationship which single parents seem to form with the child may make this an intolerable situation. On the other hand, the larger available extended family may offer needed support to these adoptions.

Though there is relatively little research on single-parent adoptions, and though that research has limitations, it probably makes a good beginning. It does provide confirmation of the strength of single-parent homes. As the characteristics of the children of the world who need adoptive placement change, so too do the unanswered questions.

CONCLUSION

What we do know about single parents provides a good base to continue to work with single-parent adoptions. We need to know more, though, about which children will particularly benefit from single-parent homes. For these children, single parents will not be 'marginal' parents, but will be the first choice. Single-parent homes may have particular strengths for children from deprived backgrounds, for there is a concentration on nurturing evident in these homes. The relative simplicity of relationship patterns may be easier for a child from a troubled succession of birth and foster homes to negotiate. Certainly the capacity to manipulate and oppose one parent against the other, which troubles many placements, is aborted in the single-parent home.

We know that the main stress in single-parent homes is economic, and that adoption allowances are important in strengthening these placements. From the point of view of waiting children, the growing willingness of adoption agencies to make placements with single parents opens new opportunities for rich family life.

However, single parents would appear to have fewer resources than couples in parenting children who present complex disciplinary problems. They lack the day-to-day support of a partner. Thus they face the responsibility of day-to-day decision-making alone, and decisions about how to handle the behaviour of acting-out children can be difficult. They do not have a family member routinely available to provide respite from the demands of childcare.

It is clear that single adoptive parents need support systems in place as they undertake their difficult task. Agencies would do well to provide individualized counselling service to the new adoptive family for as long as is needed, as well as being available to help the family access such counselling at any point necessary during the child's development. This includes a responsibility to educate the specialist services of the community about the unique issues of the adoptive family, so that help will be appropriate. Adoption allowances or subsidies can aid in providing the income to support a child. There is also a need for support groups for single adoptive parents.

Though there is much still to be learned about single-parent adoption, it is time for a change in thinking about single persons as adoptive parents. In making adoptive placements, these are not homes in which to place children for whom two-parent homes cannot be found. Research shows sufficient strength in these homes for successful parenting. They do not need to be compared with two-parent homes. Rather, they are homes in which to place children whose background and experiences are such that they can best use the unique strengths of a home with one parent.

Five key points

1. Available evidence suggests that single parents are able to successfully raise children placed in their homes for adoption.
2. Single-parent homes may be particularly appropriate for children who need concentrated nurturing and/or a simplicity in relationship patterns.
3. Reservations about single-parent homes mean that often complex children, for whom it is difficult to find homes, are placed in them.
4. The main stress on single-parent homes is low income; adoption allowances may be important.
5. Single parents who have adopted articulate the need for post-adoption agency services and support groups.

CHAPTER 11
Post-placement services

Traditionally, the granting of an adoption order signalled the closure of a case. Formal contact between the parties to adoption and the placing agency usually ceased within a year of placement; adopters were wished well and birth parents advised to put all that had happened behind them and start life anew. Occasionally, some level of contact with a placing social worker was sustained, particularly if the person remained in post for a long time. Generally speaking, this was the exception. To say the picture has changed would be an exaggeration. Although the necessity and importance of post-adoption work is increasingly recognized, the inadequate and fragmented nature of current provision, particularly by statutory agencies, is also acknowledged (Hughes, 1995b; Watson and McGhee, 1995). Yet in recent years, thousands of people have used post-adoption services and, by so doing, challenged many long-held assumptions about the effect of adoption on people's lives. This, in turn, has informed adoption law and practice.

By way of introduction, this chapter begins by looking at some of the main factors which have contributed to the development of post-adoption services. Following this, post-adoption issues in relation to each party to adoption will be examined in greater detail. This is followed by an overview of the range of services currently available. In conclusion, some future trends in post-adoption provision will be discussed.

THE DEVELOPMENT OF POST-ADOPTION SERVICES – MAIN FACTORS

Adoption, in the United Kingdom and partly in North America, is now mainly focused on children whose personal situations and family backgrounds are extremely complex. They are likely to bring legacies of loss and trauma into placement and it may be extremely difficult for the adoptive parent to nurture, support and develop a close relationship with them. Such placements are constantly vulnerable to disruption. In these circumstances it is regarded as necessary to give adoptive parents the right to on-going services by adoption agencies. There has also developed an increasing awareness of the needs and feelings of birth parents and a realization that, in the past, service provision has been woefully inadequate.

More recently, open adoption, be it by an exchange of letters between the adoptive and birth family or face-to-face contact, has moved practice into a new arena (see Chapter 4). This often requires the continuing involvement of an adoption agency to facilitate arrangements, preserve confidentiality and offer advice and support.

Increased legal rights for adopted people have resulted in the return of adult adoptees to agencies in search of information about their birth families and the circumstances of their adoption. This has provided practitioners, policy-makers and legislators with an opportunity to review the outcome of a significant number of adoption arrangements. It has also challenged the longstanding assumption that adoption involving infants is invariably straightforward and does not dispose participants to seek post-adoption services.

Achievements of self-help groups in promoting solidarity, drawing attention to issues of common concern and campaigning for change, has helped highlight the cause of each of the parties to adoption. Organizations for adoptive parents, such as Parent to Parent Information on Adoption Services in the United Kingdom and the North American Council on Adoptable Children in the United States, have a long and respected role in promoting good practice. Since the mid-1980s the voice of adopted people and their birth families has also been strengthened by the creation of self-help groups. Other groups which have mobilized include those of birth grandparents who have lost grandchildren to adoption and people who have been placed transracially. Although such organizations exercise a wide remit, they often actively campaign for improved post-adoption provision and provide complementary post-adoption support, usually by linking people with volunteers, organizing group meetings and circulating newsletters. Along with professionals in the adoption field, self-help groups can find themselves in a symbiotic relationship with the mass media, who have a seemingly insatiable interest in adoption and related issues. The overall result is a constantly high profile for the subject.

An encouraging development in recent years relates to the empowerment of individuals, with a greater emphasis on rights and the availability of complaints procedures. Legal changes are also relevant, especially those which have given access to personal information. Adoption, both domestic and overseas, has come under scrutiny in relation to equal opportunities, poverty and children's rights. As the long-term implications of placement are assimilated, the incidence of adoption-related issues in mental health and child and family psychiatric services has generated professional interest across a range of disciplines. Extreme behaviours and personal trauma, which can be adoption-linked (e.g. genetic sexual attraction, post-traumatic stress disorder, and attachment and behavioural problems), are now internationally recognized and documented. There is an increasing awareness that adoption is a life-long process and one which may vary in meaning and intensity. It forms an integral part of the person's psyche and, therefore, a request for services may be appropriate at any time.

UNDERSTANDING THE PERSPECTIVE OF SERVICE USERS

Birth parents

Traditionally, birth parents have been regarded as women who parted with their babies for adoption in a climate of secrecy and stigma. They were part of an era which provided little choice for those who conceived a child outside marriage. If the mother resided in the family home, a procedure would probably be activated which involved the mother leaving temporarily in order to give birth to the baby (see Chapter 5). A number of women who encountered this response to their situation have subsequently sought post-adoption services.

More recently, parents whose children were adopted following a period in the care system are also requesting post-adoption services. Their situation has many similarities with that of the relinquishing birth parent, although there are also some important differences. A small-scale evaluation of two series of groups for birth parents provides some significant insights into participants personal circumstances. One group comprised women who had 'volunteered' to relinquish their children for adoption, the other was made up of mothers whose children were 'lost' to them through the care system (Scourfield and Hendry, 1991 and 1994). The authors contrasted the situations of the two groups of women and noted that, after adoption, the relinquishing birth mothers were mainly in employment, with a fair degree of job satisfaction, and part of a settled, long-term relationship. They had parted with their baby within days of the birth or, at most within a few weeks. For them, the child existed as a memory of a tiny infant and the intervening years were a complete blank.

In contrast, the birth mothers whose children had been in the care system prior to adoption had very different personal circumstances. None were in employment and half of the group were not in a settled relationship. They had often cared for the child for months and even years prior to their final entry to care and they mourned the loss of someone they had seen grow and change.

As the balance is gradually redressed and more parents who have lost children through the care system come forward, post-adoption services are required to consider the needs of both groups. Although personal circumstances between 'care' and relinquishing birth parents may vary, many of the emotions are the same. Two main points to emerge from research are:

- Parents feel extremely angry about unilateral decisions made *for* them, although the focus of their anger may be different. For one young single woman it might be her parents, who refused to let her keep her baby, for another birth parent it might be the court who decided that the parent was unfit to care for their child.
- Feelings of grief and bewilderment, as parents reflect on their loss. For some this will have a continuing effect on their mental or physical health and can result in post-traumatic stress disorder (Wells, 1993).

In addition, there are implications for other relationships. Parents may feel a deep personal isolation, especially if those around them avoid referring to the child or do so inappropriately. The parenting of other children may be affected, as parents live in fear that they, too, may be 'lost'. As explored more fully in Chapter 5, separation from children, through whatever means, can leave unanswered questions and a sense of anguish.

'It's like you've lost them, but they are not dead ... I don't have a grave to visit ... I can't tell anyone ... people blame you, they don't understand ... all I can do is search ... I look at children of similar age to mine, so I can try and imagine what they look like ... how big they are. Every time there is a disaster or a child reported in an accident I worry ... I constantly worry ... I don't even know if my children are dead or alive ... it's a living hell.' (Donna, whose children were adopted from the care system, quoted from literature prepared by Parents Without Children, Durham)

A common theme in many research studies (see, for example, Bouchier, Lambert and Triseliotis, 1991) is the inability of services to focus on the needs of birth parents. These feelings may be further compounded by staff changes, lack of choice regarding their worker's race or gender and, in some instances, closure of agencies and movement of records (see Stafford, 1993). Parents can feel torn between wanting to complain about the service they receive and the fear of alienating the 'all-powerful' agency. These emotions are particularly important when post-adoption services are needed, because of the psychological barriers they place on parents returning to the agency. Additional complexities may arise from stress, problems with language or learning difficulties. Many parents are left wondering whether they will ever see their child again and, if so, what sort of relationship could be established; who could advise about this; what steps could be taken to enable (or, in some instances, prevent) a reunion taking place?

Adoptive parents

In the same way that the situation and experience of birth parents has changed over time, so too has that of the adoptive parent. Children with varied characteristics are today adopted by many different types of families. Within the course of one family's adoption experience, changes in law and policy may fundamentally alter the task. Additionally, the problems of adopted children tend to surface at different times in the child's development (and sometimes repetitively). Post-adoption services may thus be needed at varied times throughout the lifetime of the adoptive family.

First, consideration will be given to some key post-adoption issues linked with those adoptive parents who had 'traditional' infant placements, and which may present today for any family adopting a very young child. Until comparatively recently, adoptive parents were encouraged to approach childraising in a way that would closely resemble that of a biological parent. The unique aspects of adoption and the particular tasks of the family in recognizing and acknowledging differences (Kirk, 1964) were not discussed. Agencies usually discussed the importance of telling children that they were adopted, but beyond that did little to inform and guide adopters. Often the provision of a 'thumbnail sketch' of a child's birth mother (sometimes with a paragraph on the father) had more to do with emphasizing the child's fitness for adoption than anticipating the adopted person's future need for information. As a result, generations of adopted people have been unable to turn to the parents who raised them for answers to questions which are now regarded as their right to ask (Triseliotis, 1973; Haimes and Timms, 1985). In this and other ways, earlier practice often failed to adequately equip adoptive parents for their task. There is concern that many intercountry adoptions may follow this model today, similarly failing to equip parents.

Adoptive parents may expect of themselves that they are able to cope alone, perhaps with the help only of those professionals who normally guide parents through childraising, such as physicians and teachers. Having been deemed competent and suitable to parent, a return to the agency may be construed as a sign of failure. Hartman (1984) comments:

> In infant adoption, post-placement services were rather minimal. They often consisted of perfunctory visits for a period of up to a year for the purposes of monitoring how things were going with the new family. It was anticipated that young couples with their new babies would not have any particular difficulty.

Hartman goes on to refer to the 'searching nature of the home study', suggesting that in their anxiety to prove themselves as good parents, adopters were *'unlikely to talk with the agency worker about problems, concerns, insecurities and anxieties as they emerged'*. Post-adoption services thus need to help adoptive parents, particularly if they adopted some years ago, to review their attitude to further involvement with an agency and enable such an approach to be seen as a positive step, rather than a declaration of inadequacy.

Again, because the uniqueness of adoption was not stressed, families have often approached family counsellors who are unfamiliar with adoption and its special difficulties. Though this is of particular significance in relation to families adopting older children with special needs, it is of significance for all adopting families. Groze (1996, p. 77) writes about special needs adoption, but his words apply to all adoption:

> Frequently, adoptive families seeking services for themselves and their children have been discouraged to find that service providers do not have accurate adoption information. Nor do

they have a framework for understanding adoption issues. Often, the adoptive family is viewed as dysfunctional, leaving resourceful, competent adoptive parents with feelings of guilt and blame.

These ideas mean, of course, that the adoption agency assumes responsibility for the provision of post-adoption services, or for training others to provide those services, throughout the life of the adoptive family.

Many people who adopt infants are unable to have children biologically. By parenting someone else's child and securing that child's position as a legal member of the family, the impact of infertility on parents' lives can be masked. It was not until the 1970s and 1980s that a deeper understanding of the long-term impact of infertility was more widely considered (Eck-Menning, 1988; Johnstone, 1992) and the inter-relationship between this type of loss and adoption more meaningfully explored. The notion of a 'fantasy birth child' in a family created by adoption can be a powerful and pernicious force if parents are struggling to come to terms with negative feelings about the actual son or daughter who joined them through adoption.

For some adopters, the initial close bonding with a much-wanted infant and anxiety that the birth parent may 'change their mind' prior to the granting of the adoption engender caution in the mind of the adopter. A fear that the child could be lost to the adopters if contact is renewed can continue, even when the adopted person has reached adulthood.

It has been suggested that today's adopters may in some respects have more in common with foster-carers than their counterparts of earlier decades, a theme which is explored more fully in a recent report on post-placement services (Hughes, 1995b). Certainly, the children placed are more likely to have spent time with members of their birth family and to continue these relationships at some level following placement. They are also likely to have experienced maltreatment and, perhaps, frequent moves. However, the adopting family does not have agency support automatically, as does the foster family, a major differences which often causes foster parents to hesitate about adopting (Meezan and Shireman, 1985). The adopting family attracts those expectations of competence and self-sufficiency explored in the above paragraphs.

As highlighted in earlier chapters, many of the children now placed for adoption would previously have been regarded as 'un-adoptable' and spent their growing years in foster homes or residential care. In these situations they were not exposed to the continuity and intensity of life in an adoptive family. Slowly, it has been acknowledged that when placed in adoptive homes these children may present many difficulties. It is recognized that stability, understanding and unconditional love will not always override the effects of early trauma. These children who continue to present serious problems are described by Cline (1992) as being 'onions'. In contrast to 'apples' whose quality of early nurturing allows them to develop a core of trust, some children whose early lives are characterized by abuse, frequent moves, and whose pain and distress goes unrecognized, comprise a series of onion-like layers. When these are peeled away there is no healthy core. Parenting such children can have a devastating effect on their adoptive families, who find that the youngsters remain unattached and unreachable many years into placement.

A particular frustration for the families is the way the children can often superficially attach to others and function adequately in a different setting, for example at school, or when visiting the wider family. This compounds the difficulties parents can face when they describe the child's behaviour to others in an effort to obtain help. Often they are left feeling that they are the originators of the problem and that the issues they raise are trivial. Services provided by a practitioner who does not understand adoption and works from a family systems approach can compound the problem. A proportion of couple relationships do not survive the parenting of these attachment-disordered children, whose experiences have helped them develop a life-long pattern of 'divide and rule' (Parent to Parent Information on Adoption Services, 1995). Not surprisingly, some of the placements disrupt, leaving a legacy of sadness, guilt and failure, and yet another devastating move for the child.

It must also be noted that most adoptions of 'special needs' children provide satisfaction to the adopting family and are considered successful. Groze (1996) in a two-year follow-up study of special needs adoptions finds that 70 per cent of families rate the adoption as having positive effects on the family in both years. Sharma *et al.* (1996) found few differences between the self reports on a number of dimensions of adopted adolescents and a control group of non-adopted adolescents. However, this research did find that age at adoption most clearly differentiates overall adoptee adjustment. There is an urgent need for research that will begin to identify the pre-adoptive and the current family characteristics of 'special needs' children who are successful in adoptive homes, and the same characteristics of those whose problems prove intractable.

In an effort to sustain vulnerable placements and enhance family functioning, attention is being given to packages of support for adoptive parents and their children. This has not come about speedily or easily and, unfortunately, many families still struggle on with the minimum of support. By the mid-1980s it was already known that the availability of services was essential and also that many problems would not be apparent until the child was some years into placement (Macaskill, 1984). Yet over a decade later there is still considerable discussion about the form this support should take, by whom it should be provided and, in some cases, where the financial responsibility rests (Hughes, 1995b).

Whilst there can be no blueprint for the range of services needed after adoption, research and practice has helped to define the broad parameters, which are outlined below.

Easy access to skilled and experienced adoption practitioners

Some agencies operate a telephone service, so families are sure when they can obtain advice. Other options need to include speedy access to workers at time of crisis, a programme of individual counselling for parents and adoptees and the opportunity for group counselling. Sometimes support will be needed over specific issues, such as the disclosure of abuse, court appearances and sharing difficult background information with the child.

Links with others in a similar situation

Adoptive parent support groups, often organized around a particular issue (such as single-parent or transracial adoption), have been consistently found helpful by parents. Probably contact with others struggling with similar problems both normalizes the adoptive situation, freeing energy for coping, and provides ideas of things which have worked for other adoptive parents.

Therapeutic services

Some adoption agencies employ therapists to work with adoptive family members. More usually services are mobilized from within the community. As the importance of skilled multi-disciplinary support is seen as essential in many cases, post-adoption services are often in the position of identifying resources and liaising on behalf of families (Hobday and Lee, 1995). However, in many areas, there is a paucity of such services and, even where they exist, therapists may lack the framework and the experience in working with adoption. There is a continuing role for post-adoption services in establishing good links with other disciplines and, where appropriate, providing information and training on current adoption practice and the unique issues of adoptive families.

Direct work with families

Some agencies will be in a position to allocate post-adoption referrals within their staff team. It can be helpful for families to receive a service from practitioners who know them and understand the background of their child.

Financial and practical support

Financial subsidy is identified by adoptive parents as a crucial support (Rosenthal, Groze and Morgan, 1996). It is usual for needs to be identified and funding authorized prior to placement. However, need often emerges many years after placement. Sometimes adoptive parents and their children will be eligible for financial help from a variety of sources, particularly if the child has a disability. It is helpful if social workers can advise and support families who are negotiating with other agencies and if adoption agencies have systems whereby requests for financial and practical help can be considered at any stage of the placement.

Respite care

This has traditionally been used to assist parents and carers of a child with a physical or mental disability. Increasingly it is recognized that adoptive placements involving emotionally damaged children may not survive without some respite arrangements. Rosenthal, Groze and Morgan (1996) found that two-thirds of the adoptive parents of children with emotional or behavioural problems needed respite care. Agencies need to ensure that the minimum of anxiety is caused to the child by respite care and may first wish to consider family members for this task.

Advice on educational matters

Families may need help in identifying a suitable school, particularly if the child has special needs or the parents have no previous experience of educational resources in their area. Parents may need support in work with teachers on educational planning, securing extra classroom help for their child, or a special school place. It can be useful for a post-adoption service to identify key professionals in education who are in a position to give advice and mobilize resources.

On-going liaison with the placing agency

Returning to the agency post-adoption can be made easier if some link has been maintained. Newsletters, publicity leaflets, events for adopters and children, are all low-key but effective ways of reminding families that the door is still open and they have a right to services. As Hartman (1984, p. 3) summarizes:

> A reconceptualization of post-placement services in this new revolution in adoption requires that post-adoption services be available on an 'as needed' basis throughout the growing up period of the child.

Increasingly, the conceptual framework within which such placements are made is one of 'through care' (Hughes, 1995b). This perspective can affect the earliest contact between prospective adopters and an agency. Applicants are encouraged to approach adoption knowing that long-term support will be available. Obviously, not all contemporary adoptions will require the kind of service package outlined above. Some placements will progress quite satisfactorily without post-adoption input; alternatively, families may take a low-key approach and choose to intermittently avail themselves of the counselling, group meetings, and other types of mainstream support offered by many agencies and discussed later in this chapter.

Adopted children

Children themselves will often need direct help after adoption. For those placed as infants, questions about genetic identity and the circumstances of the loss of their birth parents may arise, as has been explored in earlier chapters. For those placed as older children, having experienced both poor care and later separation from birth family and foster family, the emotional and behavioural difficulties outlined in the preceding section may be expected to develop. It is not the interactions within the family which have produced these issues (though these interactions may modify or exacerbate the difficulties) but rather the experiences of the children prior to adoption, and the experiences unique to adoption.

Just as, for many children, love and time alone do not suffice, so, for many, work just with parents or with the family unit (as in family therapy) does not suffice. The children need direct help with their own issues, from practitioners sensitive to the particular needs of adopted children.

All adopted children have experienced loss of their birth families, and need to have opportunity to grieve for this loss. The need to rework this grief and loss may arise at varying times (and repetitively) during the life of an adopted child (Reitz and Watson, 1992). While the techniques of the life story book and related ideas for helping a child come in contact with his past (see Chapter 6) are useful, it must be remembered that these issues may arise in adolescence as well as childhood.

The child with multiple placements prior to adoption has, of course, additional losses which must be grieved. This child may have learned that trust and attachment lead only to painful separation, and so may be wary of forming any new relationships. Whether this is a learned inability to attach, which can be overcome, or whether this is indeed the child described as the 'onion' in the preceding section, can only be determined after long and careful work. Additionally, of course, the maltreatment which the child may have experienced will have left its residue of hostility and distrust. The family must be supported and helped to manage the child and family life; the child must be helped to uncover and work through, to the extent possible, the issues which are blocking development.

Open adoption with contact brings its own issues in direct work with children. Managing visits of birth parents or other birth relatives is probably quite like supporting children through visits while they are in foster care, though these issues have not been examined in the clinical literature.

It is crucial in direct work with children that adoptive parents be seen as partners in the endeavour to help these youngsters. The tendency to 'blame' parents when children have difficulties has too often extended to adoptive families. *In these families, parents are the best hope of the children*, and their skills and strengths must be utilized. Groze (1996, p. 77) in a plea for 'adoption-sensitive professionals' writes:

> Often, the adoptive family is viewed as dysfunctional, leaving resourceful, competent adoptive parents with feelings of guilt and blame. In addition, a framework of individual dysfunction where the child's genetic and pre-adoptive experiences are blamed does little to ameliorate adoptive family stress.

Adopted adults

An understanding of adoption as experienced by adult adoptees has been assisted by provision in the 1975 Children Act (later to form part of the 1976 Adoption Act), which allowed people over 18 years of age to have certain birth record information. This, effectively, created the possibility for any adopted person, whether or not they knew their birth name, to obtain a copy of their original birth certificate. Furthermore, they were authorized to obtain from the court which granted the adoption order the name of the adoption society or local authority (if any) that took part in the adoption proceedings. The shift towards greater openness of birth records in England was based on Scottish experience, and a number of other countries have followed (see McWhinnie, 1967; Triseliotis, 1973). In the USA access to birth records by adoptees is still surrounded by controversy, and policy on the matter varies by state.

Two factors related to this legal change are pertinent to the development of post-adoption services for adult adoptees. First, the legislation was made retrospective and, second, attendance at a counselling session was mandatory for those adopted prior to the passing of the Act in 1975 (for more detailed discussion, see Hodgkins, 1991). This legislation was influenced by similar provisions in Scotland and Finland.

In the wake of these legal changes, certain themes have been identified. For example, many adopted adults have had a satisfactory experience of adoption and consider that they have a good relationship with their adoptive parents. Nevertheless, adoption is a lifelong status that can engender a number of feelings, such as loss, rejection, a fear of intimacy, a poor self-image, guilt and grief (see Verrier, 1994; Van Gulden and Bartels-Rabb, 1995). Some people will have been denied opportunities to discuss their adoption and lack of information can result in fear and fantasy. Others may feel very isolated, experiencing a sense of dual identity as they try to reconcile their two families.

While some people are content with a minimum of information, others have an overwhelming urge to take their search as far as possible and ultimately meet their birth family. There can be various 'triggers' for this, such as the death of adoptive parents (adopters no longer feel disloyal when pursuing enquiries) or the birth of a child and the arousal of curiosity about family characteristics. Reunions can be helped by skilled intermediary work (see pp. 240–2).

The task of searching can be a complex one and many people will need practical advice as well as emotional support. Whether this support is provided by someone with personal or professional experience of adoption, it needs to allow the adopted person to take matters at their own pace and in the direction of their choice. The outcomes of reunions are many and various; they can differ over time and between parties. Reunions can remain a secret and lead to feelings of guilt and compromised loyalties (see Feast *et al.*, 1994; Moran, 1994). However, even if the outcome is less than satisfactory, people are usually glad they took the step (see Barnardos, undated).

Occasionally reunions can lead to distorted and illegal relationships if the parties are sexually attracted. The term commonly used to describe this outcome is genetic sexual attraction and it can involve any combination of individuals who are biologically related, e.g. mothers and sons, brothers and sisters. Whilst not unique to people whose lives are affected by adoption, intimacy of this kind has been linked to those who experienced long periods of separation from each other.

Various theories exist to explain genetic sexual attraction, including the impact of meeting someone who strongly resembles oneself, feeling particularly close and comfortable in the company of another person, or being part of a biological relationship which has developed very suddenly and where the usual incest taboos are absent. Factors associated with personality, health and personal circumstances can make people particularly vulnerable, for example, being isolated, having low self-esteem and difficulty in asserting oneself. Some birth mothers or fathers reunite with someone who bears a strong physical resemblance to the other parent, their former lover, a situation which can be exacerbated if there is a narrow age gap between the parties.

In recent years the acknowledgement and understanding of sexualized relationships following reunion has increased. The Post-Adoption Centre in London has studied the issue in depth and produced a discussion paper on the subject (Post-Adoption Centre, 1994).

For some people, adoption is not the only problematic issue. For example, many transracially adopted children not only lack a black role model in the family but also live in predominantly white neighbourhoods. In Burnell (1993), a group of black adults adopted as children by white parents summarized their experiences and feelings. This paper usefully explores the inter-relationship between race and adoption. At times the co-existence of the issues brought a particular dynamic to the discussion (Burnell, 1993, p. 4):

Because of the realities of racism and the complexity of the trans-racial experience, it seemed to take longer for the group to accept or recognise the deep and painful feelings intrinsic to the adoption experience. The trans-racial element complicated and sometimes clouded the process of personal resolution and adjustment to the impact of adoption. It presented the black or mixed parentage adopted adult with a more complex and difficult experience to understand and integrate. Conversely and paradoxically, the trans-racial nature of the adoption also appeared to have sensitised and developed an awareness of adoption issues in these adults which would not, in our opinion, be found in white adopted adults. This more complex task has produced sensitive and resourceful adults, able to address and tackle the issues of adoption and race, which society at large has failed to do and which many people never begin to consider.

The inter-relationship between race and adoption impacts in various ways on people's post-adoption experience. There are several reasons why services may be inadequate in their ability to meet the needs of those who are transracially adopted.

Underpinning much of the difficulty is the white image often associated with statutory and voluntary adoption agencies, which can mean that black people are either deterred from establishing the range of services on offer, or hesitate to use them. We do not know whether transracially adopted young people, who seem to move with comfort in the white world, have this difficulty. Adoption records may be inadequate in relation to race and culture. Instances where an adoptee's birth father was black can result in very sparse information on record, with general statements, such as 'West Indian' or 'Asian', to describe a person's origin. Contemporary domestic adoptions may be characterized by much fuller records, but that information will doubtless be lacking for some children placed on an intercountry basis. From the post-adoption perspective, it is known that the need to find birth family members may be great (see Burnell, 1993). In order to advise on strategies for tracing, the counsellor must be familiar with the adopted person's racial and cultural background.

Sadly, there are instances when a person's racial background was the factor leading to their adoption and they may experience further racism and rejection as they try to make contact with birth relatives in adult life.

THE ORGANIZATION OF POST-ADOPTION SERVICES

The availability of post-adoption services has increased significantly since the mid-1980s, although the overall picture is still fragmented and variable. Developments have been largely the result of particular initiatives by self-help groups or adoption agencies, either individually or in partnership. The lack of detailed legislative requirements and the resource implications for hard-pressed agencies have also affected the development of services. All parties to adoption may seek services from the wider statutory sector, for example, health or education. Overall, it is very difficult to gauge how many people whose lives have been affected by adoption seek help and advice at some point, particularly as the fact of adoption may be clouded by other issues.

We know little about why those seeking a post-adoption service approach one agency rather than another. Many factors could play a part, including the availability of services, the wish to avoid social services or the placing agency and, perhaps, a belief that the standard of service will be higher if it is purchased. Choice implies an awareness of services and for some people it can be a struggle to identify even one appropriate source of post-adoption help.

Broadly speaking, the key components of a quality post-adoption service can be identified. These include a prompt and courteous response, the respect of confidentiality, sensitivity towards racial, cultural and religious issues, the availability of staff, the experience and specialist knowledge of staff (including awareness of services offered by other agencies), choices in terms of the workers to whom enquirers are allocated and the availability of those with personal experience of adoption, some of whom may be volunteers. Another important aspect of a quality post-adoption service is to ensure that matters proceed at the pace of the person making the enquiry and in accordance with their wishes and need, not those of the agency or its staff. As post-adoption work is, by its very nature, indefinite and inconclusive, it should also be open to the enquirer to return for further services should these be required. An example would be advising an adopted person who is searching for their birth parent. Once a reunion has taken place, there may still be a need for post-reunion counselling some months, or even years, following the first meeting. It is only now, as post-adoption work becomes better established, that its open-ended nature is fully appreciated. Often resources limit the way an agency works but, ideally, there should be a choice for the enquirer about where they are seen, even if this incurs the worker travelling long distances. This may be particularly important for parents whose children were adopted from the care system and who need to be seen on their own terms and in their own territory.

A common core of agency provision usually includes the following:

Counselling

This is fundamental and may take place in person or on the telephone. The service may include siblings by birth and by adoption, grandparents and other relatives. It is increasingly recognized that the partners of both adopted people and birth parents may have their lives dramatically affected by adoption, particularly if there is a reunion.

Group support

Post-adoption services often arrange group meetings and workshops for members of the adoption 'triangle'. Another important development has been the growth of self-help groups.

Tracing advice

Adopted people wishing to make contact with their families find they are faced with a multitude of systems through which they must find a path. Although tracing can be exciting and enjoyable, it can be costly, frustrating and deeply disappointing. While it is not unknown for people who are searching to find the person they seek very quickly, there are many others who will need months or even years to achieve their aim. Some will be faced with rejection. It is usual for agencies to offer an intermediary service once the adopted person has identified the whereabouts of a birth family member. Some will also be proactive on the part of birth family members wishing to trace (see Feast and Smith, 1993 and 1995).

Staff of the Post-Adoption Centre in London see the task of the intermediary as that of negotiator familiarizing the two parties with each other and offering support throughout the process (see Post-Adoption Centre, 1990).

Letter-box arrangements

This has implications for professional and administrative resources and frequently occasions debate – for example, on whether agencies should open correspondence (see Watson and McGhee, 1995).

Issues for the future

Areas of development in post-adoption are likely to include the following:

- The move towards openness in adoption and a variety of post-placement contact arrangements will require additional staff time, clear policy statements and administrative systems; also the development of skills relating to negotiation and conciliation by counsellors.
- The increasingly complex backgrounds of children placed for adoption will necessitate flexible packages of support if these placements are to survive. There are also implications for intermediary work if children choose to reunite with birth families on reaching adulthood.
- Services need to take into account the circumstances of disabled adopted children and their families. Although it is many years since disability rendered children 'un-adoptable' we are still at the beginning stage of identifying and providing appropriate services for the adult years.
- There will be a need for agencies to link as widely as possible with organizations and individuals whose skill and experience can support members of the adoption triangle. Workers may find they are frequently in the role of 'broker' as they identify resources and liaise on behalf of their clients.
- Agencies are likely to be under increasing pressure from birth families, both to obtain up-to-date information on children currently in placement, and to be proactive in establishing whether adult adoptees have a wish for contact.
- In sharp contrast to may other countries, intercountry adoption in the UK has, so far, only involved a small number of children. The Adoption Bill, which is very likely to provide for its regulation, could lead to an increase of such placements and thought has to be given to the post-adoption needs of this group of children, some of whom will have been placed transracially.

- Some agencies will need to give increased attention to services for black children and their families. Service-users of all racial and cultural backgrounds should feel comfortable with the post-adoption support they are offered. Progress has been made in recruiting and preparing families from the black community but, as yet, an ethnically sensitive service is not always available post-adoption.
- Agencies will need to consider an approach to budgetary management which addresses the long-term nature of post-adoption need. The placements of today cannot be closed at the point the adoption order is made, either professionally or financially.

At times it is difficult to feel optimistic about the future of post-adoption work. Many agencies are operating in a climate of frequent organizational change, pragmatic planning and time-limited funding. All too often post-adoption provision is accorded low priority. Service-users can be faced with vastly different responses from agencies when requesting assistance and sometimes within an agency there will be variations in the approach of individual workers. Practitioners may feel frustrated by the lack of policy, procedural guidance and a strong legislative framework to guide their work. Managers too can be daunted by increasing demand and limited resources in a field which is not traditionally associated with income-generation.

Five key points

- Post-adoption services are seen as increasingly necessary, although provision is often pragmatic, inadequate and underfunded.
- Post-adoption services may be needed by any of the parties to a placement at any stage in their lives.
- Adoption cases are now likely to involve children who have been in the care system and who will be adopted following a court decision. Post-placement services are developing to meet the needs of these children and their families.
- Adopted adults and their birth families may search for each other and reunite. This can have implications for many relationships and skilled counselling and intermediary work can be important.

- Agencies are having to adjust their structures, policies and procedures to accommodate the open-ended nature of current adoption practice.

CHAPTER 12
Concluding comments

In the preceding chapters the authors have attempted to develop the theory which lies behind the good practice of adoption, first in relation to basic services to birth parents, children, adopted adults and adopting parents, and then as regards specific and controversial aspects of adoption. One of the bases of theory is research, and the review of research has been quite comprehensive. Values are another base of theory, and there has been an attempt to explore the values of the community which have impact on adoption, as they are and as they have changed. As for the practice, wisdom and experience which also work toward the development of theory, the authors can only hope that their many years in varied aspects of adoption work have provided some of these ingredients. Theory informs policy and helps to shape the law. Practice takes place within this framework. It is our hope that the practitioner will find in this book not only ideas about 'what' to do, but exploration of the 'why'.

As we move into the twenty-first century, several important issues dominate adoption policy and practice, including: open adoption; the adoption of children with special needs; own-race and transracial adoption; single-parent adoption; intercountry adoption; and post-placement services to all parties involved in adoption. Though policy and practice should ideally be based on the child's best interests, these are not always clear. Research in the field of adoption has expanded considerably during the last thirty or so years and has in fact helped to illuminate child development generally, but we do not yet have research in all aspects of children's lives to guide policy and practice. Because of ethical and political constraints some of this knowledge may never be developed.

Though the emphasis in the last years has been on the development of adoption services in which the needs of children were dominant, there are signs now that we may be entering, or have already entered, a period when adoption is becoming once again a more adult-centred activity. Recent developments that inform this view include:

- The emphasis of recent British childcare legislation on alternative orders to adoption which, if inappropriately applied, could lead to less permanent arrangements for some children badly needing permanency.
- Recent British government efforts to deregulate adoption and allow full freedom to market forces, a condition already operating to a large extent in the United States where independent adoption is extensive.
- The devaluing of the contribution of adopters in non-traditional type families, including those who are single people, gay or lesbians.
- The shift in the latest government thinking (Department of Health, 1993a; Adoption Bill 1996) away from the notion that 'eligibility to adopt should be judged primarily according to the needs of a particular child' to notional concepts of what makes a good adoptive parent.
- The move towards giving the wishes of the adoptive parents greater weight than those of the child.
- Aspects of intercountry adoption policy, such as the approval of adoption agencies to engage solely in intercountry adoption. Experience from other countries suggests that this usually leads to the promotion of intercountry adoption.
- The composition of adoption panels suggested in the White Paper (Department of Health, 1993a), including the representation of one or more 'successful' adoptive parents, but not of birth parents or adopted people.

These tendencies are of great concern to those who value adoption primarily as a service for a child in need of a home, and must be carefully monitored in the coming years.

It is now evident that, whilst psychological parenting is a reality and the vast majority of adoptees searching for their origins are not looking for new parents, nevertheless the family of origin remains important to the adopted child. The new openness in adoption should facilitate the comfortable handling of issues of adoption and identity. The authors welcome the new definition of adoption that includes linking together two families through the child. Such openness presents new challenges, and will demand new practice skills, as the needs of child, birth parents and adopting parents are mediated.

In this push toward openness, intercountry adoption represents a different trend, in some ways a push backward to more closed infant adoptions. Adopting parents will find it hard to present their children with as much information as possible about their birth families, and with knowledge and comfort regarding their own ethnic background. Many of these adoptions are transracial, adding another dimension and challenge. Guidelines which accompanied the recent Adoption Bill (1996) toned down the importance of matching in such matters as race and ethnicity that featured in earlier guidelines. Yet such matching can be crucial to the long-term welfare of the child.

Though the adoption of older children and children with disabilities opened opportunities for adoption for many children, a continuing problem in the United States and Britain has been the long stay of black children in the care system, and the under-representation of these children in adoptive placement. A long history of adoption services staffed by white workers, focused on placing white infants, has left a large number of older black children in foster care or residential homes. This situation has led to outreach programmes which attempt to recruit black families, but there are criticisms about the commitment and comprehensiveness of these programmes. Transracial adoption, another solution, remains very controversial. One development to be expected is the linking of open adoption (with contact) with transracial adoptions. It will be important to follow the experiences of these placements.

Independent adoptions, which are possible in the US and in which a lawyer or doctor acts as intermediary, or in which birth parents and adoptive parents reach an agreement on their own, are defended as the 'deregulation' of an essentially private, family matter. A broadly similar approach is followed in intercountry adoption, a process that is almost wholly adult-centred. Such processes introduce high adoption fees, creating discomfort as distinctions between fees for services and payment to acquire a child become blurred. This is a process open only to the better-off. Calls to relax legal requirements for independent or third party placements have been muted, though not unheard, in the UK. However, the commitment of a placing agency to the welfare of the child, the adoptive family, and the relinquishing parents, is for the lifetime of the adoption. This commitment is absent from independent adoptions.

Many of these issues are reflected in the new Adoption Bill (1996), which was published in March 1996 as this book was being completed. Views were being sought from interested parties and organizations before a final Bill went to Parliament. A large part of the Bill was based on the Adoption Acts 1976 (England and Wales) and 1978 (Scotland). Most of the principles of these Acts were retained but the language was updated. For example, the child's interests continue to be paramount. Intercountry adoption occupies a large part of the Bill. Its provisions are based on the Hague Convention (1993), which the UK signed in 1994 but has not ratified yet. The intention is to ratify the Convention as soon as a new Adoption Act is implemented, not simply passed by Parliament. Among other things, the Bill places a duty on local authorities to provide or arrange for home study reports of British adopting parents.

SOME MAIN NEW PROVISIONS OF THE ADOPTION BILL (1996)

Under the 1976 Adoption Act the need to safeguard and protect the welfare of the child throughout his childhood is the first consideration. The Bill provides that the *paramount* consideration of the court or adoption agency is to be the child's welfare, in childhood and later.

No child can be placed for adoption by an adoption agency except with the consent of the parent or guardian or under a placement order. Parents will give separate consents, first to a child being placed for adoption and then to an adoption order, though the two consents can be given at the same time. Natural parents will have their rights reduced. Previously the courts could force a mother to give up a child for adoption only if they could prove she was acting unreasonably. Under the 1996 Bill the courts need only decide it is in the child's welfare to make her hand the child over.

Freeing orders will be revoked in England and Wales and replaced by placement orders, but freeing will be retained in Scotland. In the consultation papers that preceded the Bill, placement orders had a mixed reception, with many expressing fears that they would lead to placement delays. As a compromise and subject to further consultations, the Bill provides that placement orders will only apply to those cases where the child is already subject to a care order and there is an adoption plan, or where the parents are objecting to an adoption order. In other words, where the above conditions exist, no child can be placed for adoption unless there is first a placement order. A placement order will not restrict a placement to named prospective adopters even where they are known to the agency. This new process is meant to provide opportunities to birth parents to defend themselves. As with its predecessor, the freeing order, a placement order will mean that adopters will not carry anxieties about possible parental withholding of consent. Much, in our view, will depend on whether long court delays can be avoided, as was the case with freeing orders, and on whether the majority of children will be adequately catered for by these fixed provisions.

Contrary to initial speculations, the Bill does not allow for private home studies on behalf of would-be adopters. These will still have to be carried out by an approved adoption agency. At the time of writing an agency had applied and was about to be approved as an Intercountry Adoption Agency. An important point for all adoption agencies is how far they have the resources required to provide not only for the assessment and preparation of would-be adopters but for a through-service to the post-placement stage and beyond.

Another major provision that features in the Bill is for all adopted people to have the right of information about their adoption when they reach the age of 18. Whilst this has always been the case in Scotland, the Bill will go further by providing that at the age of 18, or after, an adopted person can apply to court for a pack of information about his or her background. A similar pack is to be provided to the adopting family to pass on, but if the parents fail to do so, the child can apply to court to be provided with the same pack.

A welcome feature of the Bill is the provision for an independent complaints procedure for all the parties involved in adoption.

A court or adoption agency, in coming to a decision relating to a child, will need to consider the value to the child of any relationship with relatives and other persons continuing. Though the guidelines to the Bill acknowledge the importance of open adoption and of adoption with contact for some children, at the same time the guidelines rightly urge caution on the matter. The overall emphasis is on co-operation between the parties. The Bill itself does not provide for an adoption order with a condition of contact. Contact, apparently, will be treated as a separate issue under the Children Act 1989 (England and Wales) and 1995 (Scotland).

Attempts to develop similar comprehensive adoption legislation at the federal level in the United States have, for years, failed, and there is no indication that the current attempt will succeed. Many issues in adoption are controversial, communities differ in their values, and in the federal system it is difficult to get agreement. Perhaps there are advantages in the experimentation which this more multi-faceted system allows. But it is probable that in this system the centrality of the welfare of children is less well protected.

What are the principles of good practice which guide the practitioner through these complex issues, and through the implementation of law and regulation? First, respect for birth parents, adopting parents, the child, and the adult adoptee, and ability to assess and attempt to meet their needs, and to find and work with their strengths. Second, knowledge of the theory of adoption, and related theories of human behaviour. Third, comfort with the policies, laws and regulations of the agency in which adoption is practised, and a sense that they fit the values of the practitioner and of the community. And, finally, but most important, a firm conviction that the focus of adoption is on meeting the needs of the child, and that these needs are best met in an appropriate family.

BIBLIOGRAPHY

Abbot, G. (1938) *The State of the Child*. Chicago: University of Chicago.

Adcock, M. (1980) 'Dilemmas in planning long-term care' in Triseliotis (ed.) (1980).

Ahlijah, F. (1990) 'Intercountry adoptions: in whose interests?' MSc dissertation, University of Oxford.

Aldridge, J. (1994) 'In the best interests of the child' in Gaber and Aldridge (eds) (1994).

Altstein, H. and Simon, R.J. (eds) (1991) *Intercountry Adoption: A Multinational Perspective*. New York: Praeger.

Asian Families Adopt (1995) Video. Leicester: Leicestershire Social Services.

Assarnow, J.R. (1988) 'Children at risk of schizophrenia: converging lines of evidence', *Schizophrenia Bulletin* 15(4), 613–28.

Association of Black Social Workers and Allied Professions (1983) 'Black children in care: evidence to the House of Commons Social Services Committee'. London.

Atkinson, D.R., Morten, G. and Sue, D.W. (1989) *Counselling American Minorities: A Cross-Cultural Perspective* (3rd edn). Dubuque, IA: Wm C. Brown.

Bach, R.P. (1988) quoted by Textor, R.M. (1991) 'International adoptions in Germany' in Altstein and Simon (eds) (1991).

Bagley, C. and Young, L. (1979) 'The identity, adjustment and achievement of transracially adopted children: a review and empirical report' in G. Verma and C. Bagley (eds) *Race, Education and Identity* (pp. 192–219). London: Macmillan.

Bagley, C., Young, L. and Scully, A. (1993) *International and Transracial Adoptions*. Aldershot: Avebury.

Banks, N. (1992) 'Techniques for direct identity work with black children', *Adoption and Fostering* 16(3), 19–24.

Baran, A. and Pannor, R. (1990) 'Open adoption' in D. Brodzinsky and M.D. Schechter (eds) *The Psychology of Adoption* (pp. 316–31). New York: Oxford University Press.

Barn, R. (1993) *Black Children in the Public Care System*. London: Batsford.

Barnardos (undated) *Original Thoughts: The Views of Adult Adoptees and Birth Families Following Renewed Contact*. London: Barnardos Research and Development Section.

Barth, R.P. (1991) 'Adoption of drug-exposed children', *Children and Youth Services Review* 13(5/6), 323–42.

Barth, R.P. and Berry, M. (1988) *Adoption and Disruption: Rates, Risks and Responses*. New York: Aldine de Gruyter.

Barth, R.P., Courtney, M., Berrick, D.J. and Albert, V. (1994) *From Child Abuse to Permanency Planning*. New York: Aldine de Gruyter.

Bartholet, E. (1991) 'Where do black children belong? The politics of race matching in adoption', *University of Pennsylvania Law Review* 139, 1163–256.

Bartholet, E. (1993) *Family Bonds: Adoption and the Politics of Parenting*. Boston: Houghton Mifflin.

Bebbington, A. and Miles, J. (1989) 'The background of children who enter local authority care', *British Journal of Social Work* 19(5), 349–58.

Bee, H. (1995) *The Growing Child*. London: HarperCollins.

Belbas, N.F. (1987) Staying in touch: empathy in open adoptions', *Smith College Studies in Social Work* 57(3), 184–98.

Benson, L.P., Sharma, R.A. and Roehlkepartain, C.E. (1994) *Growing up Adopted: A Portrait of Adolescents and Their Families*. Minneapolis: Search Institute.

Berrick, J.D., Barth, R.P. and Needell, B. (1994) 'A comparison of kinship foster homes and foster family homes: implications for kinship foster care as family preservation', *Children and Youth Services Review* 16(1/2), 33–64.

Bianchi, S.M. (1995) 'The changing demographic and socio-economic characteristics of single-parent families' in S. Hanson, M. Heims, D. Julian and M. Sussman (eds) *Single-Parent Families: Diversity, Myths, and Realities* (pp. 71–98). New York: Haworth Press.

Bohman, M. (1970) *Adopted Children and Their Families*. Stockholm: Proprios.

Bohman, M. (1978) 'Some genetic aspects of alcoholism and criminality', *Archives of General Psychiatry* 35, 269–76.

Bohman, M. and Sigvardsson, S. (1980) 'Negative social heritage', *Adoption and Fostering* 101(3), 25–31.

Bohman, M. and Sigvardsson, S. (1990) 'Outcome in adoption: lessons from longitudinal studies' in D.M. Brodzinsky and M.D.

Schecter (eds) *The Psychology of Adoption*. New York: Oxford University Press.

Bond, M. (1972) *Paddington Bear*. London and Glasgow: Collins.

Borgman, R. (1981) 'Antecedents and consequences of parental rights. Termination for abused and neglected children', *Child Welfare* 60(6), 391–404.

Borland, M., O'Hara, G. and Triseliotis, J. (1991) 'Permanency planning for children in Lothian Region' in Social Work Services Group (ed.) *Adoption and Fostering*. Edinburgh: Scottish Office.

Bottomley, V. (1991) Opening Address to the International Conference on Adoption held in Edinburgh in September, 1991.

Bouchier, P., Lambert, L and Triseliotis, J. (1991) *Parting with a Child for Adoption*. London: British Agencies for Adoption and Fostering (BAAF).

Bourguignon, J.P. and Watson, K. (1987) *A Manual for Professionals Working with Adoptive Families*. Springfield, IL: Illinois Department of Children and Family Services.

Bowlby, J. (1951) *Maternal Care and Mental Health*. Geneva: World Health Organisation.

Bowlby, J. (1969) *Attachment and Loss*. Vol. 1: *Attachment*. New York: Basic Books.

Bowlby, J. (1973) *Attachment and Loss*. Vol. 2: *Separation*. New York: Basic Books.

Bowlby, J. (1979) *The Making and Breaking of Affectional Bonds*. London: Tavistock.

Bowlby, J. (1980) *Attachment and Loss*. Vol. 3: *Loss: Sadness and Depression*. New York: Basic Books.

Bowlby, J., Ainsworth, M.D.S., Boston, M. and Rosenbluth, D. (1956) 'The effects of mother–child separation: a follow-up study', *British Journal of Medical Psychology* 49, 211–47.

Boyne, J., Denby, L., Kettering, J.R. and Wheeler, W. (1984) 'The shadow of success'. Unpublished research report. Westfield, CT: Spaulding for Children.

Branham, E. (1970) 'One parent adoptions', *Children* 17(3), 103–7.

Bridge Child Care Consultancy Service (1991) *'Needs Game': An Assessment Game for Children, Young People, Parents and Professionals*. London: Bridge Child Care Consultancy Service.

Bridge Child Care Consultancy Service (1994) *My Life in Words and Pictures*. London: Bridge Child Care Consultancy Service.

British Agencies for Adoption and Fostering (1984) *In Touch with Children*. London: BAAF.

British Agencies for Adoption and Fostering (1991) *Intercountry*

Adoption: A Survey of Agencies. London: BAAF.

Brodzinsky, D.M. (1984) 'New perspectives on adoption revelation', *Adoption and Fostering* 8(2), 27–32.

Brodzinsky, D.M. (1993) 'Long-term outcomes in adoption', *The Future of Children* 33(1), 153–66.

Brodzinsky, D.M., Schechter, M.D. and Henig, R.M. (1992) *Being Adopted.* New York: Doubleday.

Brown, G.W. and Harris, T. (1978) *The Social Origins of Depression.* London: Tavistock.

Burnell, A. (1993) *Thoughts on Adoption by Black Adults Adopted as Children by White Parents.* London: Post-Adoption Service.

Butler, B. (1989) 'Adopting an indigenous approach', *Adoption and Fostering* 13(2), 27–31.

Cadoret, R. (1990) 'Biologic perspectives in adoptee adjustment' in D. Brodzinsky and M. Schecter (eds) *The Psychology of Adoption.* New York: Oxford University Press.

Cadoret, J. and Garth, A. (1978) 'Inheritance of alcoholism in adoptees', *British Journal of Psychiatry* 132, 252–9.

Canadian Royal Commission on New Reproductive Technologies (1993) *Proceed with Care.* Ottawa: Ministry of Government Services.

Caplan, L. (1990) 'A reporter at large: an open adoption: I and II', *The New Yorker*, 21 and 28 May.

Capron, C. and Duyme, M. (1989) 'Assessment of effects of socio-economic status on IQ in a full cross-fostering study', *Nature* 340, 552–4.

Carstens, C. and Jullia, M. (1995) 'Legal, policy and practice issues for intercountry adoption in the United States', *Adoption and Fostering* 19(4), 26–33.

Cattanach, A. (1992) *Play Therapy with Sexually Abused Children.* London: Jessica Kingsley.

Cederblad, M. (1982) *Children Adopted from Abroad and Coming to Sweden After Age Three.* Stockholm: Swedish National Board for Intercountry Adoption.

Cederblad, M. (1984) *A New Country, A New Home.* Stockholm: Liber Forlag.

Chambers, C. (1989) 'Cutting through the dogma', *Social Work Today* 21(6), 14–15.

Charles, M., Parvez, S., and Thoburn, J. (1992) 'The placement of black children with permanent new families', *Adoption and Fostering* 16(3), 13–19.

Checkland, S.G. and Checkland, E.O.A. (1974) *The Poor Law Report of 1834.* London: Pelican.

Chestang, L. (1972) 'The dilemma of biracial adoption', *Social Work* 17, 100–15.

Children's Legal Centre (1989) *Childright*, November.

Cicchetti, D and Toth, S. (1995) 'A developmental psychopathology perspective on child abuse and neglect', *Journal of American Academy of Child and Adolescent Psychiatry* 34(5), 541–65.

Cipola, J., Benson-McGown, D. and Yanulis, M.A. (1992) *Communicating Through Play*. London: BAAF.

Clarke, A.M. (1981) 'Adoption studies', *Adoption and Fostering* 104(2), 17–29.

Clarke, A.M. and Clarke, D.B. (eds) (1976) *Early Experience: Myth and Evidence*. London: Open Books.

Cline, F. (1992) *Hope for High Risk and Rage Filled Children*. Colorado: Evergreen Consultants Publications.

Close, M. (1983) 'Child welfare and people of color: denial of equal access', *Social Work Research and Abstracts* 19(1), 13–20.

Commission for Racial Equality (1990) *Adopting a Better Policy: Adopting and Fostering Ethnic Minority Children: The Race Dimension*. London: Commission for Racial Equality.

Corrigan, M. and Floud, C. (1990) 'A framework for direct work with children in care', *Adoption and Fostering* 14(3), 28–32.

Costin, L.B., Bell, C.J. and Downs, S.W. (1991) *Child Welfare Policies*. New York: Longman.

Craig, M. (1991) 'Adoption: not a big deal'. Unpublished report. Edinburgh: Scottish Adoption Society.

Crompton, M. (1996) *The Religious and Spiritual Needs of Children and Their Families in Receipt of Personal Social Services*. London: Central Council for Education and Training in Social Work.

Cross, W.E., Jr (1987) 'A two-factor theory of black identity: implications for the study of identity development in minority children' in J. Phinney and M. Rotheram (eds) *Children's Ethnic Socialization* (pp. 117–33). Newbury Park, CA: Sage.

Crowe, R.R. (1972) 'The adopted offspring of women criminal offenders', *Archives of General Psychiatry* 126, 534–59.

Dalen, M. (1988) 'Intercountry adopted children: under-achievers at school?' Paper presented at the International Conference on Adoption, Melbourne, Australia.

Dalen, M. and Saetersdal, B. (1987) 'Transracial adoption in Norway', *Adoption and Fostering* 11(4), 44–6.

Davis, D.F. (1995) 'Capitalizing on adoption', *Adoption and Fostering* 19(2), 25–30.

Davis, S., Morris, B. and Thorn, J. (1984) 'Task-centred assessment for foster parents', *Adoption and Fostering* 8(4), 33–7.

Department of Health (1985) *Decisions in Child Care*. London: Her Majesty's Stationery Office (HMSO).

Department of Health (1991) *Children Act Regulations and Guidance*. Vol. 9: *Family Placements*. London: HMSO.

Department of Health (1992) *The Family Placement of Children*. Circular letter. London: HMSO.

Department of Health (1993a) *Adoption: The Future* (White Paper). London: HMSO.

Department of Health (1993b) *Planning for Permanence?* London: HMSO.

Department of Health and Welsh Office (1992) *Review of Adoption Law: Report to the Ministers of an Independent Working Group: A Consultation Document*. London: Department of Health.

De Vries, A.K. (1988) Quoted by R.A.C. Hoksbergen in Altstein and Simon (eds) (1991).

Deykin, Y.E., Pratti, P. and Ryan, J. (1988) 'Fathers of adopted children: a study of the impact of child surrender on birthfathers'. *American Journal of Orthopsychiatry* 58(2), 240–8.

Dominick, C. (1988) *Early Contact in Adoption*. Research Series 10. Wellington, NZ: Department of Social Welfare.

Donati, T. (1995) 'Single parents and wider families in the new context of legitimacy' in S. Hanson, M. Heims, D. Julian and M. Sussman (eds) *Single Parent Families: Diversity, Myths and Realities* (pp. 27–42). New York: Haworth Press.

Dougherty, S.A. (1978) 'Single adoptive mothers and their children', *Social Work* 32(4), 311–14.

Duncan, W. (1993) 'The Hague Convention on the protection of children and co-operation in respect of intercountry adoption', *Adoption and Fostering* 17(3), 9–13.

Dutt, R. and Sanyal, A. (1991) 'Openness in adoption or open adoption: a Black perspective', *Adoption and Fostering* 15(4), 111–15.

Eck-Menning, B. (1988) *Infertility: A Guide for the Childless Couple*. New York: Prentice Hall.

Eekelaar, J. and Clive, E.M. (1982) *Custody After Divorce*. Oxford: Centre for Sociolegal Studies.

Erikson, E.H. (1963) *Childhood and Society* (2nd edn). New York: Norton.

Erikson, E.H. (1968) *Identity: Youth and Crisis*. New York: Norton.

Etzioni, A. (1964) *Modern Organizations*. Englewood Cliffs, NJ: Prentice-Hall.

Fahlberg, V. (1988) *Fitting the Pieces Together*. London: BAAF.

Fahlberg, V. (1994) *A Child's Journey Through Placement*. London: BAAF.

Falk, L. (1970) 'A comparative study of transracial and inracial adoptions', *Child Welfare* 49, 82–8.

Familymakers (1983) *Finding out About Me*. Kent: Familymakers Homefinding Unit.

Fanshel, D. (1972) *Far from the Reservation*. Metuchen, NJ: Scarecrow Press.

Fanshel, D. and Shinn, E.B. (1978) *Children in Foster Care*. New York: Columbia University Press.

Farmer, E. and Parker, R. (1991) *Trials and Tribulations: Returning Children from Local Authority Care to their Families*. London: HMSO.

Feast, J., Marwood, M., Seabrook, S., Warbur, A. and Webb, L. (1994) *Preparing for Re-union*. London: The Children's Society.

Feast, J. and Smith, J. (1993) 'Working on behalf of birth families', *Adoption and Fostering* 17(2), 33–40.

Feast, J. and Smith, J. (1995) 'Openness and opportunities: review of an intermediary service for birth relatives', *Adoption and Fostering* 19(3), 17–23.

Feigelman, W. and Silverman, A. (1983) *Chosen Children: New Patterns of Adoptive Relationships*. New York: Praeger.

Feigelman, W. and Silverman, A. (1984) 'The long-term effects of transracial adoption', *Social Services Review* 58, 588–662.

Fein, E and Maluccio, A. (1992) 'Permanency planning: another remedy in jeopardy?' *Social Service Review* 66, 335–48.

Finch, S. and Fanshel, D. (1985) 'Testing the equality of discharge patterns in foster care', *Social Work Research and Abstracts* 21(3), 3–10.

Finkellor, D. (1986) *A Sourcebook on Child Sexual Abuse: New Patterns of Adoptive Relationships*. New York: Praeger.

Fish, A. and Speirs, C. (1990) 'Biological parents choose adoptive parents: the use of profiles in adoption', *Child Welfare* 64(2), 129–40.

Fisher, M., Marsh, P., Phillips, D. with Sainsbury, E. (1986) *In and out of Care: The Experience of Children, Parents and Social Workers*. London: Batsford.

Fitzgerald, J. (1991) 'Working with children who have been sexually abused' in D. Batty (ed.) *Sexually Abused Children*. London: British Agencies for Adoption and Fostering.

Flaks, K. (1995) *Research Issues in Gay and Lesbian Adoption*. Washington, DC: Child Welfare League of America.

Flango, V.E. and Flango, C.R. (1993) 'Adoption statistics by state', *Child Welfare* 72, 311–19.

Fratter, J. (1991) 'Parties in the triangle', *Adoption and Fostering* 15(4), 91–8.

Fratter, J. (1995) 'Perspectives on adoption with contact: implications for policy and practice'. PhD thesis, University of Cranfield.

Gabel, S. (1988) *Filling in the Blanks: A Guided Look at Growing up Adopted*. Indianapolis: Perspectives Press.

Gaber, I. and Aldridge, J. (1994) *Culture, Identity and Transracial Adoption: In the Best Interests of the Child*. London: Free Association Books.

Gardell, J. (1980) *A Swedish Study on Inter-country Adoption*. Stockholm: Liber Tryck Gunnarby.

Giddens, A. (1992) *Modernity and Self-Identity*. Cambridge: Polity Press.

Gill, O. and Jackson, B. (1983) *Adoption and Race*. London: Batsford.

Glendinning, C and Millar, J. (1992) *Women and Poverty in Britain*. Hemel Hempstead: Harvester Wheatsheaf.

Glidden, L.M. (1991) 'Adopted children with developmental disabilities', *Children and Youth Services Review* 13(5/6), 363–76.

Goffman, E. (1963) *Stigma: Notes on the Management of Spoiled Identity*. London: Prentice-Hall.

Goffman, E. (1969) *The Presentation of Self in Everyday Life*. London: Penguin.

Goldstein, J., Freud, A. and Solnit, A.J. (1973) *Beyond the Best Interests of the Child*. New York: Free Press.

Goldstein, J., Freud, A. and Solnit, A.J. (1980) *Before the Best Interests of the Child*. New York: Burnett Books.

Golombok, S., Spencer, A. and Rutter, M. (1983) 'Children in lesbian and single parent households: psychosexual and psychiatric appraisal', *Journal of Clinical Psychology and Psychiatry* 24(4), 551–72.

Goodwin, D.W., Schulsinger, E., Moller, N., Hermansen, L., Winocur, C. and Guze, S.B. (1973) 'Drinking problems in adopted and non-adopted sons of alcoholics', *Archives of General Psychiatry* 31, 164–9.

Gottman, J.S. (1990) 'Children of gay and lesbian parents', *Homosexuality and Family Relations: Marriage and Family Review* 14(3/4), 177–96.

Greenfield, J. (1995) 'Intercountry adoption: a comparison between France and England', *Adoption and Fostering* 19(2), 31–6.

Grow, L. and Shapiro, D. (1972) *Black Children, White Parents: A Study of Transracial Adoption*. New York: Child Welfare League of America.

Groze, V. (1991) 'Adoption and single parents: a review', *Child Welfare* 70(3), 321–32.

Groze, V. (1996) 'A one- and two-year follow-up study of adoptive families and special needs children', *Children and Youth Services Review* 18(1/2), 57–82.

Groze, V. and Rosenthal, J.A. (1991) 'Single parents and their adopted children: a psychosocial analysis', *Families in Society: The Journal of Contemporary Human Services* 9(2), 67–77.

Gunnarby, A., Holfvander, Y., Sjolin, S. and Sundelin, C. (1982) 'Utlandska adoptivbarns halsotillstand och anpassning till svenska forhallanden', *Ulakartidningen* 79(17), 1697–705.

Haimes, E. and Timms, N. (1985) *Adoption, Identity and Social Policy*. London: Gower.

Hardy, B. (1968) 'Towards a poetic fiction', *Novel* 1(2), 5–14.

Harrison, D. (1991) 'Single adoptive parents', *Newsletter*, Western Region, Children's Services Division.

Hartman, A. (1979) *Finding Families*. New York: Sage.

Hartman, A. (1984) *Working with Adopted Families Beyond Placement*. Washington, DC: Child Welfare League of America.

Haworth, G. (1995) Private communication. (Ms Haworth is Director of Overseas Adoption Helpline, based in London.)

Heegaard, M. (1991) *When Something Terrible Happens* (workbook). Minneapolis: Woodland Press.

Hene, B. (1988) *Language Development of Inter-country Adoptees*. Sweden: University of Goteborg.

Hetherington, E.M. (1979) 'Divorce: a child's perspective', *American Psychologist* 34, 851–8.

Hill, M., Lambert, L. and Triseliotis, J. (1989) *Achieving Adoption with Love and Money*. London: National Children's Bureau.

Hill, M., Lambert, L., Triseliotis, J. and Buist, M. (1992) 'Making judgements about parenting: the example of freeing for adoption', *British Journal of Social Work* 22, 373–89.

Hobday, A. and Lee, K. (1995) 'Adoption: a specialist area for psychology', *The Psychologist* 8(1), 33–5.

Hodgkins, P. (1991) *Birth Records Counselling*. London: British Agencies for Adoption and Fostering.

Hogan, P. (1988) 'Preparing children for family placement through the use of groups' in Triseliotis (ed.) (1988).

Hoksbergen, R.A.C. (1991a) 'Inter-country adoption coming of age in the Netherlands' in Altstein and Simon (eds) (1991).

Hoksbergen, R.A.C. (1991b) 'Understanding and preventing "failing adoptions"' in E. Hibbs (ed.) *Adoptions: International Perspectives*. Madison, CT: International Universities Press.

Hoksbergen, R.A.C., Juffer, F. and Waardenburg, B.C. (1987) *Adopted Children at Home and at School*. Lisse: Sweets and Zeitlinger.

Holfvander, Y., Bengstsson, E., Gunnarby, A., Cederblad, M., Kats, M. and Stromholm, S. (1978) (in Swedish), quoted in Cederblad (1982).

Holmes, E. (1980) 'Assessing parental relationships', *Adoption and Fostering* 105(4), 23–8.

Horne, J. (1981) 'Groupwork with adopters', *Adoption and Fostering* 106(4), 21–4.

Horowitz, J.A. (1995) 'A conceptualization of parenting: examining the single-parent family' in S. Hanson, M. Heims, D. Julian and M. Sussman (eds) *Single Parent Families: Diversity, Myths and Realities*. New York: Haworth Press.

Horowitz, J.A. and Maruyama, H. (1995) 'Legal issues' in *Issues in Gay and Lesbian Adoption*. Washington, DC: Child Welfare League of America.

Horsbrugh Committee (1937) *Report of the Departmental Committee on Adoption Societies and Agencies*. London: HMSO.

Houghton Committee Report (1972) *Report of the Departmental Committee on the Adoption of Children*. London: Home Office and Scottish Education Department.

Howe, D. (1995) *Attachment Theory for Social Work Practice*. London: Macmillan.

Howe, D., Sawbridge, P. and Hinings, D. (1992) *Half a Million Women*. London: Penguin.

Hughes, B. (1995a) 'Openness and contact in adoption: a child-centred perspective', *British Journal of Social Work* 25, 729–47.

Hughes, B. (1995b) *Post Placement Services for Children and Families: Defining the Needs*. London: Department of Health, Social Services Inspectorate.

Hughes, B. and Logan, J. (1993) *Birth Parents: The Hidden Dimension*. University of Manchester: Department of Social Policy and Social Work.

Humphreys, H. (1992) Unpublished paper delivered at a conference on intercountry adoption in Manchester, 1992.

Hutchings, B. and Mednick, S. (1974) 'Registered criminality in the adoptive and biological parents of registered male criminal adoptees' in R.R. Feeve and D.A. Zubin (eds) *Generics and Psychopathology*. Baltimore: Johns Hopkins University Press.

Hutchins, D.J. and Kirkpatrick, M.J. (1985) 'Lesbian mothers/gay fathers' in D.H. Schetky and E.P. Beuedak (eds) *Emerging Issues in Child Psychiatry and the Law*. New York: Brunner/Mazel.

Iwanek, M.A. (1987) *A Study of Open Adoption*. New Zealand: Petone.

Jewett, C. (1984) *Helping Children Cope with Separation and Loss*. London: Batsford.

Johnstone, P. (1992) *Adopting After Infertility*. Indianapolis: Perspectives Press.

Jones, C.E. and Else, J.F. (1977) 'Racial and cultural issues in adoption', *Child Welfare* 58, 373–82.

Kadushin, A. (1970) *Adopting Older Children*. New York: Columbia University Press.

Kadushin, A. and Martin, J. (1988) *Adopting Older Children*. New York: Macmillan.

Kagan, R.M. and Reid, W.J. (1986) 'Critical factors in the adoption of emotionally disturbed youths', *Child Welfare* 65(1), 62–82.

Kaniuk, J. (1991) 'Strategies in recruiting black adopters', *Adoption and Fostering* 15(1), 38–41.

Kaniuk, J. (1993) 'Openness in adoption' in M. Adcock, J. Kaniuk and R. White (eds) *Exploring Openness in Adoption* (pp. 7–24). London: Significant Publications.

Kendler, K., Gruenberg, A. and Strauss, J. (1982) 'An independent analysis of the Copenhagen sample of the Danish adoption study of schizophrenia', *Archives of General Psychiatry* 39, 639–42.

Kenyon, F. E. (1970) 'Homosexuality in the female', *British Journal of Hospital Medicine*, 183–206.

Keppel, M. (1991) 'Birth parents and negotiated adoption arrangements', *Adoption and Fostering* 15(4), 81–90.

Keshet, H.F. and Rosenthal, K.M. (1980) *Fathers Without Partners*. Totowa, NJ: Rowan & Littlefield.

Kety, S.S., Rosenthal, D., Wender, P.H. and Schulsinger, F. (1968) 'The types and prevalence of mental illness in the biological and adoptive families of adopted schizophrenics' in Rosenthal and Kety (eds) (1968).

Kim, D. S. (1976) 'Inter-country adoptions'. PhD thesis, University of Chicago.

Kirk, D. (1970) 'The selection of adopters' in *Medical Group Papers*, II: *Genetic and Psychological Aspects of Adoption*. London: Association of British Agencies for Adoption and Fostering.

Kirk, H.D. (1964) *Shared Fate: A Theory of Adoption and Mental Health*. New York: The Free Press.

Kirschner, D. (1980) *The Adopted Child Syndrome: A Study of Some Characteristics of Disturbed Adopted Children*. Report of the South Shore Institute of Advanced Studies. New York: Merrick.

Knapp, M. (1989) *Measuring Child Care Outcomes*. PSSRU Discussion Paper 630. Canterbury: University of Kent.

Knitzer, J., Allen, M.L. and McGowan, B. (1978) *Children Without Homes*. Washington, DC: Children's Defense Fund.

Kornitzer, M., (1968) *Adoption and Family Life*. London: Putman.

Kuhl, W. (1985) *When Adopted Children of Foreign Origin Grow Up*. Osnabrück: Terre des Hommes.

Kvist, B., Viemero, V. and Forsten, N. (1989) 'Barn adopterade till Finland fran utomeuropeiska lander', *Nordisk Psykologi* 41(2), 97–108. (English abstract quoted in Tizard, 1991.)

Ladner, J. (1977) *Mixed Families*. New York: Free Press/Doubleday.

Lambert, L., Buist, M., Triseliotis, J. and Hill, M. (1990) *Freeing Children for Adoption*. London: BAAF.

LeProhn, N.S. (1994) 'The role of kinship foster parent: a comparison of the role conceptions of relative and non-relative foster parents', *Children and Youth Services Review* 15(1/2), 65–84.

Lidster, A. (1995) *Chester and Daisy Move On*. London: BAAF.

Lindsey, D. (1994) *Child Welfare*. New York: Oxford University Press.

London, L. (1992) 'Do all the family want to adopt?' MSc dissertation, University of Edinburgh.

Long, G. (1995) 'Family poverty and the role of family support work' in M. Hill, R. Hawthorne, K. Part and D. Part (eds) *Supporting Families*. London: HMSO.

Lowing, P., Mirsky, A. and Pereira, R. (1983) 'The inheritance of schizophrenia spectrum disorder: a reanalysis of the Danish adopted study data', *American Journal of Psychiatry* 140, 1167–71.

Ludden, B. (1992) 'Single parenting'. Presentation at Deschutes County Foster Parent Association Conference, October.

Lunken, T. (1995) 'Recruiting adoptive parents for older children', *Adoption and Fostering* 19(4), 16–20.

Maas, H. and Engler, R. (1959) *Children in Need of Parents*. New York: Columbia University Press.

Macaskill, C. (1984) *Against the Odds*. London: Batsford.

McCausland, C. (1976) *Children of Circumstance: A History of the First 125 Years of the Chicago Child Care Society*. Chicago: Chicago Child Care Society.

Macey, M. (1995) '"Same race" adoption policy: anti-racism or racism?', *Journal of Social Policy* 24(4), 473–91.

McGue, M. (1989) 'Nature–nurture and intelligence', *Nature* 340, 506–7.

Mckay, M. (1980) 'Planning for permanent placement', *Adoption and Fostering* 15(4), 53–60.

McLanahan, S. and Sandefur, G. (1994) *Growing Up with a Single Parent*. Cambridge, MA: Harvard University Press.

McNeil, P. (1986) *Adoption of Children in Scotland*. Edinburgh: Green.

McRoy, R.G. (1990) 'An organizational dilemma: the case of transracial adoptions', *Journal of Applied Behavioural Sciences* 25(2), 145–60.

McRoy, R.G. (1991a) 'American experiences and research in openness', *Adoption and Fostering* 15(4), 99–111.

McRoy, R.G. (1991b) 'Significance of ethnic and racial identity in intercountry adoption within the United States', *Adoption and Fostering* 15(4), 53–60.

McRoy, R.G. (1994) *Changing Practice in Adoption*. Austin, TX: Hogg Foundation for Mental Health.

McRoy, R. and Zurcher, L. (1983) *Transracial and In-racial Adoptees – The Adolescent Years*. Springfield, IL: Charles C. Thomas.

McRoy, R., Zurcher, L., Lauderdale, M. and Anderson, R. (1984) 'The identity of transracial adoptees', *Social Casework* 65(1), 34–9.

McWhinnie, A.M. (1967) *Adopted Children: How They Grow up*. London: Routledge & Kegan Paul.

Marcia, J.E. (1980) 'Identity in adolescence' in J. Adelson (ed.) *Handbook of Adolescence Psychology*. New York: Wiley.

Marindin, H. (ed.) (1992) *Handbook for Single Adoptive Parents*. Chevy Chase, MD: Committee for Single Adoptive Parents.

Marquis, S.K. and Detweiler, A.R. (1985) 'Does adoption mean different? An attributional analysis', *Journal of Personality and Social Psychology* 48(4), 1054–66.

Marsh, P. and Triseliotis, J. (eds) (1993) *Prevention and Reunification in Child Care*. London: Batsford.

Marshall, R. (1990) 'The genetics of schizophrenia' in R.R. Bentall (ed.) *Reconstructing Schizophrenia*. London: Routledge.

Maughan, B. and Pickles, A. (1990) 'Adopted and illegitimate children growing up' in L. Robins and M. Rutter (eds) *Straight and Devious Pathways from Childhood to Adulthood*. Cambridge: Cambridge University Press.

Maxime, J. (1992) *Black Like Me* (workbooks). London: Lion Publications.

Maxime, J.E. (1993) 'The importance of racial identity for the psychological well-being of black children'. Paper given at the Association of Child Psychology and Psychiatry, 15 July.

Mead, G. (1934) *Mind, Self and Society*. Chicago: University of Chicago Press.

Meezan, W. and Shireman, J. (1980) *Adoption Services in the States* (DHHS Publication, No. OHDS 80-30288). Washington, DC: US Department of Health and Human Services.

Meezan, W. and Shireman, J. (1985) *Care and Commitment: Foster-parent Adoption Decisions*. Albany, NY: State University of New York Press.

Millham, S., Bullock, R., Hosie, K. and Little, M. (1986) *Lost in Care*. Aldershot: Gower.

Mitchell, A. (1985) *Children in the Middle*. London: Tavistock.

Moran, R. (1994) 'Stages of emotion: an adult adoptee's post-reunion perspective', *Child Welfare* 73(3), 249–60.

Mullender, A. (1988) 'Groupwork with black children in white homes: groupwork with transracial foster parents' in Triseliotis (ed.) (1988).

Mullender, A. (ed.) (1991) *Openness in Adoption*. London: BAAF.

Munsinger, H. (1975) 'The adopted child's IQ: a critical review', *Psychological Bulletin* 85, 623–59.

National Committee for Adoption (1989) *Adoption Factbook: United States Data Issues, Regulations and Resources*. Washington, DC.

Nelson, K. (1985) *On the Frontiers of Adoption: A Study of Special Needs Adoptive Families*. Washington, DC: Child Welfare League of America.

Nelson, K.E. and Landsman, M.J. (1992) *Alternative Models of Family Preservation*, Springfield, IL: Charles C. Thomas.

Ngabonziza, D. (1991) 'Moral and political issues facing relinquishing countries', *Adoption and Fostering* 15(4), 75–80.

Nystrom, C. (1990) *'Emma Says Goodbye'*. Oxford: Lion Publications, 1990.

Oaklander, V. (1978) *Windows on Our Children*. Utah: Real People Press.

Oppenheim, C. (1993) *Poverty: The Facts*. London: Child Poverty Action Group.

Pannor, R. and Baran, A. (1984) 'Open adoption as standard practice', *Child Welfare* LXIII, 245–50.

Pannor, R., Baran, A. and Sorosky, A.D. (1974) 'Birth parents who relinquished babies for adoption revisited', *Family Process* 17(3), 329–37.

Parent to Parent Information on Adoption (1995) *Making Sense of Attachment Disorder*. UK (no place of publication given).

Parents Without Children (1995) *Project Papers*. Durham: Parents Without Children.

Parkes, C.M., Stevenson-Hinde, J. and Marris, P. (eds) (1993) *Attachment Across the Life Cycle*. London: Routledge.

Partridge, S., Hornby, H. and McDonald, T. (1986) *Legacies of Loss, Visions of Gain: An Inside Look at Adoption Disruption*. Portland, ME: University of Southern Maine.

Pennie, P. (1995) Reported in *Adoption UK* 73, 24.

Pennie, P. and Best, F. (1990) *How the Black Family Is Pathologized by the Social Services Systems*. London: Association of Black Social Workers and Allied Professions.

Post-Adoption Centre (1990) *Feeding the Hungry Ghost*. London: Post-Adoption Centre.

Post-Adoption Centre (1994) *Genetic Sexual Attraction*: Discussion Paper 11. London: Post-Adoption Centre.

Pringle, M.K., (1972) *The Needs of Children*. London: Hutchinson.

Pruzan, V. (1977) 'Fodt i udlandet-adopteret i Danmark', Copenhagen: *Socialforsknings institutet* 77. Quoted in Cederblad (1982).

Ratansi, A. (1992) 'Racism, culture and education' in J. Donald and A. Donald (eds) *Race, Culture and Difference*. London: Sage Publications/The Open University.

Raynor, L. (1971) *Giving up a Baby for Adoption*. London: British Association for Adoption and Fostering.

Raynor, L. (1980) *The Adopted Child Comes of Age*. London: George Allen & Unwin.

Redgrave, K. (1987) *Child's Play: 'Direct Work' with the Deprived Child*. Cheadle: Cheshire: Boys' and Girls' Welfare Society.

Registrar General for England and Wales (1969) *Adoption Orders 1969*. London: HMSO.

Registrar General for Scotland (1992) *Adoption Orders*. Private circulation.

Reitz, M. and Watson, K.W. (1992) *Adoption and the Family System*. New York: Guilford Press.

Rhodes, P. (1992) *Racial Matching in Foster Care*. Aldershot: Avebury.

Richards, M. (1995) 'Changing families' in M. Hill, R. Hawthorne, K. Part and D. Part (eds) *Supporting Families*. London: HMSO.

Richardson, D. (1981) 'Lesbian mothers' in J. Hart and D. Richardson (eds) *The Theory and Practice of Homosexuality*. London: Routledge.

Rickets, W. and Achtenberg, R. (1987) 'Adoption and foster-parenting for lesbians and gay men: creating new traditions in family' in F.W. Bozett and M.B. Sussman (eds) *Homosexuality and Family Relations: Marriage and Family Review* 14(3/4), 83–118.

Rohrbaugh, J.T. (1989) 'Choosing children: psychological issues in lesbian parenting', *Women and Therapy* 8(1/2), 51–64.

Rorbech, M. (1991) 'The conditions of 18 to 25-year-old foreign-born adoptees in Denmark' in Altstein and Simon (eds) (1991).

Rosenthal, D. and Kety, S.S. (1968) *The Transmission of Schizophrenia*. Oxford: Pergamon.

Rosenthal, J. (1993) 'Outcome of adoption of children with special needs', *The Future of Children* 3(1), 77–88.

Rosenthal, J. and Groze, V. (1992) *Special Needs Adoption: A Study of Intact Families*. Westport, CT: Praeger.

Rosenthal, J.A., Groze, V., and Morgan, J. (1996) 'Services for families adopting children via public child welfare agencies: use, helpfulness and need', *Children and Youth Services Review* 18(1–2), 163–82.

Rowe, J. (1966) *Parents, Children and Adoption*. London: Routledge & Kegan Paul.

Rowe, J., Hundleby, M. and Garnett, L. (1989) *Child Care Now*. London: British Agencies for Adoption and Fostering.

Rowe, J., Hundleby, M. and Keane, A. (1984) *Long-Term Foster Care*. London: Batsford.

Rowe, J. and Lambert, L. (1973) *Children Who Wait*. London: BAAF.

Ryan, T. and Walker, R. (1993) *Life Story Work*, London: BAAF.

Ryburn, M. (1992) 'Contested adoption proceedings'. Research report. University of Birmingham: Department of Social Work.

Ryburn, M. (1994) *Open Adoption: Research, Theory and Practice*. Aldershot: Avebury.

Sachdev, P. (1989) *Unlocking the Adoption Files*. Toronto: Lexington.

Saetersdal, B. (1989) 'What became of the Vietnamese "baby life children"?' in Proceedings of Conference on Permanence for Children, Melbourne, Australia.

Schaerlaekens, A. and Dondeyne, N. (1985) 'Taalaanpassing bij buitenlandse adoptiekinderen', *Kind en Adolescent* 6(4), 203–18.

Schaffer, H.R. (1990) *Making Decisions About Children*. Oxford: Blackwell.

Schecter, D.M. (1960) 'Observations of adopted children', *Archives of General Psychiatry* 3, 21–32.

Schiff, M., Duyme, M., Dumoret, A., Stewart, J., Tomkiewicz, S., and Feinasgold, J. (1978) 'Intellectual status of working class children adopted early into upper-middle-class families', *Science* 200, 1503–4.

Schorr, E. (1988) *Within Our Reach*. New York: Anchor Press.

Schwartz, I., Ortega, R., Guo, S. and Fishman, G. (1994) 'Infants in non-permanent placement', *Social Services Review* 68(3), 405–16.

Scourfield, F. and Hendry, A. (1991) 'Unfinished business – the experience of a birth mothers' group', *Adoption and Fostering* 15(2), 37–40.

Scourfield, F. and Hendry, A. (1994) 'Unanswered questions', *Community Care*, 14 May.

Seglow, J., Pringle, M. and Wedge, P. (1972) *Growing up Adopted*. London: National Foundation for Educational Research.

Selman, P. (1993) 'Services for intercountry adoption in the UK: some lessons from Europe', *Adoption and Fostering* 17(3), 14–19.

Sharma, A., McGue, M.K., Benson, P.L. and Peter, L. (1996) 'The emotional and behavioral adjustment of United States adopted adolescents: Part II, Age at adoption', *Children and Youth Services Review* 18(1–2), 101–14.

Sherley, J. *et al*. 'Ethnic differentials in foster care placements', *Social Work and Abstracts* 19(4), 41–5.

Shireman, J.F. (1988) 'Growing up adopted: an examination of major issues'. Unpublished report from Regional Research Institute for Human Services, Portland State University.

Shireman, J. and Johnson, P. (1975) *Adoption: Three Alternatives. A Comparative Study of Three Alternative Forms of Adoptive Placement*. Chicago: Chicago Child Care Society.

Shireman, J. and Johnson, P. (1976) 'Single persons as adoptive parents', *Social Services Review* 50(1), 103–16.

Shireman, J. and Johnson, P. (1985) 'Single parent adoptions: a longitudinal study', *Children and Youth Services Review* 7(4), 321–34.

Shireman, J. and Johnson, P. (1986) 'A longitudinal study of black adoptions: single parent transracial, and traditional', *Social Work* 31, 172–6.

Shireman, J. Johnson, P. and Watson, K. (1987) 'Transracial adoption and the development of black identity at age eight', *Child Welfare* 66, 45–55.

Silber, K. and Dorner, P.M. (1990) *Children of Open Adoption and*

Their Families. San Antonio, TX: Corona Publishing Company.

Simon, R.J. and Altstein, H. (1977) *Transracial Adoption*. New York: John Wiley.

Simon, R.J. and Altstein, H. (1981) *Transracial Adoption: A Follow-up*. Lexington, MA: Lexington Books.

Simon, R.J. and Altstein, H. (1987) *Transracial Adoptees and Their Families: A Study of Identity and Commitment*. New York: Praeger Press.

Simon, R.J. and Altstein, H.H. (1991) 'Intercountry adoptions: experiences of families in the United States' in Altstein and Simon (eds) (1991).

Simon, R.J. and Altstein, H. (1992) *Adoption Race and Identity: From Infancy Through Adolescence*. New York: Praeger.

Small, J. (1986) 'Transracial placements: conflicts and contradictions' in S. Ahmed, J. Cheetham and J. Small (eds) *Social Work with Black Children and Their Families*. London: Batsford.

Small, J. (1991) 'Ethnic and racial identity in adoption within the United Kingdom', *Adoption and Fostering* 15(4), 61–8.

Smith, C. (1984) *Adoption and Fostering*. London: Macmillan.

Social Services Inspectorate (1995) *Moving Goal Posts: A Study of Post-adoption Contact in the North of England*. London: Social Services Inspectorate.

Sokoloff, B.Z. (1993) 'Antecedents of American adoption' in R.E. Behrman (ed.) *The Future of Children: Adoption*. Los Altos, CA: David and Lucile Packard Foundation.

Sorgedrager (no date) quoted in R.A. Hoksbergen (1991) 'Intercountry adoption coming of age in the Netherlands' in Alstein and Simon (eds) (1991).

Sorich, C.J. and Siebert, T. (1982) 'Towards humanizing adoption', *Child Welfare* 61, 207–16.

Soul Kids Steering Group (1977) *The Soul Kids Campaign*. London: Association of British Adoption Agencies.

Stafford, G. (1993) *Where to Find Adoption Records*. London: BAAF.

Stebbing, M. and Edwards, M. (1992) 'Adopting a child from abroad' in Marindin (ed.) (1992).

Stein, L. and Hoopes, J. (1985) *Identity Formation in the Adopted Adolescent*. New York: Child Welfare League of America.

Stein, T.J. (1991) *Child Welfare and the Law*. New York: Longman.

Stolley, K.S. (1993) 'Statistics on adoption in the United States' in R.E. Behrman (ed.) *The Future of Children: Adoption*. Los Altos, CA: David and Lucile Packard Foundation.

Stone, M. (1981) *The Education of Black Children in Britain*.

London: Fontana.

Strathclyde Social Work Department (1991) 'The outcome of permanent family placement' in Scottish Office (ed.) *Adoption and Fostering*. Edinburgh: Central Research Unit Papers.

Striker, S. and Kimmel, E. (1979) *Anti-Coloring Books*. London: Scholastic Publications.

Sullivan, A. (1994) 'On transracial adoption', *Children's Voice* (Child Welfare League of America) 3(3), 3–6.

Sullivan, A. (1995) 'Policy issues in Child Welfare League of America' in *Issues in Gay and Lesbian Adoption*. Washington, DC: Child Welfare League of America.

Taylor, C. (1989) *Sources of Self*. Cambridge: Cambridge University Press.

Textor, R.M. (1991) 'International adoption in West Germany: a private affair' in Altstein and Simon (eds) (1991).

Thoburn, J. (1994) *Child Placement: Principles and Practice*. Aldershot: Avebury.

Thoburn, J., Murdoch, A. and O'Brien, A. (1986) *Permanence in Child Care*. Oxford: Blackwell.

Thoburn, J. and Rowe, J. (1988) 'A snapshot of permanent family placement', *Adoption and Fostering* 12(3), 29–34.

Thom, M. and MacLiver, C. (1986) *Bruce's Story*. London: Children's Society.

Tienari, P. (1991) 'Interaction between genetic vulnerability and family environment: the Finnish adoptive family study of schizophrenia', *Acta Psychiatrica Scandinavica* 84, 460–5.

Tizard, B. (1977) *Adoption: A Second Chance*. London: Open Books.

Tizard, B. (1991) 'Intercountry adoption: a review of the evidence', *Journal of Child Psychology and Psychiatry* 32(5), 743–56.

Tizard, B. and Phoenix, A. (1989) 'Black identity and transracial adoption', *New Community* 15, 427–38.

Tizard, B. and Phoenix, A. (1993) *Black, White or Mixed Race*. London: Routledge.

Tolfree, D. (1995) *Roofs and Roots: The Care of Separated Children in the Developing World*. Aldershot: Gower.

Tremitiere, B.T. (1984) 'Adoption of children with special needs in the client centred approach', *Child Welfare* 58, 681–5.

Triseliotis, J. (1970) *Evaluation of Adoption Policy and Practice*. University of Edinburgh: Department of Social Administration.

Triseliotis, J. (1973) *In Search of Origins*. London: Routledge & Kegan Paul.

Triseliotis, J. (ed.) (1980) *New Developments in Foster Care and*

Adoption. London: Routledge and Kegan Paul.

Triseliotis, J. (1983) 'Identity and security in long-term fostering and adoption', *Adoption and Fostering* 7(1), 22–31.

Triseliotis, J (1984) 'Obtaining birth certificates' in P. Bean (ed.) *Adoption: Essays in Social Policy, Law and Sociology* (pp. 38–53). London: Tavistock.

Triseliotis, J. (1985) 'Adoption with contact', *Adoption and Fostering* 9(4), 19–24.

Triseliotis, J. (ed.) (1988) *Groupwork in Adoption and Foster Care*. London: Batsford.

Triseliotis, J. (1991a) 'Adoption outcome' in D.E. Hibbs (ed.) *Adoption: International Perspectives*. Madison, CT: International Universities Press.

Triseliotis, J. (1991b) 'Maintaining the links in adoption', *British Journal of Social Work* 21, 401–14.

Triseliotis, J. (1991c) 'Inter-country adoption: a brief review of the literature', *Adoption and Fostering* 15(4), 46–52.

Triseliotis, J. (1993a) 'Social work decisions about separated children' in H. Ferguson, R. Gilligan and R. Torode (1993) *Surviving Childhood Adversity: Issues for Policy and Practice*. Dublin: Trinity College, Department of Social Studies.

Triseliotis, J. (1993b) 'Inter-country adoption: in whose best interests?' in M. Humphrey and H. Humphrey (eds) *Inter-country Adoption*. London: Routledge.

Triseliotis, J. (1994) 'Setting up foster care programmes in Romania', *Community Alternatives* 6(1), 75–92.

Triseliotis, J. (1995) 'Adoption: evolution or revolution?' in S. Shah (ed.) *Selected Seminar Papers 1994/95*. London: BAAF.

Triseliotis, J., Borland, M., Hill, M. and Lambert, L. (1995) *Teenagers and the Social Work Services*. London: HMSO.

Triseliotis, J. and Hall, E. (1971) 'Giving consent to adoption', *Social Work Today* 2(7), 24–8.

Triseliotis, J. and Russell, J. (1984) *Hard to Place: The Outcome of Adoption and Residential Care*. London: Gower.

Triseliotis, J., Sellick, C. and Short, R. (1995) *Foster Care: Theory and Practice*. London: Batsford.

United Nations (1989) *The Charter: The Convention on the Rights of the Child*, Article 21, adopted by the UN Assembly on 20 November.

Van Gulden, H. and Bartels-Rabb, L. (1995) *Real Parents, Real Children*. Crossroads Publishing Company.

Varley, S. (1992) *Badger's Parting Gifts*. London: Random Century.

Verhulst, F., Althaus, M.S. and Bieman, H. (1990) 'Problem

behaviour in international adoptees. I. An epidemiological study; II. Age at placement', *Journal of the American Academy of Child and Adolescent Psychiatry* 29, 94–103, 104–11.

Verrier, N.N. (1994) *The Primal Wound.* Gateway Press.

Vondra, J.I. (1990) 'Sociological and ecological factors' in R.T. Ammerman and M. Hersen (eds) *Children at Risk: An Evaluation of Factors Contributing to Child Abuse and Neglect.* New York: Plenum Press.

Vroegh, K. (1991) *Transracial Adoption: How It Is 17 Years Later.* Chicago: Chicago Child Care Society.

Walby, C.M. (1992) 'Adoption: a question of identity'. Thesis submitted to the University of Wales for the degree of MSc.

Wallerstein, J.S. and Kelly, J.B. (1980) *Surviving the Break-up.* London: Grant McIntyre.

Ward, M. (1981) 'Parental bonding in older child adoptions', *Child Welfare* 60, 24–34.

Warner, S.B. (1992) 'Lower threshold for referral for psychiatric treatment for adopted adolescents', *Journal of the American Academy of Child and Adolescent Psychiatry* 31, 512–17.

Watson, K. (1994) 'The history and future of adoption'. Keynote address, North American Council on Adoptable Children. Reprinted in *Family Matters* (Oregon's Special Needs Adoption Newsletter), February, 1–2, 7.

Watson, L. and McGhee, J. (1995) *Developing Post-Placement Support.* Edinburgh: BAAF.

Wedge, P. and Mantle, G. (1991) *Sibling Groups and Social Work.* University of East Anglia: Department of Social Work.

Wells, S. (1993) 'What do birth mothers want?', *Adoption and Fostering* 17(4), 22–32.

Wells, S. (1994) *Within Me, Without Me.* London: Scarlet Press.

Wender, P., Rosenthal, D., Kety, S., Schulsinger, S. and Elner, J. (1974) 'Crossfostering: a research strategy for clarifying the role of genetic and experiential factors in the aetiology of schizophrenia', *Archives of General Psychiatry* 30, 121–8.

West, J. (1996) *Child Centred Play Therapy.* London: Edward Arnold.

White, R. (1993) 'Adoption and openness: the legal framework' in M. Adcock, J. Kaniuk and R. White (eds) *Exploring Openness in Adoption* (pp. 91–104). London: Significant Publications.

Wiehe, V.R. (1976) 'Attitudinal change as a function of the adoptive study', Chicago: *Smith College Papers in Social Work* 46, 127–36.

Wilhelm, H. (1985) *I'll Always Love You.* London: Hodder & Stoughton.

Winkler, R. and Van Keppel, M. (1984) *Relinquishing Mothers in Adoption*. Melbourne: Institute for Family Studies.

Witmer, R.T. (1963) 'The purpose of American adoption laws' in H. Witmer, E. Herzog, E. Weinstein and M. Sullivan (eds) *Independent Adoptions: A Follow-up Study* (pp. 19–43). New York: Russell Foundation.

Worell, J. (1988) 'Single mothers: from problems to policies', *Women and Therapy* 7(4), 3–13.

Zaar, C. (1984) *A New Country, a New Home*. Stockholm: Swedish National Board for Intercountry Adoptions.

Zastrow, C. (1977). *Outcome of Black Children/White Parent Adoptions*. San Francisco, CA: R & E Research Associates.

AUTHOR INDEX

SUBJECT INDEX